£1.00
5

THE
PLAYMASTERS

From Sellouts to Lockouts-An Unauthorized History of the NBA

ELDON HAM

CONTEMPORARY BOOKS

Library of Congress Cataloging-in-Publication Data

Ham, Eldon L., 1952–
    The playmasters : from sellouts to lockouts, an unauthorized
history of the NBA / Eldon Ham.
        p.   cm.
    Includes bibliographical references (p.).
    ISBN 0-8092-2602-2
    1. National Basketball Association—History.   2. Basketball—
Economic aspects—United States.   I. Title.
GV885.515.N37H26   2000
796.323'64'0973—dc21   99-37967
                                                        CIP

Cover and interior design by Nick Panos
Cover photograph copyright © Henry Horenstein/Photonica

Published by Contemporary Books
A division of NTC/Contemporary Publishing Group, Inc.
4255 West Touhy Avenue, Lincolnwood (Chicago), Illinois 60712-1975 U.S.A.
Printed in the United States of America
International Standard Book Number: 0-8092-2602-2
00 01 02 03 04 05 MV 19 18 17 16 15 14 13 12 11 10 9 8 7 6 5 4 3 2 1

To family and friends, past and present

CONTENTS

ACKNOWLEDGMENTS

No book comes to fruition without the direct and indirect efforts of many. I am particularly grateful for the perseverance of my editor, Ken Samelson, and the faith of my publisher without whom *The PlayMasters* would still be an abstract idea.

I would like also to acknowledge friends and family, to whom this work is dedicated, for without the inspiration and support of others the efforts of any author would likely be in vain. I owe a special thanks to Stats, Inc., Skokie, Illinois, for supplying home and away games statistics, and to Dan Druggan, a former student of mine who contributed to my research efforts.

Most of all I am indebted to those who made the NBA—the good, the bad, the spectacular, and the inane. Without the legacies of Abe Saperstein, Julius Erving, Wilt Chamberlain, James Naismith, Magic, Bird, Jordan, and others, the NBA would still be a pipe dream waiting to happen. And without the egos, guts, imagination, and machinations of present and past playmasters extraordinaire, the history of the NBA would remain a dull chapter in the history of sports.

Finally I would like to thank the Chicago-Kent College of Law for its continued faith and support over the past quarter century, without which both my legal career and this book would remain a fiction.

INTRODUCTION

Is the NBA really a business?

This is a curious question in an era of multi*billion* dollar marketing and television deals, yet a necessary first step to unlock the surreal world of what professional basketball has become.

Technically, yes—the NBA is a business—but the innuendo is all wrong, for the business of basketball has become an *Alice in Wonderland* aberration, complete with its own mad hatters and loony caterpillars on and off the court. But unlike the looking-glass images of *Alice*, basketball's perverse inner core *can* be understood—for the NBA itself is real, not fictional, and in turn must be a product of real explanations, tangible motives, and discernible history yielding a wealth of clues about its modern identity and ultimate destiny. Therein lies the opportunity for *The PlayMasters*: dissecting the hidden bowels and heart of the NBA to both celebrate its grand history, from Mikan to West to Magic and Jordan, and explore how today's NBA juggernaut is in danger of drowning in its own stellar successes.

Indeed, why would the Chicago Bulls run six-time world champion coach Phil Jackson out of town, practically tarred and feathered as the brunt of management contempt, a futile first in a series of collapsing dominoes that would ultimately dismantle the once and glorious world champion dynasty?[1] In this day and age of sports dissension in which recalcitrant players have mutinied against coaches en masse as they did in Orlando—or singularly, as did Latrell Sprewell when he physically assaulted Golden State coach P. J. Carlesimo—would not a quiet, successful leader at peace with himself and his players be treated like gold? Perhaps, if only the NBA were a typical business. Alas, it is not, for the NBA is a sports macrocosm of money, marketing, collusion, show business, and—above all—a swarm of id-driven egos racing out of control in what appears to be a reckless quest for self-identity. Overblown egos are becoming the black hole of pro sports, sucking the life from otherwise vibrant and exciting enterprises such as today's NBA.

But where in the world did this megamarketing machine come from, how does it work, and what is its future? Moreover, to what extent will it bend the rules to perpetuate itself—and at what cost?

The National Basketball Association is a unique amalgam of talent, owners, and tradition, standing not alone as an island but as the inevitable product of all that has come before—and yes, one *can* become the proverbial fly on the wall to steal an inside glimpse. Many of the obscured answers to the NBA phenomenon are really hidden in plain view, begging to be discovered simply through the application of contemporary logic to the history of human nature in general and sports thinking in particular.

From playing tactics to player rights, antitrust to television ratings and money, today's NBA is a product of strategic, economic, and marketing evolution. Even the essence of the game itself is a function of evolutionary forces, such as the vaunted triangle offense, a sophisticated triple-post motion attack that deploys speed and discipline to frustrate NBA defenses. The triangle offense never could have evolved without the NBA three-point line pulling offenses and defenses from the basket. The three-point line altered how offenses are run, neutralizing strong, immobile centers like George Mikan and even the athletic Wilt Chamberlain by rewarding speed, grace, spacing, and discipline—the crucial formula of modern basketball exploited by the Chicago Bulls of the 1990s and occasionally a few others before them (like some of the Celtics and Knicks teams of old), running circles around other teams overly reliant upon low-post muscle. In turn, the three-point line itself had evolved from the old American Basketball Association (ABA) efforts to add new layers of excitement to an otherwise predictable floor game to better compete with the staid rival NBA; and the ABA adopted it from the old ABL, where Globetrotters owner Abe

Saperstein had invented it in the first place. And so it has gone, and still goes, on and on.

It is a long, long journey from the crude stone and hoop games of the ancient Mayan Indians to the above-the-rim act of Julius Erving and those who have followed, but those changes did not result from one quantum leap in athletic history. Rather, they progressed slowly, step by imperceptible step, from Roman gladiators to James Naismith to the high-flying ABA and the eventual marketing juggernaut of Michael Jordan's modern NBA.

Just what *did* the NBA of Jordan & Company become? It was nothing if not dynamic. Whatever the pinnacle of pro basketball may be now, profound changes are surely in the offing—not only because change is always inevitable, but because pent-up forces of ego, money, and politics have begun to reinvent the NBA, either propelling it to a new strata of marketing entertainment or pushing it over the edge of reason. There is, after all, a fuzzy gray line between marketing savvy and greed, between confidence and insolence. Players, owners, coaches, and pundits are equally capable of succumbing to history's great equalizers: ego and greed. Which road will the post-Jordan NBA travel? No one can yet say for sure. But the road now traveled, very real and daunting, is the same fateful passage that once doomed the 1980 Russian Olympic hockey team, Sonny Liston, the Colts in Super Bowl III—and even inspired the demise of such diverse historic failures as the *Titanic* and the Roman Empire long before that.

Arrogance.

Not just greed. Simple greed is too easy and especially too clichéd. The purported greed of athletes and owners is well publicized, critiqued, and overused. Profit motives have a pervasive place in history and were behind the *Titanic* and the Roman Empire, to be sure—but both were ultimately sunk by human obsession, not just money. Arrogant sports egos have historically spun out of control, from Ty Cobb to Marge Schott to Howard Cosell, possibly including certain top brass members of Chicago's curious Bulls of the 1990s. A prime example of wayward sports egos can be found across town and one decade removed from the lofty Bulls, harboring a lesson or two for the NBA or any other sports empire that takes itself too seriously: the 1985 Chicago Bears, perhaps the greatest football dynasty that never was. Those 18–1 victors of Super Bowl XX were a ruthless gridiron machine bent not just on winning, but on destroying the opposition. Not only did those Bears whip a good Cowboys team in Dallas 44–0 with an 11-sack devastation, they wreaked havoc all year—including the postseason, in which they stomped their opponents (Giants, Rams, and Patriots) by a combined score of 91–10. They were the Mike Tyson of football, a veritable plague of fear and destruction behind such defensive stars as Richard Dent, Dan Hampton, Mike Singletary, Otis Wilson, Wilber Marshall, William Perry, Steve McMichael, and Dave Duerson. The offense was no slouch either, sporting the likes of Walter Payton, Jim McMahon, Willie Gault, and Dennis McKinnon behind an All-Pro offensive line that included Jay Hilgenberg, Jimbo Covert, and Keith Van Horne.

Yet instead of relishing and nurturing their thoroughbred team, the first thing management did was fire assistant coach Buddy Ryan, a defensive wizard who enjoyed the respect and love of his battle-tested troops. Ryan was replaced with the venerable Vince Tobin, a passive football man who once announced that his defensive scheme was actually designed to give up yards. As fate would have it, Tobin's first team in 1986 statistically exceeded the season points-allowed mark; but linebacker Otis Wilson confided to me that every player had to work twice as hard since the Tobin game plan was more coverage oriented than the attack mode of his predecessor Ryan, thus running Bears defenses all over the field in pursuit of fleet receivers and elusive scat-backs. This scheme took its toll, wearing on the players and eroding their emotional, take-no-prisoners approach to the game. Instead of growing stronger all year from a feeding frenzy of sacks and winning, the Bears ran out of physical and emotional fuel, first floundering in the playoffs and then missing the postseason altogether.

To make matters worse, after failing to repeat the Super Bowl after the 1986 season, the Bears began to systematically displace their time-tested stars. Marshall and Gault were soon dumped, and

McMahon was run out of town. Bears player personnel guru Bill Tobin, largely credited for a series of stellar drafts, was also let go—so as other battle-weary players such as Payton and Hampton retired, they would not be replaced by equivalent stars for a whole decade and counting (although Neal Anderson did hold his own in Payton's shadow for awhile until his beaten and bruised body could carry the load no longer).

The once-invincible Monsters of the Midway crumbled, sliding a little further each year, until finally a 5–11 team quit playing for its one-time idol, Coach Mike Ditka. The team has never recovered (though one day it perhaps will), and the glory days of the '80s are long gone as Bears teams of the '90s languish in sub-mediocrity. But why did this happen? How could management of any enterprise, much less a highly visible pro football team, commit such obvious suicide? And what, if anything, can the NBA playmasters learn from this reversal of Bear fortunes?

The answer perhaps can be found in the mirror: "We have met the enemy, and the enemy is us,"² which is precisely why such a football story is apropos to launching a surgical dissection of the National Basketball Association. The NBA does not exist in a vacuum, and there is always much to be learned from history and, in this context, sports history. But in particular, there is a geographic and cultural irony in remembering those Bears in light of the crosstown phenomenon that paradoxically defines all that is right and much of what is wrong with the contemporary NBA—the Bulls. With a winning team, everyone gets credit: the point guard, the bench, the coach, the general manager—even the owner. The problem stems from the overwhelming temptation of everyone receiving credit to have it all and not share it. Therein lies the moral of sports failure. Ravenous egos killed those Chicago Bears just as surely as beauty killed the fictional beast King Kong—both human frailties, but neither rooted solely in money or greed. The world of sports seems to generate misplaced egos like no other business, and in the last quarter century the phenomenon has worsened to the point of dominating sports pages. Everyone, it seems, wants credit—*all* the credit—for winning. And, of course, the fate of such ill-advised narcissism is the cruel opposite: losing.

Losing breeds animosity in any business, but antipathy in sports can be bred by winning *or* losing. True to contemporary slang, today's sports fans are subjected to endless rounds of public "dissing," followed by a series of arguments about who is dissing whom, no matter what the cause. Warriors coach P. J. Carlesimo "disrespected" Latrell Sprewell; the Bulls "dissed" Phil Jackson; and, for refusing to tear up Scottie Pippen's contract, the Bulls allegedly "disrespected" Scottie. (Perhaps they *did* disrespect Pippen, it would appear, but not for that reason.) If we listen carefully to history and to the deliberate words, actions, and demeanors of GMs, players, and owners—not just for what they do say, but more important, for what they do not—then we will learn the truth in spite of the NBA spinmasters, showmen, and playmasters.

Will the NBA prove immune to the universal law of physics, sports, and economics—what goes up must come down—or will the league do a crash and burn à la the *Hindenburg*, Nero's Rome, the 1985 Bears, or 1994's Major League Baseball? The intentional dismantling of the Chicago Bulls during and after the labor-torn year of 1998 could be the penultimate chapter of the NBA, foretelling the ultimate reversal of NBA fortunes in the wake of dangerous egos fiddling before a smoldering league. So click off the remote, buckle up, and hang on for an insightful ride from then to now and beyond. For if the curious fate of the Jordan-less Bulls is any indication, the foreboding truth is nigh upon us.

ENDNOTES

1. Could it have been to save the coach's lofty salary, knowing, perhaps, that a labor lockout was on the way? Not only must serious fans question team motives regarding Jackson, they should also scrutinize the whole 1998–99 player lockout scenario and its inherent risks, if not folly, all while second-guessing a Bulls organization bent on alienating a virtual basketball messiah in Michael Jordan.
2. Pogo.

SURVIVAL OF THE FITTEST

PART I

1

OUTRAGEOUS FORTUNE

He is a bigger-than-life off-court persona, recognized by millions of serious and casual fans alike, male and female, young and old—especially the adoring young. When he donned the black, red, and white colors of the Bulls uniform, he became a fierce competitor with quick hands, strong legs, and lightning reflexes. A student of the game who reveled in the Bulls' complex triangle offense, a cagey veteran fending off age with superior conditioning, he was a basketball wonder who loved the fast break, stellar defense, downcourt passes, and Phil Jackson. Not the tallest player by any means, he overcame his average NBA size with nearly unprecedented determination, athleticism, heart, and uncanny court awareness.

Hollywood money isn't money. It's congealed snow, melts in your hand, and there you are.

—DOROTHY PARKER

No, no—this particular player is not Michael Jordan. Though Jordanesque in many ways, Dennis Rodman listened to his own drummer, complementing Michael with his power forward defense, rebounds, and court awareness that often generated downcourt fast breaks to the chagrin and exhaustion of broken opponents. Jordan is a virtuoso, Rodman the abrasive multiple personalities of a one-man percussion section. The two players are so different they are hardly of the same planet, yet curiously they can be described in many similar ways. How could this be? How can two athletes so different in approach and appearance have so much in common?

The enigmatic answer is at once simple and complex, as are Jordan and Rodman themselves. More important, this perceived dichotomy symbolizes today's schizophrenic NBA. Both players left the league in 1999: Jordan through a graceful (though mildly controversial) retirement, Rodman via one final meltdown that launched him from the Lakers. Together on the Bulls, Rodman had been the eccentric Thoreau to Jordan's articulate Emerson, one complementing the other, while also portraying the Jekyll and Hyde images of an adolescent league that during much of the 1990s outdueled football and baseball for the competitive heart of American sports fans. This is a league that has orchestrated itself into the marketing stratosphere, a league of image, attitude, manipulation, and dynamic modulation typified by Rodman's hair and Jordan's endorsements. This, then, is where the NBA is, but how it got here is the anatomy—the guts and the grit—of contemporary sports in America.

Big-time sports have undergone more change in the courtroom than on the playing field during the past quarter century, breeding a socioeconomic upheaval that virtually reinvented sports in general and the National Basketball Association in particular. This is nothing new, for even a cursory review of major sports headlines over the past two decades confirms such a simple truth about the business and legal machinations of pro sports. The real question, then, is not so much *what*, but *why*?

Money. Big bucks and fast jack. As player free agency and network television took hold, a modest money spigot opened in the 1970s, cascading into an unprecedented ocean of sports wealth 20 years later. Indeed the wealth, glitz, and "big screen" glamour of today's NBA is a throwback to Dorothy Parker's Hollywood of the 1930s and 1940s. With players, owners, agents, and television networks breeding a new generation of media moguls, sports dollars have acquired a showbiz surrealism, as easy to get, spend, and lose as Monopoly money. True to form, as television, endorsements, and sports marketing continued to raise the stakes, both the economic rudder and moral compass of the sports industry began to spin out of control. Winning took on new importance—at least for the players, if not the owners—and shortcuts like steroids and other performance enhancers soon infiltrated the world of big-time athletics.

Football seems to have paved the way, at least among major team sports. Former Atlanta Falcons guard Bill Fralic once told the Senate Judiciary Committee that "probably about 75 percent" of NFL linemen, linebackers, and tight ends use anabolic steroids. He may not have been far off. As recently as 1990, sixteen hundred NFL players received questionnaires about steroid use. Only 7.5 percent responded, but of that small sample 28 percent indicated they had used steroids in the prior twelve months. Of those who were offensive linemen, two-thirds reported such use. Pat Donovan, a Dallas Cowboys offensive lineman for nine years ending in 1983, has publicly suggested that steroid use among offensive and defensive linemen may at one time have reached 70 percent.

Given that NFL drug testing has tightened over the last decade, with increased numbers of better tests and significant penalties for violations, it is unlikely that NFL steroid use remains on the rise or even hovers at such lofty levels. But reports are replete with steroid and performance enhancer difficulties, from Olympian Ben Johnson to Mark McGwire, who used a questionable over-the-counter supplement during his 1998 home run rampage.

But the lure of drugs in sports is not limited to performance issues, for the temptations of money are both sweeping and disturbing. From marijuana to cocaine, unbridled sexual indulgences and lavish spending on everything from six-figure cars to multiple child support payments, the money of these new age centurions has changed the sports landscape forever. For example, the basketball and nonbasketball worlds were stunned, if not embarrassed, in the wake of Wilt Chamberlain's postretirement braggadocio about his twenty thousand or so sexual conquests. Even so, the impact of individual player indiscretions pales in comparison to the megadeals of the power broker agents, owners, and sports marketers: especially the masters of play who shape, influence, and manipulate the NBA growth explosion fueled by the mystique of one Michael Jeffrey Jordan. Indeed, do we dare say that the charismatic and powerful Mr. Jordan himself had become both player and playmaster? Just how far these playmasters will go, and to what extent they may bend the rules to perpetuate the NBA profit machine, will determine much of the league's integrity, foresight, and economic future. More bluntly, when does a carefully orchestrated pursuit of entertainment drama and competitive balance go too far, traversing an invisible but real line into the less noble world of self-aggrandizement and sports manipulation?

That is, just when does the selling of the NBA become selling *out*?

Michael Jordan and television prospered in a unique sports marriage made in money, drama, and sheer entertainment, launching the NBA starship to unprecedented success. Most pundits now agree that Jordan emerged as the greatest basketball player in history, and the timing of his arrival in 1984 could not have been better. Although Chamberlain individually may have been more dominant on the court—he once had seven 50-plus–point games in a row, and he averaged a stunning 22.9 rebounds per game for an entire career—Michael Jordan blended grace, versatility, defense, and unstoppable offense with a titanic will to win and be better than any player to lace up a pair of sneakers. With a public moniker first reduced to just "Michael" and now simply the initials "MJ" in deference to Jordan's cult status among fans, MJ is clearly "the man" on, and now off, the court.

From the mid-1980s until the labor lockout of 1998, NBA insiders such as longtime commissioner David Stern, Rod Thorn, key owners like Jerry Reinsdorf, and a host of others masterfully bought peace with the players and marketed the NBA for what it is—a high-flying entertainment product. Along the way, a league organization first content to tolerate MJ, superagent David Falk, and Phil Knight's Nike empire soon unabashedly collaborated with the sports marketing behemoth that Jordan's image had become. Soaking up licensing dollars from Chicago Bulls merchandise and a ratings explosion whenever Jordan appeared on national television, the whole league prospered.

Ironically, if not deservedly, Michael Jordan often made more money as a Bull than the whole organization did. According to *Forbes*, the 1998 Bulls made $8.6 million on revenues of $112.2 million. The Bulls paid Jordan about $35 million that year. The

Bulls, on the other hand, have experienced payrolls as high as $60 million or so, not counting office and support personnel, GM Jerry Krause, or owner Jerry Reinsdorf, leaving perhaps $40 million for overhead, other expenses, and eventually profits. Result? MJ made about nine times what the Bulls investors made in 1998.

Therein lies the economic rub that exacerbates the inherent sports ego problem. Not only did Michael probably make 100 or 200 times what his general manager made, he eventually cost his employer a good $20 million a year of bottom-line results (although he still did wonders for the league as a whole). Without Michael, the 1999 Bulls saved all his salary and likely made over $40 million net. With a team salary cap in the range of $32 million during his last year, MJ exceeded the whole cap structure all by himself—a phenomenon made possible by the "Larry Bird Rule," which until 1999 softened the cap ceiling by allowing teams to overspend for the purpose of retaining their own free agent veterans. Of course Michael deserved his due, for without him, could the Bulls expect to sell out every single game? Certainly not—so there became a negotiated quid pro quo nestled amidst the respective ledgers of management and superstar.

The NBA teams collectively made a fortune from the overall Jordan effect, and that definitely included the Bulls. But how much of $3 billion in annual gross merchandising sales will remain without Jordan in the NBA? The licensing revenue to the league from those sales is in the $210 million to $270 million range, yielding perhaps $7 million per team. Even if post-Jordan licensing drops by half—a decrease that steep is possible but unlikely—the Bulls, *sans* Jordan, might perceive themselves the big winners, losing only about $3.5 million per year from reduced licensing royalties but gaining over $35 million by saving the Jordan salary burden. The league as a whole, though, would lose 30 times that figure: over $100 million annually, a significant difference.

The same analysis could be made for league television revenues, but the real wild card for the Bulls lies with projected ticket sales. *With* Jordan, the Bulls sold out—more than twenty-three thousand fans every game for 41 regular season contests, plus a handful of exhibitions and, lately, a number of playoff games. But what happens *without* Michael? No one can yet know for sure because season tickets had already been sold for 1999 before his retirement. Some number between contemporary average attendance on a league-wide basis and the old pre-Jordan Bulls attendance might be appropriate, but even this could be exacerbated by fan discontent. If history perceives Michael's retirement as graceful and on his own terms, the immediate negative results may not be so dramatic. However, if the public believes Michael was run out of town by management in the way it apparently dumped mentor Phil Jackson, the results could be staggering. If attendance eventually drops by ten thousand per game, the Bulls lose over $30 million a year just on the tickets, not counting concessions, lost TV revenue, diminished merchandising, and all the rest. Coincidentally, or maybe not so coincidentally, MJ's recent salary was precisely in this range, suggesting he was paid exactly his worth.

So is Michael's fortune so outrageous? Probably not. Certainly it holds up against mathematical and economic scrutiny. And besides, there have been years when Mike Tyson has made more, and MJ's income is dwarfed by other sums in the entertainment business, where Oprah Winfrey, Steven Spielberg, and James Cameron often top the $100 million mark—even $200 million in some cases. That is the key: entertainment. Pro sports personalities are in the entertainment business, so the salaries they command should be viewed accordingly.

But Michael Jordan is an icon, a class of one. And therein lies part of the problem: what worked for MJ may not pass the logic test when applied to others or other settings. In the spring of 1998, *Chicago Tribune* sports columnist Lacy Banks wondered as much in his essay on misplaced sports wealth, noting that the lowly Washington Wizards had inked monster multiyear contracts with Juwan Howard and Chris Webber for over $160 million. If ever an NBA fortune were outrageous, that might be it. No offense to the players who, rather appropriately, would argue they earn what they are worth through arm's-length bargaining, but those deals are perfect examples of the NBA machine—management and players alike—losing grip on reality.

Banks went on to note that power forward Derrick Coleman, then in the fifth season of a six-year deal worth $40.7 million, had done little more than change teams and get three coaches fired. The jury may still be out on Kevin Garnett, a legitimate star and potential bright light for the NBA future, but his league record $126 million contract extension is still suspect. As Banks observed, Garnett himself may not have been the best player on the Minnesota Timberwolves, let alone the whole league.

Ironically, these stratospheric salaries are the direct result of Jordan's influence. Without the frenzied fan interest generated during the 1990s and the influx of television and marketing money, the NBA spending spree could not have happened.[1] So what is wrong with making money, big money? Not a thing—except maybe perspective. The huge dollars spawn huge problems from narcissistic players fathering children out of wedlock from coast to coast à la Shawn Kemp, or players from the Magic to the Warriors turning on their respective coaches—to wit, one Latrell Sprewell.

Sprewell was hauling in almost $100,000 per game when he was suspended over the now infamous December 1, 1997, choking incident involving his Warriors coach, P. J. Carlesimo. An arbitrator eventually reduced the original one-year suspension to 68 games, still costing Latrell an aggregate of $6.4 million in lost salary. Do big player dollars fuel big egos? Sure they do, but it cuts both ways. Coaches who earn more than neurosurgeons and see themselves on television more than Johnnie Cochran can also fall victim to fame's allure. General managers and owners are not immune, either.

The Warriors hired P. J. Carlesimo during the summer of 1997. Latrell was team captain at the time, a position he was proud to hold, as he would later testify during his suspension appeal. Their relationship was strained from the start, as Carlesimo apparently failed to contact Sprewell all summer. Finally Latrell met his new coach at training camp in October. According to the written opinion and transcript of the Sprewell arbitration case, Carlesimo was a hardnosed, often inflexible, and sometimes theatrical coach, especially where inflammatory words were concerned. Immedi-

ately he was on the case of player Donyell Marshall with a relentless in-your-face verbal assault, on one occasion calling him a
"fucking idiot." In the midst of a difficult Lakers game on November 9, 1997, with the Warriors trailing terribly, teammate Bimbo
Coles relented out loud, "I'm gonna foul out of this motherfucker." Latrell laughed, causing Carlesimo to bench him, after
which Sprewell called his coach a "fucking joke."

With the rest of the league at war with itself, its coaches, and
its stars, much of the league's wealth was necessarily carried on the
shoulders of Mr. Jordan and the Chicago Bulls, but for the most
part MJ himself steered clear of cheap-shot controversies and
on-court dissension. He has not avoided controversy altogether by
any means, defending himself against Nike labor policies, abruptly
retiring only to return near the end of his second season away, and
staunchly supporting Phil Jackson even though the embattled
coach was clearly on his way out. In the wake of other team controversies and coaching mayhem, the latter issue is perplexing.
The six-time world champion had embraced a coach whom not
only he respected, but who also commanded the respect of the
other team members. Even Dennis Rodman once responded to a
question about Jackson by referring to the now former Bulls coach
as "the coolest cat I ever played for."

Egos and money. Money and egos. The two are so inextricably
wound in the NBA that making sense of playmaster motives is an
intellectual challenge. But perhaps without the money, the egos
would be of little consequence. Could Mickey Mantle or Oscar
Robertson have had less of an ego than Karl Malone, Patrick
Ewing, Wilt Chamberlain, or Jordan himself? Unlikely, yet athletes
of another era could hardly afford the luxury of spouting off, let
alone punching out coaches. Money has become the great equal-
izer. With many, if not most, players earning more than their
respective coaches, and some players perhaps rivaling the take of
entire teams, the athletes have the power and affordable luxury to
take chances on and off the court—all of which begs the cliché
"role model" question of the 1980s and 1990s.

Are professional athletes role models to others? Yes. *Should*
they be?

Why not? After all, the role model badge is historically and socially inevitable. Other people are role models—police officers, for example—and their exalted status is simply accepted as going with the territory. Like it or not, movie stars are role models, too, as are astronauts and athletes. Being a role model only implies a certain civil duty toward others, and denying the position only increases career risk to the movie star, athlete, or public figure. Even President Clinton seemed surprised at being a role model, complete with all the incumbent implied duties that go with it, but he knows all too well the consequences of taking his position too lightly. The same is true of movie stars—any substantial fall from public grace jeopardizes entire careers. That is nothing new, or even lofty pontificating, it is a fact—a severe dose of reality. By no means are professional athletes any exception. They do not have to relish the role, or be nice, or even be civil. But if they choose aberrant behavior, they must risk the consequences of public scorn, which, in turn, can quickly translate into reduced demand, lost dollars, and a diluted career.

The exception that proves the rule is again the enigma otherwise known as Dennis Rodman. Until he arrived with the Bulls, Rodman was largely perceived as a malcontent at best and a thug at worst. In a Bulls uniform, his image radically improved, ranging from eccentric to loose cannon, but even his oddest of antics failed to trip up his surprising public acceptance. Moreover, his crackpot, different-drummer persona has actually become an asset, transforming the power forward into a world champion antihero with psychedelic hair, multiple personalities, and the all-attitude nickname "Rodzilla." Sometimes lost in all the hyperbole is another lingering Rodman quality: he became an exceptionally good basketball player whose attributes, as we have seen, could sometimes be mistaken for Jordan's.

The style of a Dennis Rodman drives opposing players to prosaic distraction. Sometimes he distracts his own team (as the 1999 Lakers learned) or the officials, fans, and opposing coaches, even himself on occasion. No wonder. Dennis *is* a walking distraction—period. Still, his on-court performance was tireless and relentless, as the Rodman of the 1990s wore down the bodies, minds, and confidence of opponents while he jumped, tipped, and snared rebounds like no other contemporary player. But there was much more to the player Rodman, at least as a Bull—much, much more. His game had become a heads-up brand of basketball second to none. Rodman knows the game cold and competed as a remarkably cerebral player manning the high post or low post or triggering the fast break. His rebounding technique is one of a kind, always in good technical position and frequently tipping the ball straight up to himself one, two, sometimes three times before snaring the missed shot. But Dennis was still Dennis, daring the fine line between eccentricity and lunacy, potentially jeopardizing the outcome of games and risking the support of his teammates.

This, then, is where Rodman leaves off and Jordan begins, for MJ was always in control, perpetually focused. Not that Michael is infallible, unemotional, superhuman, notwithstanding his less humble alias spawned by the Chicago media: Superman. He most certainly is, and has all the incumbent shortcomings of, a mere mortal. But his unrelenting will to win historically channeled his emotional energies in one direction only: victory. Other great players have taken over individual games and have tried to carry their teams singlehandedly, sometimes succeeding, sometimes not. Still, no one has ever done it the way Michael could. Michael Jeffrey Jordan challenged himself to win and willed others to win on and off the court. Failure was not a viable option; it sometimes presented itself in small doses, but never enough to derail championships during any full MJ season beginning with his first NBA ring.

If a team could be beaten on a given night, Michael surgically dissected how to do it. For some games it was with relentless offense, for others it was with tenacious defense. Sometimes he won by making all the right passes, occasionally by a cold, almost cruel pass to an open teammate thrust into the spotlight of history for a last-second attempt à la John Paxson in 1993 or Steve Kerr against the Jazz in Game Six of the 1997 NBA Finals. Often, though, it was Michael himself with the buzzer-beater heroics, nailing a last-ditch bucket against the Cavaliers in what now feels like another era. One of his best efforts was the last great act of the 1998 Utah series, when Jordan stopped on a dime, shook loose (some say pushed off), and squared up to launch a two-point dagger, snuffing out the proud Jazz, who had expected more after their gallant showing the year before.

But 1998 was not to be the year of the Jazz, for Jordan the legend overcame Jordan the man once again, snaring victory as only he can snare it—dramatically, decisively. In all of sports, there have been few competitors so fierce as Jordan; so relentlessly determined is MJ that luck is afraid to scorn him. With his closed-eyes free throws, shrugs of on-court wonderment, and a tongue-wagging lay-it-on-the-line attitude, few athletes have ever matched Jordan's drive to tempt both fate and himself. One noteworthy exception may have been the singular Muhammad Ali, who belittled opponents, challenged himself, and found ways to overcome the impossible time and again. Ali's antics could not have been lost on Michael, so perhaps it is no coincidence that Jordan and Ali embarked upon a series of joint commercial endorsements during the 1997–98 season. They have much in common, those two, probably the two most universally recognized athletes in world sports history. True, Babe Ruth may have been as big in his day at least in North America, but the Babe would never have been widely recognized in China, Africa, or the Philippines. The world-wide universe of the true superstar would not be invented for another half century, but when it did materialize it came fast and loud.

Jordan's predecessor Ali reinvented the athlete as a world figure, masterfully working television and the reporter-turned-straight-man Howard Cosell until Ali the legend grew bigger than life. But Muhammad paved the way to fame and power, not wealth—at least not the megawealth of today's athletes. (He and George Foreman signed for $5 million each to "rumble in the jungle" for the famous Zaire fight, a princely sum but one that is still dwarfed by the winnings of Tyson and the marketing deals of Jordan, Tiger Woods, and others.) Still, Jordan took the trail blazed by Ali to new heights, building a marketing empire worth hundreds of millions to himself and as much as $10 billion to a sports-entertainment industry balanced on the strength of his shoulders. In this,

Michael did what Ali could not. White America was not ready for "the Greatest" in 1964, but by the early '70s after his victory against the federal government,[2] Ali's popularity grew, slowly at first and then accelerating as the man became a myth, and then the myth became reality: Ali indeed was the greatest. Still, much of America was not ready for a brash African American athlete as quick with his wit as with his lightning feet and stinging hands. Ali the legend could not capitalize on the endorsement windfall that would not invade pro sports until the early 1980s, missing out on millions of dollars that otherwise would surely have followed such a worldwide persona.

Alas, the issue has come full circle to the lure and power of money in the 1990s. Regardless of the dollars, Jordan has secured his place in history; but other would-be stars measure their self-esteem by contract dollars, sometimes demanding more than the next guy just to feed compulsive egos. The money is so large, distant, and esoteric that it loses genuine meaning for many young athletes who grew up in modest homes. After the mansion is secured and the Ferrari parked in the driveway, the dollars are really just a means of keeping score in a game of athlete one-upmanship. For some players, the profound dignity and grace of Michael Jordan is lost in their own accounting, a shame for those otherwise proud athletes who could achieve so much more—and a very poor placebo for lesser players, who briefly sported loftier contracts until Michael scored a series of new deals with the Bulls. What they forget is that MJ was underpaid for many years, but he honored his contract and played his heart out, setting a great example that was probably lost on many.

Management, too, has its own shortcomings. And these are potentially the most serious of all. Where players use money to measure self-worth and esteem, management is guilty of measuring and allocating credit: adulation for winning, blame for losing. This is the essence of NBA schizophrenia, a magic carpet ride where winning is a drug and adulation the addictive high that goes with it. A case in point: there is no other logical way to explain the Jerry Krause riddle. By apparently running Phil Jackson out of town, Mr. Krause divested the Bulls of all key personnel not handpicked by himself—with the one, solitary, towering exception of Mr. Michael Jordan—that is, until MJ followed suit. Mr. Krause, then, laid it all on the line. Could he dare instigate the departure of Jordan directly? The carnage around Jordan suggests Krause wanted him out, but why?[3] In the world of today's NBA, the answer is simple: ego. If Jerry "the Sleuth" Krause can win without Jordan, does he believe history will anoint him to the esoteric Hall of Genius somewhere near Red Auerbach, who won championships with three different Celtics teams?[4]

No one should aspire to be the next Red Auerbach, for the "next" one does not exist. Michael was not the "next" anybody when he exploded into the NBA, and there may be no "next" Michael Jordan. Greatness is achieved by being different, innovative, and—above all—opportunistic. The NBA was a big man's game when Michael arrived, and he changed it. Heavyweight boxers were slow and deliberate until Ali arrived to combine middleweight speed with deceptive power. If anything, in retrospect the "next" Babe Ruth probably turned out to be Jordan, and therein lies the folly of predicting or manipulating the "next" of anything. The odds strongly suggest the next Michael Jordan may not be a basketball player at all. The "next" greatest, the next to capture the hearts of America, will explode out of another dimension, previously invisible until destiny chooses otherwise. Will it be Tiger Woods? Sammy Sosa? A football player? A new tennis star?

The tomfoolery of the Bulls' apparent scorched earth approach to basketball is that it fights opportunity at every juncture. Auerbach respected his players; to be a Celtic was to join a great family. Auerbach built new teams around revered, though aged, stars. To be a Celtic was a great thing during many green-and-parquet dynasties. This is the one characteristic of all perpetual winners: respect. John Wooden had it and gave it, as did Dean Smith, Vince Lombardi, and Tom Landry. With the greatest competitor in the history of basketball, and the best mentor of players great and small in its cerebral, honest coach, the Bulls are—or at least were—a team drenched in opportunity. But this was all lost on the Bulls organization, for there is one crucial element missing from team management's attitude toward its bread and butter, the players and coaches in the trenches: respect. Cross Krause, and you're out. That's it. Ask former Bulls trainer Chip Schaefer, former coach and mentor to Phil Jackson, Scottie Pippen, and even Michael Jordan, supporter of both Jackson and Pippen.

The Celtics were a warm family lavished in tradition and respect. The recent Bulls have become, at best, a dysfunctional family. They are a Tennessee Williams play, mired in self-pity, drunk with power, and compulsively married to form over substance. The near-term future of the Bulls is bleak, not because Krause cannot find a good player here and there—he can—but the trick will be to maintain the respect of that player once he proves himself. History would discourage optimism in this regard.

There is much more to the story of the NBA than the Chicago Bulls, of course, but the travails of those Bulls are symbolic of what the NBA has become. The whole league is in danger of becoming the "next" Citizen Kane (remember those nexts—they come from nowhere), driven by self-destructive egos on and off the court. Will "Citizen" Krause awaken one day pining for his own lost "rosebud"? Will the NBA wake up to appreciate its successes in spite of its egos? Ironically, the true *outrageous fortune* lies not with player salaries, but with the grand success of the whole league, a success that is in serious jeopardy because the power broker playmasters calling the shots are lost in a forest of magnificent athletes and marketing successes. To make matters worse, the scorched earth approach of the Bulls is not confined to Chicago. For the first time, the owners blinked and blinked hard, imposing a 1998 labor lockout, effectively burning their own field of dreams and money in a power struggle against the players. Maybe they won; maybe they did not.

Outrageous.

Indeed, could the slings and arrows of Hamlet's "outrageous fortune" possibly be more prophetic?

ENDNOTES

1. The 1999 labor agreement placed a firm cap on spending for players, negating much of the Larry Bird Rule, while the league as a whole got a grip on spiraling veteran salaries.
2. On April 28, 1967, Ali refused induction into the armed forces, citing his religious beliefs against the Vietnam War. His boxing title was immediately revoked, and the United States Government prosecuted Ali for draft evasion. Ali was eventually vindicated after a series of court battles and appeals, after which he regained the world championship by defeating Jerry Quarry in a three-round TKO in October 1970.
3. Mr. Krause was asked to comment for this book. He declined.
4. From management's perspective the motive could have been money—not altogether irrational since Michael's salary had become almost four times the net income of the whole organization—but still the peculiar carnage displayed in the ouster of Jackson, Jordan, and Pippen was curious at best.

2

A LEAGUE IS BORN

Baseball was a half-century old (more or less, depending upon who gets credit for inventing the pastime) when Dr. James A. Naismith tacked up a pair of peach baskets in December of 1891, hoping to invent a new indoor sport at a YMCA college in Springfield, Massachusetts. As a teacher of boxing, wrestling, canoeing, and swimming at the Y, Naismith was no stranger to the sports world. In addition to teaching, he actually played on the school football team and, remarkably, is credited with inventing the original football helmet—demonstrating, one supposes, a proclivity toward invention.[1]

Luck is the residue of design.

—BRANCH RICKEY

Basketball was not the magical result of sudden creative inspiration; rather, it was more a function of necessity being the proverbial mother of invention. Naismith had been ordered by school administrators to invent an indoor athletic contest that could be played by artificial lighting to occupy a particularly rowdy YMCA class during winter months. After endless experimentation with variations of rugby and soccer, both of which were much too rough, Naismith decided to raise the scoring goal to perhaps dilute some of the physical force necessary to score via ground-based goals. Armed with his ball of choice, an American soccer ball, Naismith summoned a school janitor to retrieve a pair of 18-inch boxes to tack onto the gym's upper balcony railing. No boxes were available, but the now famous peach baskets emerged and were affixed to the railing, which, as history and luck would have it, were exactly 10 feet from the floor. Thus the all-time standard basketball rim height the world over was a function of pure accident, fiat, luck: peach "baskets," not boxes, inspired the name *basketball* (not *boxball*, thankfully), and the 10-foot rim was dictated by the height of a random railing somewhere in Springfield, Massachusetts. And, of course, none of this would have occurred in the first place had the 1891–92 YMCA class been better behaved in winter months.

Naismith sketched out 13 original rules, several of which were designed to mitigate the inevitable rough play. In an obvious counter to the roughness of football and rugby, one such rule prevented running with the ball. Another rule defining the concept of the "foul" was more direct:

> No shouldering, holding, pushing, tripping, or striking in any way the person of an opponent shall be allowed; the first infringement of this rule by any person shall count as a foul, the second shall disqualify him until the next goal is made, or, if there is evident intent to injure the person, for the whole of the game, no substitute allowed.

Naismith, then, was both the original and ultimate playmaster, dictating the guts of the game from dribbling, defining and penalizing fouls, creating a 10-foot basket, and even prescribing the approximate size of today's ball. And given the original purpose of the game—to occupy and control rowdy students during the winter months—there is an ironic legacy of subtle manipulation that would follow the game from its inception to the volatile 1990s, one day inviting constant tampering to control players and fans and to maximize entertainment value and eventually profits at the pro level.

With Naismith's innovation, the turn-of-the-century playmasters were off and running. Soon the notion of backboards emerged, not to enhance scoring but to control the crowds. Old gymnasiums were often built with a ring of protruding balconies to maximize capacity, thrusting some spectators near the baskets, where they took pleasure in interfering with the shots. Thus, the backboard was implemented as a barrier to rowdy fans and not as a conduit for making a wider array of shots as it is used in the modern game.

Early changes emerged quickly as the game itself evolved into the five-man team approach. At first the famous peach baskets did not have holes, so the problem of retrieving the ball was significant. Apparently obsessed with ball retrieval, early basketball games were played with a net or other form of cage around the perimeter of the entire court, thus the odd, now antiquated nickname *cagers* for basketball players.

The cage was a wire mesh or net device 12 feet high (or much more in some cases) completely engulfing the court. It was first used by what appears to be the first pro basketball team, a group from New Jersey with an excruciatingly unimaginative name: the Trenton Basketball Team. The cage certainly kept all balls in play, but that was clearly not its only purpose. During the 1890s basketball had taken on a decidedly rough personality, and the net served three other distinct purposes: one, to protect the courtside crowd; two, to enhance physical play as players bounced off the cage, somewhat like pro ice hockey; and, three, to speed up the action as a side benefit to keeping the ball in play at all times. Derisive nicknames notwithstanding (the first device was called the "Trenton monkey cage"), the cage idea caught on rapidly.

Basketball quickly gained popularity and eventually spread to many other schools. Within five years of basketball's invention, the first intercollegiate game employing the 10-man format took place with Penn losing to Yale 32–10. Six years after that landmark contest, a child was born in England who would one day change the game forever with flair and style: Abe Saperstein. A youthful Saperstein would eventually find his way to America, but, as fate would have it, he was destined to grow to no more than 5 feet in height. Despite of his lack of stature, or perhaps even because of it, Abe proved to be a fierce competitor in at least three high school sports, one being basketball. Saperstein longed to continue in college, but the University of Illinois refused the diminutive player an opportunity to try out, even though many early players were of average height. Not to be denied, he eventually landed a position on a team of semipro cagers called the Chicago Reds.

By 1926, a 23-year-old Saperstein found himself running an all-black collection of basketball players known simply as the Savoy Big Five (another remarkably uninspired title), taken from the team's home court in Chicago's Savoy Ballroom. In early January the following year, Abe took his band of Savoy athletes on the road, if one could call it that, to perform in tiny Hinckley, Illinois, a country burg too far removed from the Windy City to be regarded a suburb—even today. About 300 spectators turned out for the show, launching Abe's traveling team with a windfall gate share of $75.

Abe took the money and the team on the road again, scraping together bookings around the Midwest, often in small towns peppered throughout Illinois, Michigan, and Ohio. Although Abe passed away in 1966, the team was still at it in 1998, playing its twenty-thousandth game at the Tri-County High School gym before 3,500 jam-packed enthusiastic fans in nondescript Remington, Indiana, a farm community hiding somewhere between Indianapolis and Chicago. In between, the team hit 114 different countries (maybe more?), befitting of its one label that stuck: the Globetrotters (decidedly more creative than its first name, Saperstein's New York, later modified to Saperstein's Harlem New York).

At first its ambitious label didn't mean much—the team failed to travel farther than western Pennsylvania during the entire decade of the 1930s—but Abe combined "Harlem" with "Globetrotters," achieving an ironic Big Apple tag for his Chicago barnstormers. Stocked with very talented athletes performing at peak athletic levels, today's Globetrotters are more for entertainment than competition, basketball exhibitions instead of league play (although on a recent European tour they were 15-0 in legitimate games). But at one time they were dominant in all facets of the sport, playing up to 175 games a year and winning almost all of them. In fact, the paucity of close games inspired the players to develop flashy styles, take chances, and develop routines that not only evolved into the contemporary Globetrotter motif but set the stage for the glitzy brand of fast-paced modern streetball and eventual NBA play. This, then, is the real legacy of the Globetrotters: combining superior athletic performance with entertaining competition. Show business. Glamour—the now distant forerunner to a modern National Basketball Association entertainment dynamo.

The Globetrotters were a legitimate contender during the '30s and '40s, losing by four points in a world championship tournament in 1939 and then winning it all over the Chicago Bruins of the National Basketball League the following year. By 1951 they went truly international with their unique brand of uptempo ball, flashy dribbling, and vaudeville shtick, entertaining fans across oceans and continents as ambassadors of basketball, goodwill, and America itself.

Although the stylish Globetrotters were the flashiest pro team, they certainly were not the first or necessarily even the best, especially during the Roaring Twenties. Soon after the Trenton Basketball Team had emerged in 1896, the first pro league was developed in 1898. There was even an early team called the "Globe Trotters" (actually the Basloe Globe Trotters, so named for their owner) and a provincial New York bunch named the Original Celtics. (Did they think there would be other Celtics—thus the adjective "original"?)

Indeed these Original Celtics would be the dominant team of the 1920s, an era of big-time sports in America with even bigger household names: Ruth, Dempsey, Red Grange, and Bobby Jones, to name a few. Actually, these Celtics trace their history to a Manhattan settlement house for teenagers in 1914. In 1918, James A. Furey, an experienced promoter, acquired the team and hired manager Frank McCormack. The team proceeded to dominate the competition, going 65–4 under Furey and McCormack's stewardship, drawing New York crowds of four to five thousand per game. Their best competition in those days was provided by the rival New York Whirlwinds, an innovative team that was the very first to sign a player from the college ranks: Barney Sedran, a towering 6′4″ star from the City College of New York. The Whirlwinds were organized, owned, and controlled by one of the biggest boxing promoters of the era, one Tex Rickard, the man behind many of the Jack Dempsey million-dollar fights. Rickard helped promote a three-game championship between the Celtics and Whirlwinds in 1921, the first game drawing an impressive eleven thousand fans who saw the Whirlwinds prevail 40–27. The Celtics won the second game by two points, but the teams left it at that, failing to play the rubber game of the series.

Basketball was taking over America. By the middle of the decade, some 93 percent of all high schools had organized teams. However, except for the Celtics and Whirlwinds, many pro teams began to struggle. One likely explanation was the double dribble. Most pro leagues allowed the players to bulldoze the ball upcourt, using the double dribble where necessary. The effect was rugby-like assault that even included head-butting (long before the technique was briefly resurrected by Dennis Rodman). The game became awkward and slow, sometimes resembling a scrum more than a basketball contest by the onset of the 1930s.

Meanwhile, the college game continued to evolve, emphasizing ball movement and passing, speed and agility. Then, in 1925–26, a new pro league surfaced adopting the style of college play, dumping the double dribble and placing a renewed premium on a clever passing attack. The smoother method of play was more entertaining, developing an identity, a sense of basketball purity just beginning to find itself. This new American Basketball League (ABL) was the death knell to the older rough-and-tumble approach. Although new on the block, the ABL did not lack sports marketing savvy. The ABL's first president was Joseph F. Carr, president of the National Football League. The NFL, though still in its own infancy at five years and counting, was nonetheless a good proving ground for those interested in this new pro basketball league.

Other notables in the ABL hierarchy included NFL founder and Chicago Bears owner George Halas, George Preston Marshall (a future owner of the Washington Redskins), and department store mogul Max Rosenblum of Cleveland, respectively spearheading three of the original ABL basketball teams: the Chicago Bruins, the Palace Five, and, of course, the Cleveland Rosenblums. (Anyone who believes only modern owners sport large egos evidently never heard of the Rosenblums. So far the modern sports era has yet to endure the likes of, say, the New York Steinbrenners, Chicago Reinsdorfs, or Atlanta Turners.)

The remainder of the ABL teams included such memorable franchises as the Brooklyn Arcadians, Buffalo Bisons, Fort Wayne Caseys, an American Legion entry called the Detroit Pulaski Post, and the Boston Whirlwinds. The New York Celtics also joined the new league, which by 1927 had expanded into two divisions. The formidable Celtics ran up a 40–9 division record to win the East, while the Fort Wayne Hoosiers took the West over the nifty Rosenblums. The Celtics eventually won the championship that year, taking three of four from the Hoosiers.

As the new league grew, it continued to refine itself and its approach to basketball. For the 1927–28 season, it adopted a five-foul disqualification rule to further check on court roughness. The following year, the Rosenblums won the title, and major stars were beginning to make good money, sometimes approaching five figures for the year. But fate finally caught up in 1929, when the stunning October stock market crash ushered the decade-long Great Depression. As the 1930s emerged, pro basketball attendance dwindled. Five-cent movies were cheaper entertainment, not to mention more uplifting given the harsh times. Hollywood prospered in the 1930s with a decade of blockbuster musicals chiefly because the public ratcheted down its entertainment spending to the best value available: movies.

Meanwhile, the pro basketball teams managed to degenerate into wrestling matches under the basket. Loose ball fouls did not exist as a violation, so all the pushing and shoving away from the ball produced a good deal more mayhem than legitimate basketball (a harbinger of things to come in the modern NBA?). A team called the Brooklyn Visitations was especially nasty, trotting out villain Willie Scrill—perhaps the original Charles Barkley or Rodman—who proceeded to push and shove from the opening jump. Borrowing from both football and wrestling, the nastiest pros would employ straight arms and headlocks, reducing the sport to shambles.

By 1933, fate and rough play had finally done in the old ABL, although regional variations would attempt a modest go at it from time to time. College ball did not die, however, for its ticket prices remained modest and, most significant, the play remained fast, clean, and entertaining. The pro game had become a dribbling scrum of sorts, while amateur play embraced crisp passing and speed.

As in many sports and indeed most industries, racism was another factor contributing to the legacy of basketball as the Depression years wore on. In stark contrast to professional baseball, there were no "negro leagues" in basketball. As a result, two all-black barnstorming teams emerged in the 1930s: the Renaissance Five and the Harlem Globetrotters. Although the fragmented regional leagues that survived were all white, the black barnstormers were not relegated to playing each other. The white teams were eager to take them on, for the public loved the excitement and drama of white versus black competition—perhaps for the wrong reasons—and attendance soared for these games.

The 1930s moved forward with little change in the pro basketball landscape. Although the Depression ended by the early 1940s, America was soon distracted by World War II, a preoccupation that would linger nearly four years. But then four vectors of history and social change converged all at once during the later half of the decade, all of which would contribute to the birth of a contemporary NBA. First, World War II ended in 1945, unleashing a pent-up public demand for entertainment, fun, economic growth, and unprecedented prosperity. In 1945, Branch Rickey signed African American Jackie Robinson to begin play in the Dodgers farm system. Robinson would be named Rookie of the Year as a Brooklyn Dodger in 1947, quashing racial concerns at least about the *abilities* of black athletes but, of course, not eliminating racism itself. And, of direct significance to basketball, a very big young man who had been recruited to play basketball by first-year coach Ray Meyer at Chicago's DePaul University turned pro in 1946: George Mikan. The 6'10" Mikan had become the original basketball superstar at DePaul under the watchful, caring tutelage of Meyer. The youthful Mikan would become an All-American three times, collegiate player of the year twice, and the national scoring leader twice. He was MVP of the prestigious NIT tournament in 1945, scoring 120 points in three games, including a crushing defeat of runner-up Rhode Island in the championship game.

Remarkably, Mikan singlehandedly matched the scoring total of Rhode Island's entire team in that game—53 points—as DePaul rolled to victory 97–53.

George Mikan began his pro career with the Chicago American Gears of the embryonic National Basketball League (NBL). After the Gears collapsed, he moved on to the Minneapolis Lakers of the same league. Leading the league in scoring and the Lakers to the championship, Mikan was awarded the league MVP.

Mikan's NBL had been formed in 1937. A resurrected ABL was put back together briefly in 1945, but it folded for good by 1947, with one franchise hanging on to merge into the Basketball Association of America (BAA), a rival league formed in 1946. The NBL, which was first called the Midwest Basketball Conference, was an amalgam of company teams such as the Akron Goodyear Regulars and the Fort Wayne General Electrics, plus a variety of owner-operated teams identified by the names of their founders: the Indianapolis Kautskys, the Whiting Ciesars, and the Warren Hyvis Oils. The owner and coach for the latter was Gerry Archibald, a part-time player for the team who had more than his share of basketball blood in his veins: he happened to be the son of Lyman W. Archibald, one of the malcontents in Dr. Naismith's original basketball class of 1891–92.

Archibald would soon move his franchise to Detroit as the Detroit Eagles. They did very well there, losing the Eastern Division title to none other than the Akron Firestone Nonskids, a team obviously in need of a better name and a more imaginative creative department. World War II depleted the crop of available players, so necessity inspired the NBL to integrate and utilize black players to fill the ranks, a practice first deployed by the Chicago Studebakers. Although named for a now defunct automobile, the Studebakers were not backed by the car company but, rather, the UAW union chapter at the Chicago facility. All the integrated Studebaker players worked at the car plant, which, by this time, had converted over to wartime production, exempting all the players from the military draft. The integrated teams encountered the typical racial strife of the times, not so much internally but in their interaction with the many communities on the road. Eating together in restaurants, even in the North, was often problematic, and staying together in hotels was sometimes impossible. Nonetheless, the teams and league plodded along, playing basketball and scratching out a living.

As the war ended, teams began to proliferate. The NBL expanded out of the Midwest with the addition of the Rochester Royals, a decent team stacked with good former college players and sporting a number of players who would later acquire fame, if not fortunes, in and out of basketball. This group included none other than Red Holzman, who would later coach the NBA Knicks to two world championships; the lanky, lean, muscled Chuck Connors who would later headline TV's "Rifleman" series; and Otto Graham, the eventual All-Pro quarterback of the Cleveland Browns.

Just before George Mikan entered DePaul University, the pro teams were not especially tall, though they were headed in that direction. In 1937, there were only 6 players above 6′5″ in the whole 13-team league; by 1940 there were 9 such players scattered throughout fewer teams. By 1946, 25 players topped the 6′5″ level, inspiring occasional cries to raise the basket height, none of which succeeded.[2] At 6′10″ George Mikan was certainly big, although he was not the first big man around; but he did evolve into the first big center to combine adequate (but not spectacular) athleticism with a fundamental knowledge of the game and a superior competitive attitude. Those combined attributes would not only make him the first basketball superstar, they would help propel the entire NBA in its early years, much the way Red Grange did for the NFL and as Julius Erving did for the ABA two decades after Mikan.

Although he began with the Gears for a hefty $60,000 over five years, Mikan's lasting fame would come as a Minneapolis Laker. In 1949, the NBL and the BAA merged, combining players, teams, and even acronyms to become the NBA: the first and only National Basketball Association. Although 9 of the original 17 teams would fail by 1954, the survivors began to earn dividends from an emerging new medium capable of generating big sports dollars: television. By 1960, NBA franchises were commanding $200,000, a hefty sum for the fledgling league.

The roots of many current NBA teams can be found in the annals of the BAA. Each of the original BAA teams was owned by a local stadium or arena. For example, the Boston Celtics were originally owned by Boston Garden, which also operated the National Hockey League Boston Bruins. The Chicago Stags were likewise owned by the Chicago Stadium, which also had the NHL Blackhawks. Other teams could be found in Cleveland, Detroit, Philadelphia, and New York, the latter called the Knickerbockers. Those Knicks started out with a bang at Madison Square Garden as more than seventeen thousand fans witnessed a ten-point loss to the Chicago Stags. All 11 teams that started the season stayed afloat long enough to finish the year, although average attendance figures ran as low as three thousand per game with actual paid attendance significantly lower than that.

True to form, the venerable George Mikan would lead the Minneapolis Lakers to the first "combined" NBA title in 1949–50. One of Mikan's teammates would gain greater fame, if not fortune, in the football arena: Bud Grant, who would eventually coach the Minnesota Vikings football team to four Super Bowls. The Celtics, though, were slowly building the foundation for a dynasty, landing legends Bob Cousy and Billy Sharman. With the pro sports color barrier already broken by Jackie Robinson, the NBA began adding black players in 1950. Although white owners were somewhat reluctant to step on the toes of Abe Saperstein, whose Globetrotters were a huge draw when they played the white BAA and NBA teams, the NBA owners could not resist the vast pool of black talent. In particular, the Knickerbockers coveted Globetrotter star Sweetwater Clifton, a big man with a bigger attitude.[3] Eventually the Knicks won over Sweetwater, and so the age of raiding superstar free agents was well under way. The first time a black player actually appeared in a regulation game was October 31, 1950: Earl Lloyd for the Washington Capitols. Sweetwater and the others were soon to follow, by a matter of only days in some cases.

One footnote to history: by 1961, the Globetrotters and the NBA had come full circle. Abe Saperstein made an effort to purchase an NBA franchise but was turned down by the league.

ENDNOTES

1. During his gridiron days Naismith found himself playing next to a future football legend, Amos Alonzo Stagg.
2. Had the baskets been raised, no slam-dunk NBA could have evolved, depressing the entertainment value of games. But higher baskets probably would have opened the court up to a speedier sport consisting of motion, spacing, and shooting—in effect creating the women's basketball game of the 1990s.
3. I climbed into a Chicago cab one day, perhaps in the early 1980s, only to discover the driver was none other than Sweetwater himself. A huge man, Sweetwater proved as personable as he was large, a proud man who was before his time, at least in terms of reaping the vast financial rewards that loomed ahead for modern NBA stars.

3

DR. J AND THE ABA

Al McGuire was the longtime coach of the Marquette (then Warriors) NCAA Division I men's basketball team. He was a players' coach. On the eve of his retirement in 1977, he would win a national title with a gutsy bunch of kids who could play, listen, and perform at crunch time: for, above all, they loved their vibrant coach McGuire. So they just sucked it up and bucked the odds, taking on all comers until they had captured a national title for their brassy but hamish mentor, a New York street kid at heart who sported a lovable accent thicker than the East River.

Who the hell is that kid out there?

— AL McGUIRE

McGuire later brought a rainbow of colorful words to his commentator role as a national broadcaster. He was John Madden even before Madden was, spinning whimsical tales of players and playgrounds as each game wore on. He salted each telecast with insight and playful descriptive phrases, referring to the big men down low as "aircraft carriers." As recounted by Wayne Embry, former Celtics center and later Milwaukee Bucks GM, "Who the hell is that kid out there?" was McGuire's spontaneous exclamation upon first witnessing a certain skinny, unknown New York kid with more moves than a ballet dancer.

Marquette had the misfortune of playing Massachusetts in a first-round NIT game. As McGuire watched the magical leaps, spins, and lightning moves of the mystery kid, UMass ran up a 12–0 lead on the Warriors with two-thirds of those points scored by one nearly anonymous Julius Erving. According to Embry's account, McGuire excitedly called timeout, ranting hysterically about the magical Erving, who had appeared from nowhere. "Julius who? What d'ya mean *Julius*?" McGuire exclaimed. Assistant coach Hank Raymonds muttered something about the kid hailing from New York, so McGuire grabbed one of his players from the Big Apple, guard Dean Meminger, and demanded answers.

Trouble was, nobody ever did find an answer to Julius, later known as "the Doctor," some say because he could singlehandedly cure any deficiency of points. Julius was the missing basketball link—except maybe for the "missing" part—because he was a throwback to the flashy Globetrotters and at the same time represented the future of the high-flying, slam-bam, in-your-face NBA.

A transcendental conspiracy of fate and luck once brought me a fleeting firsthand glimpse of the basketball promised land at a gala thrown by Oprah Winfrey to celebrate the birthday of her beau, Stedman Graham. Held at the Wrigley (as in Cubs and chewing gum) mansion on Chicago's near north side, the party was invaded by an army of celebrities (like Ernie Banks), wannabes, and "others" (yours truly). Crawling with Cubs, Bears, entertainers, and media moguls, it was difficult to imagine a more impressive gathering.

And then it happened. As I leaned on a magnificent banister of the first-floor grand staircase, the stately front doors opened not 30 feet away to reveal the reigning king of all celebrities: none other than His Airness, Superman, Michael J. Jordan. The silence was at once stunning and profound. The bustling commotion came to a sudden halt as all eyes turned, followed by excited whispers as news of MJ's arrival burned its way from room to room, floor to floor. Even a mansion full of diamonds, pearls, gold chains, $500 perms, and God knows what else came to such a complete standstill that the basketball messiah must have arrived—and well he did, I suppose. Meticulously dressed and wearing the patented Jordan smile, MJ glided with grace and style through the forest of onlookers, fans, colleagues, and friends.

But wait. That was not all. Who was the genteel distinguished escort with Michael, striding along, side by side, fully confident, totally at ease with his own celebrity and that of his great above-the-rim companion?

Dr. J had arrived as well. Dressed to kill and perhaps an inch taller than Michael, Julius Erving beamed as Michael's eyes glistened. It was all too fitting, these two crashing the party of the year, arm in arm not just with each other, but with history. Erving invented Michael's game. Not Michael himself, nor all of Michael's unique game, but enough of it to deserve an anointed position in the annals of basketball greatness. Could Julius have been the first Michael? Yes—but then again, no, of course. Julius was the first Dr. J, Michael the first Michael, Ali the first and only . . . and so on. But neither the NBA nor Michael Jordan would or could have been the same without the grace, speed, character, and innovation of Julius "the Doctor" Erving. He may not have invented Michael, but he did invent the best of contemporary NBA basketball, wresting it from the big man era of yesteryear.

On November 22, 1950, soon after the NBA was created, big man George Mikan scored all but three of his team's points in a one-point Lakers loss at the hands of the Fort Wayne Pistons. An impressive feat, of course, but its significance is tempered by the final score itself: 19-18, the lowest-scoring game in NBA history. But throughout the 1960s and 1970s the game would belong to the behemoths underneath, Al McGuire's aircraft carriers, who would dominate basketball until the late 1980s as the bad boy Detroit Pistons pushed, shoved, punched, and kicked their way to a pair of NBA titles.

Although Mikan invented the dominant center position, the ultimate big man was undoubtedly Wilt Chamberlain, a monstrous presence with quick feet, strong shoulders, and a fearsome, take-no-prisoners attitude. Wilt "the Stilt" Chamberlain was variously listed as 7′1″ or 7′2″ in height, weighing just under 300 pounds during the course of his NBA career. Even as a teenager in high school he had sprouted to 6′11″, the same height as today's youthful Kevin Garnett. But in Chamberlain's early days, he was an unstoppable force. Like Garnett, Wilt was drafted directly from high school by the NBA, in his case to the Warriors. Unlike Garnett, however, Wilt could not actually play pro ball directly from high school, for the NBA then had a rule against signing players until either their four-year college eligibility was exhausted or their respective college classes would graduate four years hence (if the player had failed to attend college at all).[1]

Instead, Wilt attended Kansas after graduating high school in 1955. His presence was immediately telegraphed throughout the conference with an explosive 52-point showing in his very first intercollegiate game. Chamberlain's NBA debut season with the Philadelphia Warriors in 1959 was even more impressive. Not only was he Rookie of the Year, he was the league MVP and scoring leader by a wide margin at 37.6 points per game. Second place belonged to Jack Twyman at 31.2. For good measure, Wilt added the rebounding title to his first-year collection of awards, averaging a remarkable 27 boards per game. The great Bill Russell was second at 24, still very impressive given that Dennis Rodman, the perennial leader of the 1990s, hauled down around 16 per game. (A few other good names made the 1959 list: Bob Pettit with 17 per game and Elgin Baylor with 16.4. Seventh was big man John "Red" Kerr at 12.2 rebounds per game for Syracuse. Kerr would later become the first coach of the Chicago Bulls.)

Chamberlain's feats were a quantum leap for the NBA. Everything he did was historic, and much of it still is. The guards of the day were not big and strong; they were even on the frail side, like Bob Cousy. And even most of the big men were not behemoths, although at 6′9″ or so the Celtics' tenacious Russell often gave Wilt fits. For the most part, though, Wilt was a colossus among the rank and file, rather like today's Alonzo Mourning playing in a 6′4″-and-under league.

Mikan had set the stage for the early NBA: big is better. Chamberlain then reinforced it—or, rather, reinvented it, taking the big man ideal to a new level. Consider one of the more playful trivia questions of all time: Who scored the most points ever in a regular season NBA game? Answer: Wilt Chamberlain. OK, so who scored the *second*-highest total? Answer: Wilt Chamberlain. In fact, Wilt has the top 4 scoring games (100 points, 78, and 73 twice) and 32 of the top 50. The 100-point effort against New York on March 2, 1962 (36 field goals and 28 free throws, with no overtimes), might have been the all-time quantum leap of pro basketball as the Warriors beat the Knicks 169–147. (Although New York certainly had no 100-point scorers, it did have three different players score over 30 points in the game for a combined total of 103—not a bad effort in itself.)

Wilt also holds the record for most rebounds in one game (55), but Bill Russell hangs tough at second (51) and third (49—twice). Of the top 12 rebounding games in history, Chamberlain has 8, Russell 4, the rest of the league 0. Nate Thurmond, a notable big man from the old San Francisco Warriors, sneaks into thirteenth place with 42 boards against Detroit on November 9, 1965, but then the next eight slots in a row belong to Russell and Chamberlain again.

Although there were plenty of top-notch guards in the early days from Cousy to Oscar Robertson, John Havlicek, and a few others, the beginning years were dominated by big players: George Mikan, Moses Malone, Elvin Hayes, Wes Unseld, Artis Gilmore, Willis Reed, and Bob Pettit, in addition to Russell and Chamberlain. In fact, Pettit won the first league MVP award, and guard Cousy the second; but after that, every MVP from 1958 until 1980 was awarded to a center or a big forward (including Russell five times, Chamberlain four, and Kareem Abdul-Jabbar six), except for one award to Oscar Robertson in 1964, himself a big, strong guard/small forward.

Chamberlain, then, may have become the first on-court playmaster, dominating the game and dictating the character of NBA basketball for at least 10 years himself, but influencing the game with a continuing big man mentality that would not fade until the 1980s with Magic Johnson (a big guard) and Michael Jordan, himself destined to become a playmaster. The distinction between great player and playmaster extends beyond the court and encompasses a myriad of analyses, but the conclusion can be easily summarized by one observation. When Chamberlain played, the battle cry of every other NBA team was to "find the next Chamberlain," and they looked everywhere, from Nate Thurmond to Ralph Sampson. Now it is in vogue to try to "find the next Jordan." But noticeably little psychic energy has been exhausted in searches for the next Pettit, Jerry Lucas, Patrick Ewing, or even Larry Bird. From Stackhouse to Iverson, Hill to Miner, and even Garnett, the next Jordan is perennially just around the corner—but, of course, the next MJ never quite shows up. Naturally. The next dominant player will be "the first" *someone*, for he will bring a unique style to the game, influencing basketball the way Chamberlain and Jordan did.

Shaquille O'Neal presents an interesting study. He was Rookie of the Year in 1992–93 and certainly combines size and athleticism in a way that no other center has quite managed since Chamberlain himself. But unlike Chamberlain, Shaq may have landed in the wrong era. In 1959 he actually *would have been Chamberlain.* (Among other things, they have missed free throws in common; in fact, Wilt also holds the all-time record for missed free throws in one game at 22.) But, alas, in 1993 and beyond, Shaq might really be the *last* Chamberlain, a big man caught in an emerging era of motion, speed, and passing. Time, perhaps, will tell with certainty.

Chamberlain himself had not been "the next" anyone; nor has Jordan. Who is to say, for instance, that "the next" will be a player at all? How about a revolutionary coach who changes how basketball is played? Or perhaps a different kind of player who reinvents the game, like a 7-foot guard who shoots over everyone? The last possibility might seem absurd, but in perspective is no more preposterous than a skinny guard named Michael coming from nowhere to dominate a league of 7-foot centers. If the notion of a 7-foot guard still seems ludicrous, consider the Bulls' Toni Kukoc, a 6'11" shooter whose best natural position may really be point guard. But as noted before, perhaps the next MJ will not even be in basketball. Will he be a golfer such as Tiger Woods, a pitcher like Kerry Wood, or a hitter the caliber of Sammy Sosa or Mark McGwire? Or maybe even a boxer the likes of Ali, who reinvented heavyweight boxing by combining lightning footwork and hand speed with size (6'3"). Or a football player. Gale Sayers was probably "the greatest" in the making, but a career-ending injury denied him playmaster status, even though he may have been the best pure runner of all time, combining strength, speed, and football instinct perhaps like no other before or since.

Could the next MJ be a basketball player, but not originate in the NBA? A woman, perhaps? How about a female player so remarkable that she becomes the first woman to crack the men's NBA? But if not a female player, then at least a player from another league may emerge somewhere, somehow.

Julius Erving. Again, the tables of history come full circle. As the eventual link between Chamberlain's day and Jordan's contemporary style, the Doctor himself did not surface first in the NBA. While Chamberlain ground his way to an astonishing 118 games of 50-plus points (that's nearly one and one-half *seasons*' worth) plus one string of 65 *straight* games at 30-plus, Julius Erving landed in the upstart American Basketball Association, spinning, flying, and soaring to new heights of basketball wizardry.

At the time, the big men were mired in the NBA, so the ABA had no choice but to up the tempo and, to some extent, invent a whole new game. But where did the ABA itself come from? How did it emerge from the shadows of Chamberlain, Russell, Cousy, and the NBA?

Enter Globetrotter Abe Saperstein once again. By 1961 he was a believer in the NBA, which, at the time, was selling new franchises for $200,000 each. As a longtime basketball innovator and marketing impresario, Saperstein was a natural for the NBA. But to his profound disappointment, he was turned down in his bid to acquire the rights to a team. Not being one to take defeat in stride, in 1961 Abe founded the new American Basketball League to compete with the NBA.

It was a stormy undertaking to say the least, landing Saperstein's ABL in court against the NBA when star player Dick Barnett attempted to jump leagues. Barnett was the number-one draft choice of the NBA Syracuse Nationals in 1959 and played for the Nationals through the 1960–61 season under the terms of a standard NBA player contract. In July of 1961, however, Barnett inked a different deal with the Cleveland Basketball Club, Inc., a member of Saperstein's new ABL doing business as the Cleveland Pipers. It was a one-year deal commencing September 15, 1961.

At that time, the NBA maintained pro teams in New York City, Philadelphia, Syracuse, Boston, Detroit, Cincinnati, Chicago, St. Louis, and Los Angeles. The new ABL had a presence in Washington, Pittsburgh, Cleveland, Chicago, Kansas City, San Francisco, Los Angeles, and Hawaii. Syracuse took offense to the move, suing Barnett for breach of contract and the Cleveland Pipers for interference with contract. Syracuse demanded, among other things, an injunction to prevent Barnett from playing in and for Cleveland.

During the 1960–61 season with Syracuse, Barnett was paid the princely sum of $8,500. Syracuse argued that the payment was partial consideration for an option to renew Barnett's deal for 1961–62. This was the principal bone of contention since Barnett's contract with Syracuse had expired by the time he had signed up with Cleveland in July of 1961. Barnett admitted to extensive negotiations with the Nationals for the 1961–62 season, even discussing a higher salary in the range of $11,500, but never coming to terms on either a new contract or a renewal of the old one. The March 16 agreement that *was* signed by Barnett and Syracuse contained a number of provisions, including these:

5. The Player promises and agrees (a) to report at the time and place fixed by the Club in good physical condition; and (b) to keep himself throughout the entire season in good physical condition; and (c) to give his best services, as well as his loyalty, to the Club, and to play basketball only for the Club unless released, sold or exchanged by the Club; and (d) to be neatly and fully attired in public and always to conduct himself on and off the court according to the highest standards of honesty, morality, fair play and sportsmanship, and (e) not to do anything which is detrimental to the best interests of the Club or of the National Basketball Association or of professional sports.

22. (a) On or before September 1st (or if a Sunday, then the next preceding business day) next following the last playing season covered by this contract, the Club may tender to the Player a contract for the term of that season by mailing the same to the Player at his address following his signature hereto, or if none

be given then at his last address of record with the Club. If prior to the November 1, next succeeding said September 1, the Player and the Club have not agreed upon the terms of such contract, then on or before 10 days after said November 1, the Club shall have the right by written notice to the Player at said address to renew this contract for the period of one year on the same terms, except that the amount payable to the Player shall be such as the Club shall fix in said notice; provided, however, that said amount shall be an amount payable at a rate not less than 75% of the rate stipulated for the preceding year.

These two sections are notable for three reasons. First, the absurd ends to which the top paragraph goes regarding dress codes, morality, and player conduct established a hostile environment for players under the extreme control of ownership. Second, taken together they represent the worst in legalese, fabricating a word structure that few rational humans could discern without a flowchart and a computer. Third, the last part of the second section seems to have been lifted from the Major League Baseball reserve clause, especially the part about the 75 percent renewal floor. This is interesting, if not significant, for 15 years later Dodger Andy Messersmith would finally defeat the almighty baseball reserve system by arguing the plain meaning of the words and the illogic of forcing a series of renewals at 75 percent of the original salary: eventually the salary would approach zero, an absurd reading of the clause.

Fifteen years before Messersmith, though, the Ohio courts would tackle the NBA reserve clause in the Barnett case. According to sworn testimony of Syracuse president and general manager Daniel Biasone, he told Barnett in March of 1961 that Barnett would be one of seven players protected from the upcoming NBA expansion draft necessary to create a new team in Chicago. At that time, he and Barnett discussed a $3,000 salary increase and, according to the GM, Barnett said, "You mail [the contracts] down, and I will sign them and return them." On cross-examination Biasone admitted he was "not sure" and did not know whether Barnett said "I will sign." Barnett, however, was precise in both his recollection and testimony in court:

Question: What did he say?

Barnett: Well, he called me up and said that he wanted to discuss contracts for the coming year.

Question: What did you say?

Barnett: I said I thought I was worth $3,000 more.

Question: And he said?

Barnett: He agreed. He said, "I think you are worth $3,000 more myself." I said, "Send the contracts and I will look them over."

New contracts were drawn up and signed by Syracuse and mailed to Barnett on May 26, 1961, where they remained unsigned. Biasone neither received the signed contracts back nor even heard from Barnett, so on November 6, 1961, Biasone mailed a letter to Barnett including the following language:

It is our position that your 1960-61 contract with us was renewed when we came to terms and we sent you an advance. However, to abide by the letter of the contract and to make the position of the Syracuse Nationals absolutely clear, we hereby notify you that pursuant to Paragraph 22(a) of said contract, we hereby renew the same for the period of one year ending October 1, 1962. The amount payable to you under such renewed contract is hereby fixed at $11,500.

In the meantime, Barnett met with his former coach and advisor John B. McLendon, now the coach of the Cleveland Pipers from the ABL. Although Barnett desired to play for Cleveland, he and the coach were reluctant to commit until a pending California case addressing a separate attempt to jump leagues was decided. Relying upon an eventual news report that they interpreted as favorable, Barnett and Cleveland inked a deal, leaving the Syracuse Nationals out in the cold.

Syracuse sued to enforce its reserve clause and enjoin the switch. Citing an archaic Pennsylvania case concerning old-time baseball player Nap Lajoie, the Ohio court agreed with Syracuse, forcing Barnett to stay put and denying the state of Ohio (via the

Cleveland Pipers) the talents of Dick Barnett. The court was probably wrong, adhering to old thinking that favored owner rights over player freedom, even to the point of ignoring simple contract law. There was no meeting of the minds—no contract—between Barnett and Syracuse, and the Syracuse renewal option was weak to nonexistent. Along the way, Barnett did everything he could to prevent the court from enjoining his switch to Cleveland, in some cases probably overdoing it at the expense of his credibility.

To obtain an injunction, a plaintiff must show a likelihood of irreparable harm, the potential loss of something irreplaceable by money damages. The Syracuse Nationals had the upper hand on this part of the case, for one would think Barnett would be regarded as much more than fungible property. Nonetheless, Barnett himself argued in court that he was not unique or exceptional and, therefore, there was no practical need or legal mandate to prevent him from jumping to the Cleveland Pipers. Even though Barnett was a first-round draft pick and league star, he testified in court and under oath as to the precise opposite, demonstrating a remarkable gift for the understatement:

> Question: Do you represent to this Court that you have exceptional and unique skill and ability as a basketball player?
> Barnett: No.
> Question: Do you represent to this Court that your services are of a special, unusual and extraordinary character?
> Barnett: No.
> Question: You do represent to the Court that you are a professional basketball player; is that correct?
> Barnett: Yes.
> Question: Do you think you are as good as Oscar Robertson?
> Barnett: No.

It would be difficult to imagine a contemporary player so willing to disparage himself, but it is equally amazing to find an owner talking up the very player with whom he just negotiated in the manner done by Barnett's GM at Syracuse:

Question: What is your opinion as to his ability, this is, as a guard, now, at driving?
Biasone: Terrific.
Question: What is your opinion as to his ability at play making as a guard?
Biasone: Good. He has all the abilities a good basketball player should have. He has all the talent of a great basketball player. He is terrific all the way around.

Biasone went on to testify that he would place Barnett in the top 10 list of extraordinary players in the NBA at that time. Quite a switch in perspectives, for here we have a player arguing how poor he is and a GM extolling his virtues. In a twist of logic, however, the court used Barnett's ability against him, citing Syracuse's desire to give him a $3,000 raise and the Pipers' willingness to pay $1,500 more than that. Therefore, Barnett must be good, and being good he must also be unique. The court granted the Syracuse injunction and blocked Barnett's move, but in so doing it devoted little attention to the Syracuse contract itself. Unique or not, if the contract is not enforceable in the first place, no injunction would be proper. The court also referred to a 1961 Dallas Cowboys case with a similar result, a Warner Brothers movie decision against star Bette Davis in 1937, and a 1946 Yankees case in baseball. In no decision, though, did the court thoughtfully consider the reserve restrictions themselves until 1976, when an arbitrator read Messersmith's contract and logically found that a one-time renewal meant one time only, thus toppling baseball's mighty reserve clause with nothing more than a simple interpretation of common English.

The loss to the Nationals was a serious blow to Cleveland and the entire ABL. In fact, the league would fold after 18 months, costing founder Abe Saperstein over $1 million of his own investment. All was not lost to history, however, for the ABL did manage to accomplish at least three acts of significance. First, it demonstrated that the NBA was potentially vulnerable if somehow quality players could be signed. Second, through the creative efforts of Saperstein the league also invented and adopted the three-point shot, an idea that the American Basketball Association would adopt in 1967, setting the stage for today's NBA three-point line. Third, the league gave us none other than one George Steinbrenner, the main owner of the very Cleveland Pipers ballclub that lost out on Dick Barnett. In 1973, just 12 years after the Barnett loss, Steinbrenner would buy the New York Yankees from the CBS network for $10 million.

The short-lived ABL did a crash and burn in 1961, but the historic advent of the ABA was less than six years away.

ENDNOTES

1. Upon Wilt's graduation from high school in 1955, the Philadelphia Warriors sought and obtained a special NBA ruling to allow the Warriors to draft Chamberlain early, even though they would have to wait four years to sign him.

4

SQUEEZING THE NBA

The American Basketball Association was formed in 1966 to compete with the NBA and capture a portion of a booming basketball market. As Abe Saperstein discovered but could not capitalize on when he was rejected as a potential owner, NBA franchises in 1961 had been selling for $200,000 each. By 1966 they were $1,750,000, and four years later they would climb to $3,750,000. By 1987 the value had multiplied almost tenfold as newly formed Minnesota and others would ante up $37,500,000. Today the value exceeds $200,000,000 each, over $300,000,000 for some teams—so the founders of the ABA were not wrong in their assessment of a basketball-hungry marketplace.

At Kentucky we had a rule: if Dr. J was coming down on the fast break, foul him. I didn't care if he was 20 feet from the basket. Just foul him before he took off. If you didn't foul him and Julius dunked, it was a $50 fine.

—HUBIE BROWN

Consumer demand, fate, and high-flying money players all converged at the right time to launch the ABA as a serious contender for the basketball market. Listed as only 6′6″, Julius Erving had nonetheless played center at the University of Massachusetts, where he relied upon the speed and quickness of a guard to become the remarkable force that caught the discerning eye of Coach McGuire—the hard way. The Doctor went on to average 27 points *and* 19 rebounds for his junior year, after which he left school to sign a then whopping $500,000 deal with the ABA Squires.

Like Michael Jordan, Julius could launch himself from the free throw line for a slam dunk, shoot the jumper, or explode to the basket. Unlike anyone, including MJ, Julius had a remarkable move to the hoop that defied logic and video, let alone words, but here goes: he would cut to the basket from, let's say, the right side, allowing momentum to pull him baseline behind the backboard and away from the opposing defense. At nearly full speed he would then leap in the air from behind, circle back-door while airborne, reach out with his long right arm with the ball nestled in his powerful grip, and then—while still in flight—finger-roll the ball from under the backboard for a reverse fallaway layup. With centrifugal momentum carrying his body past the left side of the basket, Julius would finally land in play at the edge of the free throw lane as the defense watched two points slip softly through the bottom of the net. It was a virtually unstoppable move.

As an ABA rookie, Julius Erving averaged 27.2 points and 15.7 rebounds per game in 1971–72. Immediately thereafter he attempted to sign with the NBA Atlanta Hawks, but the courts intervened à la Dick Barnett, forcing him to continue playing for the Squires. In his second year Erving went ballistic, averaging a hair under 32 points per game while adding a stunning 22 rebounds—both Chamberlain-type numbers. On his best days Jordan would not pull down 22 boards; and Dennis Rodman, the best contemporary rebounder, rarely did so. To *average* that many rebounds per game is staggering, but to do so while leading the league in scoring is almost a transcendental act. In a way, if you combine Rodman and Jordan, you get Erving—although, to be fair to history, both Dennis and Michael play an energetic, in-your-face defense that was not the trademark of either Julius or the ABA. And given the level of contemporary competition, there is little hope that the Doctor could average 22 boards in the 1990s, although perhaps a youthful Julius could give Michael a run for his money on the offensive end. (If anything, perhaps a modern-era Erving would be similar to Scottie Pippen—same size, great mobility, and an eye for the basket; Julius might score a little more, but Scottie is known for better defense.)

Eventually, the Squires traded Julius to the Nets for financial reasons. He continued to flourish, leading the league in scoring two out of three years, both times taking the Nets to a league championship. He shared the league MVP with George McGinnis in 1975 and won it outright in 1974 and 1976. All in all, Julius played five seasons in the ABA, averaging 28.7 points and 12.1 rebounds per game over that span. On Valentine's Day, 1975, Erving hit his career high by pouring in 63 points on 26-for-46 shooting against the San Diego Conquistadors.

San Diego was an interesting team, actually, for its coach during the 1973–74 season was Wilt Chamberlain, who had been enticed to play ball for San Diego with a then staggering salary of $600,000 for one year. Alas, Chamberlain's former team, the Lakers, went to court and successfully challenged the move as a player. So Chamberlain was relegated to the bench, where he and his marquee name were now labeled "coach." (There are those who say Chamberlain did little as coach, suggesting assistant Stan Albeck called most of the shots.)

Albeck would later do a stint as coach of the Chicago Bulls, as would Kevin Loughery, Erving's coach at New Jersey. Loughery, who had been in the NBA with virtually no firsthand exposure to the Doctor, was soon impressed not only with Erving's sheer ability, but his dependability and work ethic as well. In three full seasons with the Nets, Julius would not miss one game or even a practice. As for the on-court performance, Julius was a one-man superlative. According to Loughery, near the first half of his very first game as a Nets player, Julius slammed a thunderous dunk between two towering defenders, George McGinnis and Darnell Hillman. Published accounts quote Loughery proclaiming that slam as the best dunk he had ever seen up to then, though he would watch Julius top it a number of times over the years.

Erving the man was a remarkable individual. As sportscaster Bob Costas once observed, "There was electricity in his game and kindness in his personality that added up to a lot of charisma." Sounds a lot like Michael Jordan, actually, on and off the court, which no doubt explains how the Doctor launched a whole league into virtual parity with the more established NBA.

The playmasters of the ABA—its founders, key owners, coaches, and special players—had opened up the court with speed, scoring, and a three-point line borrowed from Abe Saperstein's innovation at the short-lived ABL. The ABA built its image around Julius Erving and a host of flashy stars, including 7'2" Artis Gilmore, George "the Iceman" Gervin, George McGinnis, Connie Hawkins, and others. All were unique, but Hawkins was an especially fascinating study of basketball evolution.

In the late 1950s—maybe the year was 1960—Hawkins, while still in high school, found himself in a pickup game against Wilt Chamberlain. Observers, including NBA player Jerry Harkness, saw a remarkably mobile Hawkins hold his own against Wilt. Regrettably, this young high school protégé would never have a chance to play college ball. While knocking heads in those New York playground games, Hawkins had the misfortune of befriending gambler Jack Molinas, who from time to time bought dinner for the youth, once even loaning him a couple of hundred dollars (which, by the way, Connie repaid).

Hawkins then attended the University of Iowa to play ball, but the association with Molinas, who had already been in court for years over a gambling and point shaving scheme, tarnished his reputation. Molinas had been an NBA player himself, suiting up for the Fort Wayne [later Detroit] Pistons in 1953 after graduation from Columbia University. But in his first season he was caught betting on the Pistons and admitted to pocketing some $400 over the course of the scheme. In 1954 the NBA suspended Molinas over the gambling episode. Between the time of his suspension and the befriending of Hawkins in 1960, Molinas actually attended the Brooklyn Law School, graduated, and became a licensed lawyer in the state of New York.

True to form, one supposes, Jack Molinas then filed suit against the NBA on behalf of himself, claiming his gambling suspension had been part of an illegal antitrust conspiracy on the part of the league. He lost—not because a league such as the NBA is incapable of antitrust shenanigans (it is, as we shall see), but because the antigambling rules implemented against Molinas were ultimately deemed reasonable in scope and application by a federal judge in 1961. Unfortunately, all the hoopla caught the attention of both the University of Iowa and the NCAA, causing Hawkins's relationship with Molinas to surface publicly. Hawkins was kicked out of

Iowa because of the scandal, even though Connie himself could not have fixed or profited by any NCAA games, for as a member of the Iowa freshman team he had yet to play in a varsity game at all. Worse still, the NBA shunned Hawkins, too, even though Connie had been convicted of nothing and, of course, did not—could not—gamble on games he could influence.

Young, talented, and highly disillusioned, Connie Hawkins looked elsewhere and was embraced by the Pittsburgh Rens of Abe Saperstein's new ABL. All Connie did was become the league's top scorer for the 1961–62 season, averaging 27.5 points per game (PPG), and leading the Rens to the ABL championship and winning the league MVP award. When the league folded the following year, Hawkins followed Saperstein to become a barnstorming member of the Harlem Globetrotters, leaving four years later to chase his dream with the Pittsburgh Pipers of the new ABA. Again he was the league's top scorer (26.8 PPG) and MVP, but this time it was the Pipers he led.

Eventually Hawkins was vindicated, partly with the help of his old friend and advocate Jack Molinas, who stood up to proclaim and verify Connie's innocence. A suit Hawkins filed against the NBA for its arbitrary blackballing action was settled in 1969 for $1 million (or perhaps $1.3 million—published reports differ) plus the right to play in the NBA. Hawkins signed on with Phoenix and immediately became the first Suns player ever named to the NBA All-Star team, averaging 24.6 points per contest, good enough for sixth place leaguewide. Now a member of the Basketball Hall of Fame, Hawkins played seven seasons with Phoenix, four of which were All-Star years, before his luck ran out as bad knees and age caught up.

Hawkins and the Doctor were not, of course, the only stars of the upstart ABA. In its prime, the ABA trotted out a bevy of athletes who could play, and play they certainly did. One such star in the making was so cool under pressure he seemed to have ice in his veins. George "the Iceman" Gervin was a spectacular street player from the ghettos of Detroit in the middle and late 1960s who clawed his way to an athletic scholarship, first at San Diego State University and then Eastern Michigan.

Gervin was averaging almost 30 points per game when his pro career was jump-started for a much different reason: he was kicked out of school for punching an opposing player in the midst of a two-team brawl in his second year on the court. With few other options, Gervin latched onto the Continental Basketball Association, a lesser pro league, where he played until being drafted by the insightful Virginia Squires during a special ABA midyear draft during the 1972–73 season, loading the Squires—who already had Julius Erving—with offensive talent. Erving was on his way to leading the league in scoring that year with a 31.9 average, and the upstart Gervin caught on fast, making the all-rookie team.

Fate and financial pressure took their toll on the Squires, so in early 1974 Gervin, like Julius, was sent to another team. While Julius went north to the Nets, George Gervin was launched southwest to San Antonio, were he came into his own as a legitimate superstar. Two years later the Spurs were in the NBA, bringing their fearless gunner along. The Iceman led the NBA in scoring four times, including a sparkling 33.1 average during the 1979–80 season. In his combined ABA–NBA career, Gervin would wind up with 26,595 total points, just 105 points behind Oscar Robertson on the all-time list and ahead of such luminaries as Elgin Baylor, Jerry West, and John Havlicek. Of the top scorers who played in both leagues, the Iceman would take third place behind Dan Issel (27,482) and Erving (30,026).

The Squires were fun to watch for a brief period, and San Antonio was entertaining with Gervin, but one of the winningest teams (at least in regular season play) was the Denver Nuggets, one of only two ABA teams (Indiana was the other) to play in the same home city for the entire life of the league—nine years. The Nuggets began life as the Rockets, actually, but changed their name in 1974, paying homage to an old 1949 NBA franchise in Denver with the same name. They were also making an effort to avoid the current NBA Rockets, already situated in Houston, perhaps not to avoid confusion so much as to eliminate a reason to reject Denver's own NBA bid a few years hence.

In the early years Denver had star Spencer Haywood, who would later leave for the NBA. But with a growing cache of players and a talented coach in Larry Brown, Denver compiled an impressive 65–19 record in 1974–75. The team had perennial trouble in the playoffs, though, often losing in the first round—except for their 60–24 campaign and a trip to the 1976 finals, where they lost to New York. That team was loaded, for just before the season the Nuggets brass first picked up standout Dan Issel, then outbid the NBA for two of its own draft picks, David Thompson and Marvin Webster. The ABA was catching the attention of the NBA, but it still had plenty of problems, one being an inability to snare a national television contract. Today the problem is less severe for upstart leagues, new sports, or even new sporting gimmicks, as the advent of superstations and specialized cable creates an abundance of television possibilities.

One of the top priorities of every ABA commissioner was bigtime television contracts, so the ABA installed a number of big names in its quest for visibility and credibility. Indeed, the first commissioner, George Mikan, was literally "big" and hoped to capitalize on his aura of basketball greatness. It didn't work, so the league eventually appointed the former head of CBS Sports, Jack Dolph, who knew television and television contracts, but who could land neither for the fledgling league. Eventually, the ABA snared NBA star Dave DeBusschere, who, as a former Knicks player, brought name recognition and NBA-type credibility, but still no national television contract.

With money, credibility, and pride on the line, it was not long before a series of legal battles ignited between and among teams, leagues, and players. Indeed, former ABA commissioner Mike Storen once commented that when he took the reins in 1973, the ABA legal bills exceeded a million dollars a year.[1] In 1972, for example, the Carolina Cougars sued William John Cunningham (Billy) over a spat with the Philadelphia 76ers. In 1967, superstar Rick Barry was sued by the San Francisco Warriors when he attempted to jump the NBA for a five-year deal to join his father-in-law, then GM of the ABA Oakland Oaks. The Warriors won, so

Barry laid low, forgoing basketball for one year, after which he did finally sign with Oakland across the bay. He remained in Oakland until the Oaks moved to Washington, D.C., causing Barry to stay with the Oakland team (which by then was the Washington Capitols). But his sojourn was not over. When the Oaks moved again, this time to Virginia, Barry objected and was traded to the Nets for cash and a first-round draft pick. After two years, Barry's ABA contract ran out, whereupon the courts ruled that he must honor his last NBA contract with San Francisco—which by this time he was happy to do, signing on with a six-year deal. Barry (the last player to shoot free throws underhand, by the way) led the Warriors to the NBA championship in 1975, along the way beating the Chicago Bulls in seven games during the semifinals, a scrappy team that featured Jerry Sloan (the legendary coach of the Utah Jazz), Norm Van Lier, Chet (the "Jet") Walker, and Bob ("Butterbean") Love.

As grueling as Barry's sequence of legal battles might have been, however, his troubles paled against a series of bigger travails with two antitrust actions launched by Spencer Haywood and Oscar Robertson. The latter suit would eventually kill a proposed ABA–NBA merger in 1970, changing the course of the two leagues over the ensuing six years, if not forever.

ENDNOTES

1. Storen would later do a brief stint in the Chicago suburbs as president of Zucker Sports Management Group, Inc., a sports agency and marketing firm that hit its stride in about 1989–92 by adding the likes of Deion Sanders and Richmond Webb to a stable of mostly football players that already included Jim McMahon and a number of stars from the Super Bowl Bears of 1985–86. I was general counsel to ZSMG at the time, moving up to chief operating officer to fill a void created by Storen's departure. The firm would occasionally do well with NBA players, with clients such as Darryl Dawkins, Rod Strickland, Dee Brown, and Eric Murdock, but the basketball players never supplanted the football stars the firm was already known for.

5

MONOPOLY WARS

The elusive NBA triple double—achieved when a basketball player registers double figures in a game for each category of points, rebounds, and assists—is a remarkable benchmark accomplishment reserved almost exclusively for superstars. Even so, Michael Jordan performed it sparingly, and the 6'9" point guard Magic Johnson had some limited success due to his size, strength, and quickness. But overall, notching a triple double is an overwhelming feat of basketball acuity that is rarely achieved by even the best of the best.

One player in the history of the NBA raised the bar so high for complete play that no player since has flirted with matching the accomplishment, a year-long effort that defies logic and even imagination. Oscar Robertson, the 6'5" 220-pound superstar guard, not only registered double-figure stats on a regular basis, he was the only player in NBA history to *average* a triple double for an entire season! During the 1961–62 campaign, Robertson played in 79 games, logging season marks of 30.7 points, 12.4 rebounds, and 11.3 assists per game. Since all assists translate into at least two points by definition, a quick math exercise shows that Oscar Robertson directly accounted for over 53 points per game (not

Participating in professional basketball as a player against the best competition which the sport has to offer is as necessary to the mental and physical well being of [Spencer] Haywood as is breathing, eating and sleeping.

—UNITED STATES DISTRICT COURT FOR THE CENTRAL DISTRICT OF CALIFORNIA, 1971 even counting the effect of his 12.4 boards) over an entire year. With Jordan-like speed and points, the strength and rebounds of a Karl Malone, plus the consistency and assists of a John Stockton, Robertson may have been the best complete package ever to play in the NBA. Indeed, if Karl Malone could become a guard, maybe he would be a modern clone of Oscar Robertson, combining pure strength with perseverance, scoring, and leadership.[1]

Although Robertson's on-court totals are staggering, they fail to reflect the profound impact Oscar the person had *in* court as well as on it, first preventing and then paving the way for a blockbuster merger of the NBA and ABA. He was, in effect, basketball's version of Curt Flood, the former Cardinals star who challenged Major League Baseball on antitrust grounds in 1970. Unlike Flood, though, Oscar was not hampered by an illogical United States Supreme Court decision holding that Major League Baseball was not a business in interstate commerce and, thus, is supposedly not subject to federal antitrust laws (and is the *only* sports league not subject to those laws). The NBA is not baseball, however, and so it was a sitting duck for antitrust attack.

Oscar's star rose early when he led his Indianapolis high school team to two successive state championships, including one run of 45 wins in a row. Later, as a University of Cincinnati Bearcat, the "Big O" set the NCAA single-game scoring record of 62 points, averaging 33.8 points and 15.2 rebounds during his three-year All-American college career. In his first 10 years in the NBA, with the Cincinnati Royals, he launched an impressive pro campaign as Rookie of the Year while leading the NBA in assists. Upon a 1970 trade to Milwaukee, where he complemented a youthful Lew Alcindor (Kareem Abdul-Jabbar), Robertson pumped in enough baskets and assists to win the NBA championship on a team only three years old. After a remarkable career on and off the court, the Big O finally retired in 1974.

In early 1970, rumors surfaced about budding merger talks between the NBA and its fierce new rival, the American Basketball Association. In fact, by May 4, 1970, the two leagues had reached an agreement subject to formal NBA ratification, scheduled for the following year. Under the merger terms, the NBA would absorb 10 of the ABA teams, leaving out the Virginia Squires because they were too close in proximity to the NBA Baltimore Bullets franchise. With bidding wars pushing skyward the star salaries of Rick Barry and others, the ABA–NBA rivalry provided the greatest boost to player earnings in basketball history up to that time. Robertson and others believed a two-league merger would quash competition and diminish salaries as a result, so he willingly became the lead name plaintiff in a federal class action suit filed in New York on behalf of all players in those respective leagues. The other names weren't chopped liver, as they say, and included Bill Bradley (the future senator), John Havlicek, Wes Unseld, Dick Van Arsdale, and Chet (the "Jet") Walker.

The players' complaint named the NBA, the ABA, and both leagues' member teams as defendants, charging all with conspiring to restrain competition for the services of professional basketball players through the college draft, basketball's reserve clause found in the uniform player contract, the compensation plan attached to the reserve clause, and various boycott and blacklisting techniques invoked against the players. Ironically, the NBA chose to merge in part because of the barrage of ABA legal actions against it for antitrust violations, and now in the Robertson suit it would face the same charges by players who believed the merger itself was an illegal restraint of trade. In May of 1970, soon after the complaint was filed, a federal district court entered a preliminary injunction halting the ABA–NBA merger in its tracks, although the court did allow the two sides to hammer out a tentative, non-binding merger for the purpose of seeking special statutory antitrust exemptions from Congress.

Congress had created precedent for such exemptions when it passed the Sports Broadcasting Act of 1961, allowing the NFL to first package all team TV rights together for joint negotiation with the networks. Undaunted, in 1966 Congress passed an amendment to the act specifically allowing the NFL to merge with the intensely competitive AFL without antitrust retribution.[2] The NBA believed it could similarly win over the Congress of 1970–71, and the court allowed just enough legal maneuvering to explore the political possibilities.

In August of 1973, the court modified its order, allowing the two leagues to negotiate a merger on the express condition that any resulting agreement specifically address the disposition of uniform player contracts, the common draft, and the reserve clause. As of February 14, 1975, no such agreement had been reached, although the Robertson court was prepared to rule on key elements of Oscar's case in the face of NBA motions to disqualify the class action and to seek antitrust protection under what has now emerged as the labor exemption to antitrust.

Robertson and the other name plaintiffs alleged that since its inception in 1946, the NBA had engaged in a "concerted plan, combination, or conspiracy" to monopolize and restrain trade and commerce in major league professional basketball by:

1. Controlling, regulating, and dictating the terms upon which professional major league basketball was played in the United States
2. Allocating and dividing the market of professional player talent
3. Enforcing its monopoly and restraint of trade through boycotts, blacklists, and refusals to deal with the players.

Those allegations were a handful, but the players were not through. They contended that the NBA's objective was the elimination of all competition in the acquisition, allocation, and employment of professional basketball players in violation of Sections 1 and 2 of the Sherman Act, the flagship federal statute proscribing monopolistic business activity in the United States.

In a nutshell, Section 1 of the Act prohibits any contract, combination, or conspiracy in restraint of trade, while Section 2 addresses illegal market power of single monopolists in a given industry. A great deal of legal wrangling goes on over the two sections. For example, if the courts deemed the NBA a single entity rather than a conspiratorial collection of individual teams, then it could not violate Section 1, which requires some form of conspiracy among two or more parties. Since one can hardly conspire with oneself, a single entity cannot logically or legally be held in violation of Section 1.

Just as baseball's Curt Flood was futilely punching his way through the major league antitrust quagmire all the way to the Supreme Court, Robertson and his army of plaintiffs were gaining in their assault on the NBA, a league of oppressive rules and restrictions that left it vulnerable to antitrust attacks. At the same time, yet another player had launched a flank attack, also suing the NBA on antitrust grounds—but with a much different twist. Superstar Spencer Haywood had locked horns with the NBA to void a league rule requiring all new players to be at least four years removed from high school, or from their respective graduating classes if they had left high school early.

The NBA four-year rule was implemented to keep college players out of the NBA, perhaps with some intentions that were good and some not so laudable. But in Haywood's case, the application of the rule produced a bizarre, even absurd result. Haywood, like Robertson, was an Olympian, although the two stars did not play on the same team. Haywood was an All-American high school player out of Detroit. He attended and starred at Trinidad Junior College during the 1967–68 season, just before his appearance at the 1968 Olympics. After winning gold, he returned to college, this time at the University of Detroit, where he played one year and again achieved All-American status.

Unlike Robertson, though, Spencer Haywood did not stick with college. Instead, on August 16, 1969, the Denver Rockets signed the 6′9″ Haywood to a pro contract to play ball in the ABA, where he sparkled as a rookie. Not only was Haywood named Rookie of the Year, he was voted MVP of the whole league, plus MVP of the League All-Star Game for good measure. In his first professional season he had led the ABA in both scoring (30 points per game) *and* rebounding (averaging an amazing 19.5 rebounds), later prompting a federal judge to officially find he had achieved the rare status of "super star." After starting the season at 9–19, Denver then went on a tear as Haywood hit stride, winning 42 of the next 56 games to finish up at 51–33 on the year.

Still just under the age of 21, Haywood renegotiated with his team and eventually signed a seemingly spectacular Denver contract worth $1.9 million. But the youthful Haywood soon learned all that glitters is not gold, for his glitzy playing contract proved to be a six-year deal that paid a signing bonus of $50,000 plus just under $50,000 in salary in each of the first and second years. The salary in the last four years was to be $75,000 annually. Since bonus and salary added up to only $450,000 in total, Haywood scrambled to find the "missing" balance of nearly $1.5 million, which was discovered as a planned stream of twenty $75,000 annual payments beginning at age 40. The unhappy Haywood hired agent Al Ross, who helped sort out the meaning of the convoluted Denver deal and steer Haywood around similar future negotiating blunders.

Upon still closer review, Ross discovered Haywood had been induced to sign a contract not only with the Denver team, but also another contract with Ringsby Truck Lines, Inc., calling for Ringsby to invest $10,000 per year for 10 years in a "growth mutual fund" under something called the "Dolgoff Plan." The fund, though, was not for Haywood to own, although Ringsby was also to purchase $100,000 of life insurance, which would be Haywood's. Haywood had the right after 10 years to request a string of annuity payments from this peculiar Dolgoff fund equal to 10 percent of the fund value as of the date of such notice, but meanwhile Ringsby had the right to collateralize the balance of the fund to secure corporate debts, so these payments were always at risk in the Ringsby business.

Haywood's guardian signed the contract on his behalf, and even obtained court permission to bind the minor Haywood under Colorado law. A court would later find that all but $394,000 of his playing contract was "illusory" and indefinite. In April of 1970 young Spencer turned 21 and shortly thereafter, on June 8, 1970, Haywood actually ratified the contract as an adult, effectively signing it all over again. By November 23, 1970, however, Haywood experienced a profound change of heart and gave written notice to the Rockets not only of his dissatisfaction, but also his desire to disavow and rescind his playing contract due to the perceived fraudulent misrepresentations made by Denver management about the size and accessibility of his compensation.

Not content to stop there, on December 28, 1970, the determined Spencer Haywood signed a six-year deal with the Seattle

Supersonics of the NBA. However, Seattle could not activate Haywood right away due to Section 2.05 of the NBA bylaws, a rule preventing teams from signing players less than four years removed from high school. The ABA had implemented a similar rule, but waived it for Haywood when he joined the league. The NBA version that stood in Haywood's way read as follows:

> A person who has not completed high school or who has completed high school but has not entered college, shall not be eligible to be drafted or to be a Player [in the NBA] until four years after he has been graduated or four years after his original high school class has been graduated, as the case may be, nor may the future services of any such person be negotiated or contracted for, or otherwise reserved. Similarly, a person who has entered college but is no longer enrolled, shall not be eligible to be drafted or to be a Player until the time when he would have first become eligible had he remained enrolled in college. Any negotiations or agreements with any such person during such period shall be null and void and shall confer no rights to the services of such person at any time thereafter.

Besides proving painful legalese can drain the excitement from even the NBA, the cumbersome four-year rule was a major obstacle for Haywood. The rule was also illogical in Haywood's particular case, producing an absurd unfair result, for even at age 21 Haywood was far, far removed from high school. He was a successful Olympian and professional basketball player already, with both a pro MVP and a sinuous million-dollar ABA contract under his belt. But the NBA was determined to avoid a bidding war for younger and younger players. And it was respectful, even fearful, of NCAA criticism that would surely tarnish the league as a greedy corrupter of our nation's students. Such a fear at the time was not unjustified.

Facing a no-win situation and a recalcitrant Seattle club that could not activate him in view of the rule, a determined Haywood turned to the federal courts in an attempt to enjoin its enforcement. Now, with one action proceeding by Haywood in California and another pushed ahead by Oscar Robertson in New York, the NBA struggled to extricate itself from a constricting legal vise of federal antitrust laws.

The federal district court in New York saw the college draft as a conspiratorial device designed to prevent competition among member NBA clubs for NCAA players who, together, comprised an exclusive source of high-level basketball talent in the United States. The court in the Robertson suit was also skeptical of the uniform player contract, which every NBA rookie or veteran player was required to sign as a condition of employment. The contract required such a player to remain with his club or its assignee exclusively until he was otherwise sold or traded. It also provided that the club was vested with the absolute right to sell, exchange, assign, or transfer the player contract to another club; and that if the player were to refuse, the club could either terminate the contract or seek an injunction to prevent the player from playing basketball for anyone else.

The reserve clause within this player contract of adhesion[3] added insult to injury, requiring all players, even superstars like Oscar Robertson, to renew their contracts for one year upon the same terms as the expiring agreement. Thus, if the team could not come to terms with its player, it had the power to force the player's hand indefinitely, forcing the athlete to either play under conditions of servitude or to retire. (This was the rule when the Robertson court made its findings in 1975—and it actually was an improvement from the players' perspective. Before 1971, the team could keep renewing at a 25 percent *reduction* in salary every year, effectively ratcheting the salary down toward zero over time.[4]) Although the NBA used its contractual and league muscle wherever it could to keep players from the ABA, still the ABA served a significant purpose in bidding up salaries in general, signing new players out of college (or otherwise, such as Haywood), and occasionally stealing one from the NBA. Robertson's lawyers argued that the new ABA, just formed in 1967, was the only viable competition for the otherwise monopolistic NBA, and any merger would be the final nail in the antitrust coffin, forever condemning the players to the whims of a league with unbridled power.

Corroborating the Robertson fears was an NBA policy of boycotts, blacklistings, and refusals to deal with certain players, strong-arm tactics aimed toward its competition. The Robertson plaintiffs contended that no NBA club would negotiate with a new player from another team, arguing that either such player would logically be under contract and not eligible or, otherwise, he would be subject to the reserve clause restrictions. Effectively, then, no player could ever switch teams without being traded unless his team owner agreed otherwise. Further, Robertson contended, if any NBA club violated these restrictions, the team itself would be boycotted, blacklisted, or otherwise penalized. Therefore, one count of the Robertson complaint attacked NBA predatory tactics as an illegal conspiracy waged against the ABA itself for the sole purpose of improperly preserving its monopoly position and acting in concert to suppress competition—the crux of antitrust law proscriptions.

Meanwhile, the Spencer Haywood case was progressing rapidly, squeezing the NBA and diluting its arguments for the Robertson court. In fact, the Haywood lawsuit would be decided in 1971, four years ahead of the eventual Robertson ruling, a lengthy written opinion that would actually cite the Haywood case as precedent for Oscar's own results.

Haywood posed a unique problem for the NBA, not only because of his extraordinary star power, but because of the unprecedented circumstances of his meteoric rise from high school. The ABA had waived its own four-year rule, actually inventing the term "hardship," according to Mike Storen, one of the top ABA brass who had engineered the Haywood signing. The actual hardship was that Haywood was the best potential breadwinner in a deserving family of one mother plus nine brothers and sisters, a virtuous motive if taken at face value. Nonetheless, the whole basketball world from the NCAA to the NBA went berserk—but in the end, the ABA aced everyone by landing Haywood anyway.

By the time Haywood had sued the NBA for refusing to waive its four-year rule, Haywood was by definition ineligible for college ball as a veteran ABA professional. By digging in and stonewalling the obvious distinction between Haywood and the customary college player who would consider leaving early for the NBA, the league shot itself in the foot. Effectively, the NBA gave the courts a free crack at interpreting the rule for everyone, not just Haywood, even though signing the veteran pro would have offended no one's sense of "decency" and "collegiate" values—the ABA had already done the offending part when it signed him in the first place.

Not only did the NBA stubbornly commit to its rule in the face of a changing world, it even came down on the Seattle club for signing him. Every NBA team that played Seattle protested every game in which Haywood played or even just suited up, regardless of whether each team had won or lost its game. The whole thing smacked of conspiracy, for what team would logically protest a game it had won except for some ulterior purpose? Further, on January 12, 1971, the NBA Board of Governors voted for drastic measures to coerce Seattle's continued cooperation in keeping Haywood off the court. In its own rendition of a proverbial full-court press, the NBA, through its commissioner, released statements to the news media calculated to intimidate both Haywood and the Supersonics management, including the threat of total expulsion from the league, including the following public pronouncement:

> The Board of Governors, by a 15–2 vote, have passed a resolution directing the Commissioner with the aid of counsel to consider bringing charges against Seattle before the Board of Governors in connection with the Spencer Haywood matter and to advise the Board of the most drastic penalties lawfully at its command if such charges should be sustained. . . . This means expulsion of the franchise through various other levels, including fines, suspending draft choices.

Harsh words on the surface, but when the text is read carefully, it reveals itself as largely hot air. Had Seattle been expelled, the resulting lawsuit by the Seattle club would likely have paled the Haywood action. In any event, this public jawboning was an attempt to try the Haywood controversy in the press, a risky tactic in most circumstances but especially so when a suspect rule is applied to bad facts. Mindful of the high stakes involved, Haywood's attorneys pressed forward with motions for a preliminary injunction and other relief, even requesting an expedited resolution prior to the March 29, 1971, college draft. As it happened, they got their decision a week early, on March 22.

To win injunctive relief, Haywood had to jump over four key legal hurdles, two of which included showing evidence linking the questionable NBA conduct to a conspiracy under antitrust laws and then showing a substantial likelihood of irreparable harm to Haywood if the preliminary injunction were not granted.[5] In addition to scrutinizing Section 2.05 of the NBA bylaws, the court took note of Section 6.03, which further delineated player eligibility for the NBA draft, summarizing the eligible categories as follows:

(a) Students in four-year colleges whose classes are to be graduated during the June following the holding of the draft
(b) Students in four-year colleges whose original classes have already been graduated, and who do not choose to exercise remaining collegiate basketball eligibility
(c) Students in four-year colleges whose original classes have already been graduated if such students have no remaining collegiate basketball eligibility
(d) Persons who become eligible pursuant to the provisions of Section 2.05 of these by-laws

Clearly the four-year theme appears throughout the NBA draft eligibility criteria. Moreover, a strand of pandering to the NCAA emerges as the bylaws pay express homage to college eligibility. Why should it matter that a player has used up his college eligibility unless, perhaps, the NBA had made a policy decision to placate NCAA authorities and, to a lesser extent, placate public opinion? There is only one viable answer remaining, and Haywood himself suggested it to the court: collegiate athletics provide a more efficient, less expensive way for the NBA to develop talent than operating a self-contained farm system, such as that maintained by Major League Baseball.

The NBA playmasters strenuously resisted Haywood's arguments, of course, posing at least two justifications for its four-year rule. First, the NBA argued that the rule was financially necessary to professional basketball. But this approach begged the issue, and, if anything, may have corroborated Haywood's belief that the league was just using the NCAA as its own private farm system. Second, the league stressed that the rule was necessary to guarantee that each prospective basketball player would be given an opportunity to finish college before embarking upon a pro career. Under the circumstances, the rule as applied to Haywood was an abomination. Haywood had no possibility of finishing college on a scholarship, for he had already been a pro in the ABA; further, Haywood argued hardship, stating that to force him to finish college would be a burden on him and his family. In short, he could not have cared less about the supposed altruism of the NBA; Haywood yearned for a pro basketball career and all its trappings. What right did a private organization have to tell him to stay in school, even if it allegedly was "for his own good"?

When NBA commissioner Walter Kennedy first disqualified Haywood and launched a campaign of threats and sanctions against the Seattle Supersonics, he sparked an immediate legal battle up and down the federal system over Haywood's demand for injunctive relief. Before its sojourn was over, Haywood's case traveled up to the U.S. Court of Appeals, which stayed a lower court injunction in favor of Haywood, then on to the United States Supreme Court, where the legendary liberal Justice William O. Douglas vacated the stay, reinstating the original injunction. In ruling for Haywood, Justice Douglas noted that only baseball was exempt from antitrust scrutiny and, since the NBA was neither baseball nor otherwise exempt, Haywood should be entitled to his injunctive relief against the NBA on antitrust grounds.

Back at the district court level, the federal trial judge addressed the blackballing of Haywood and others similarly situated as potentially a primary group boycott, which normally is an antitrust violation. The harm to a player in Haywood's position is multifaceted. Haywood, of course, was victimized by his exclusion from the primary NBA market for his talents; free market competition was also harmed, a major factor in antitrust litigation; and the pooling of their collective conspiratorial power vested the teams and league with the market power of a shared monopoly.

The NBA countered with a "rule of reason" argument, asserting a number of compelling needs for such a rule that should be balanced against the otherwise negative effects. In similar cases, for example, the NFL has prevailed against numerous attacks on its draft structure by stressing that a reasonable draft procedure is necessary to achieve competitive balance in the league, which, in turn, serves to preserve an optimum number of jobs for players and actually promotes competition.

Faced with what could have been a difficult dilemma, the court turned to one balancing issue: procedural safeguards. In many other instances where antitrust laws could be a factor, the existence of procedural safeguards for aggrieved parties has often strengthened a defendant's legal position. In a significant antitrust case against the Professional Golfers' Association (PGA) in which the plaintiff challenged the PGA eligibility standards, a 1966 decision for the defendant PGA cited the players' ability to challenge and appeal the initial eligibility findings. In the case of Spencer Haywood, however, the court noted that there were no exceptions to the four-year rule, and no appeal or other review process was offered. In other words, the rule was rammed down the throat of everyone without regard to circumstances, logic, or fairness. The ABA, on the other hand, had improvised a "hardship" approach whereby the application of the rule could be reviewed and even overturned. The NBA had no such flexibility built into its bylaws structure where the four-year rule was concerned.

With that, the court fired a shot heard 'round the basketball world, handing the NBA a startling defeat on March 22, 1971, by granting the preliminary injunction and issuing the following order:

IT IS ORDERED AND ADJUDGED that the . . . NBA [is] enjoined from applying the Constitution, By-laws, Rules and Regulations of the NBA in any manner so as to prevent or interfere with, or from taking any other action, directly or indirectly, to prevent or interfere with . . . Haywood playing professional basketball as a player on the playing roster of the Seattle Supersonics.

So just as the Oscar Robertson case was nipping at its heels, a left hook from Spencer Haywood rocked the NBA. Then, still reeling from the Haywood blow, the league braced for Oscar's own history-making assault, the finale to a great one-two punch that changed the face of today's NBA.

In its written findings issued on Valentine's Day, 1975, the Robertson decision added insult to injury by citing the Haywood case as precedent to support its conclusion that the NBA is, indeed, subject to antitrust laws, and that the players actually have standing to bring an antitrust action.[6] After setting the legal table, the court proceeded to specifically address the validity of the NBA reserve clause and related issues in a mammoth opinion running nearly 100 single-spaced printed pages. The Robertson plaintiffs argued that the clause automatically renewed itself into perpetuity one year at a time, while the NBA argued the opposite premise—namely, that the clause was a one-time device only, after which the player would become a free agent able to sign with other teams without restriction.

In a not-so-subtle twist of fate, had the parties not been pitted against each other in a federal antitrust action, it is likely they would have posed inverse arguments. One would expect that players interested in maximizing freedom of choice would normally argue the clause is a one-time provision that works only for a single renewal for one year. Conversely, the NBA should logically take the position that its clause renews itself perpetually to give maximum control to the league. The league's problem with the Robertson case, however, was that to avoid a legal trap it had to distance itself from a harsh reading of the renewal language. This left the league with a soft posture and Robertson with a more rigid interpretation, and under the circumstances Robertson was probably much closer to the truth. The whole purpose of the reserve clause was to keep players on their own respective teams for so long as their owners desired—which, as it happens, also had the effect of depressing leaguewide player salaries by suppressing competition.

Ironically, just one year later, in 1976, Dodger pitcher Andy Messersmith took Major League Baseball's mighty reserve clause to task in an historic baseball arbitration case that led to the demise of owner control over player movement. There the league strenuously argued against an NBA-type interpretation by reasoning that a one-year renewal clause in a renewed contract automatically becomes another mandatory renewal clause at the end of that year, a cycle that could stretch into perpetuity just as the baseball owners had planned. Among other flaws, however, was a baseball provision that allowed a 25-percent salary reduction for every year of mandatory renewals. This led the Messersmith arbitrator to conclude the owners' interpretation was illogical, for it would not only quash player freedom, but would also potentially cause each player's salary to approach zero over time. Accordingly, the arbitrator had no rational choice but to rule the baseball clause a one-time only device, the exact result that could have bolstered the NBA position against Robertson—but it happened a year too late.

Even that may not have saved the NBA, though, for the league had already dropped its own version of the 25-percent-reduction rule, giving more teeth to the enforceability of its reserve clause, the precise harsh reading it sought to hide from the Robertson court. Further, unlike the Messersmith case, Oscar's suit raised many issues beyond just the reserve clause question, such as the restrictive nature of the college draft and especially the anticompetitive effects of an ABA-NBA merger, the heart of the Robertson lawsuit and injunction action.

All in all, the Robertson court weighed the pro- and anticompetitive implications and ultimately ruled in favor of the Big O and the players against the league, finding, in part, as follows:

> The merger and/or agreement of non-competition between the two leagues is another mechanism whose effect would be a restraint of trade. Either would result in the total elimination of competition between the two leagues for the services of college players, free agents, or those intending to break their contracts and jump leagues. The end of the bidding war between the NBA and the ABA would mean the loss of negotiating power which NBA players obtained in 1967 [upon the creation of the ABA].

The court noted the unique structure of professional sports leagues, however, which by their very nature require a modicum of joint cooperation from the setting of playing rules, eligibility, and even (to some degree) the promotion of team parity to promote the health of the league and optimize the number of jobs available for players. Even so, it did not believe a merger in light of all the other restrictions on competition in general and player freedom of choice in particular could pass the muster of legal reason. The court continued:

> Some degree of economic cooperation which is inherently anticompetitive may well be essential for the survival of ostensibly competitive professional sports leagues [the court cited the Curt Flood case against baseball]. Without these mechanisms unrestrained price wars for the service of the most proficient players will ensue, or so runs the argument, with the wealthiest teams capturing the top talent and the poorer teams facing demise due to the loss of fans and profit. . . . Because survival necessitates some restraints, however, does not mean that insulation from the reach of the antitrust laws must follow. Less drastic protective measures may be that solution.[7]

Ultimately, the NBA and ABA did in fact merge—so what happened? Because the NBA was woefully losing the court battle, it was forced to negotiate a settlement with the players. Following extensive pretrial proceedings and negotiations, the parties reached a settlement agreement on April 29, 1976, that called for payments to the plaintiffs of $4.3 million plus a substantial modification of NBA rules and tactics. Robertson had won.

With that, the stage was set for the national basketball explosion. For just three years later, the arrival of icons Magic Johnson and Larry Bird fueled a fierce maelstrom of money, television, and entertainment muscle that first launched the NBA marketing juggernaut—none of which could have occurred without the off-court determination of Robertson and Haywood.

ENDNOTES

1. Oscar was still human, though. Norm Van Lier, the feisty Bulls guard from the 1970s, played with Robertson during Van Lier's rookie season, only to be admonished by Oscar, "Rookie, you don't touch the ball." According to Van Lier, Oscar was gone the next year and "Stormin' Norman" led the team in assists.

2. The 1966 amendment was supported by Louisiana's powerful congressmen Senator Russell Long and Representative Hale Boggs. Lo and behold, the next NFL expansion team was awarded to New Orleans in the form of the Saints.

3. *Contracts of adhesion* are those which are unduly one-sided, non-negotiable, and usually offered in a no-win situation where one party has little choice but to sign.

4. The NBA eliminated the 25 percent reduction formula in 1971. Could this have been a defensive move in view of the Oscar Robertson action filed in 1970? Oscar's suit could provide one credible explanation for the change.

5. The remaining two elements necessary to prevail on an injunction (that is, one granted preliminarily before a full trial on the merits of the whole case) include demonstrating a likelihood of future success on the merits, and showing that the plaintiff is free from his own improper conduct that would bar his claim. (Sometimes a separate fifth element of showing no potential harm to the public is also required.)

6. In later years, a "labor exemption" surfaced in antitrust cases, the effect of which was to exempt employers from antitrust activity where a union was involved and the activity in question was the mandatory subject of collective bargaining. At the time of the Oscar Robertson decision, the labor exemption under federal law applied only to unions themselves, which, without statutory exemptions, would almost always be deemed conspiracies in restraint of trade. This is precisely why the present players association expressed a desire to decertify as an approved collective bargaining unit.

7. Aside from its concise legal reasoning, it is clear the court was upset with NBA tactics toward its players. Not only did the league possess suspect powers, it wielded them with little self-restraint. The judge continued, "I must confess that it is difficult for me to conceive of any theory or set of circumstances pursuant to which the college draft, blacklisting, boycotts and refusals to deal could be saved from Sherman Act condemnation, even if defendants were able to prove at trial their highly dubious contention that these restraints were adopted at the behest of the Players Association."

6

THE KANSAS CITY FARM SYSTEM

The National Collegiate Athletic Association (NCAA) traces its storied roots to 1906, when President Teddy Roosevelt assembled a select group of university officials to study and refine the rules for playing college football. With unsophisticated equipment, roughneck playing tactics like the flying wedge, and a brute-strength running game with no forward pass, intercollegiate football was an out-of-control rugby match generating almost two dozen deaths and countless major injuries per year.

Beware the ides of March Madness.

—THE AUTHOR (WITH CREDIT TO WILLIAM SHAKESPEARE)

Roosevelt's conference evolved into the NCAA, which took immediate control over the game of football and other intercollegiate sports. At first, that control manifested itself in the standardization and regulation of rules and safety on the field, leaving other issues like scholarships and eligibility to the member schools. But after World War II, the NCAA wrestled for and won jurisdiction over the conduct of the actual member institutions and not just the game itself. At that point, the seeds for decades of tension and internal strife were sown, for that subtle shift in control would one day foster a virtual industry of litigation by students against schools, colleges against coaches, and seemingly everyone at one time or another against the NCAA. Much of the conflict was generated by perennial friction between amateurism and professionalism, a distinction now blurred almost completely by $100,000 athletic scholarships, lavish training tables, and just plain fate, spawning the inevitable role of universities as proving grounds for the pros.

No one can say for sure when the notion of using colleges to breed pro players was first conceived, but one determined young man from Wheaton, Illinois, undoubtedly boosted the idea: Red Grange. In the 1920s, college football and major league baseball dominated sports in America; but in 1924, Red Grange became the first pro football superstar-in-the-making when he led the University of Illinois to a devastating romp over national power Michigan with five touchdowns on opening day in Champaign, Illinois, including a 95-yard touchdown burst on the opening kickoff.

By that time baseball already had its own heroes, from Rogers Hornsby (who batted .424 that same year) to Walter Johnson (23 wins) and Babe Ruth (46 homers and a .378 average), but the National Football League was only four years old. In dire need of heroes, glitz, and a dose of its own lore, the NFL was tailor made for Grange.

Conceived by the legendary George Halas, the emerging NFL was still a motley collection of teams in America's heartland comprised mostly of factory workers from their corporate team sponsors like, for example, the Decatur Staleys (who would later sport a more recognizable label, the Chicago Bears). Halas's ragamuffin players were taken seriously by few staunch fans of true football in an era dominated by collegiate legends at Notre Dame, Michigan, and Army. Pro football was an afterthought in 1924, comparing to big-time college ball rather like the Continental Basketball Association of today stacks up against the NBA.

At Illinois, Grange had become a virtual legend. Donned "the Galloping Ghost" by Grantland Rice, Red Grange would rewrite the Big Ten recordbooks before launching the NFL as an entertainment dynamo. In 1924, Grange's first varsity year, Calvin Coolidge was elected president, J. Edgar Hoover was appointed director of the FBI, Buster Keaton starred in Hollywood, and a newfangled company adopted three innocuous initials for its name: IBM. Grange was bigger than all of them at the time, bigger than life almost, during a year in which America's bestselling authors included Ernest Hemingway, Thomas Mann, and E. M. Forster, and the whole country was hooked on the catchy new tune "Tea for Two."

Everyone grew to know Grange's athletic exploits in short order, but one man recognized the value of his persona, a star power that would change the sports landscape forever. That visionary was George Halas, who, in short order, let his money do the talking. Grange would sign on with the Bears for a whopping $100,000 per year guaranteed deal, bringing instant credibility to the struggling NFL.[1] Almost immediately the Bears were on the map, drawing thirty-six thousand fans to Wrigley Field for a Thanksgiving Day game against the Cardinals, followed by a New York gate exceeding sixty thousand for a game against the Giants.

As Grange's professional star power grew, so did the avarice of his manager, a colorful but opportunistic character by the name of C. C. Pyle. Eventually Pyle induced Grange to abandon the Bears to build an entirely new league around his seemingly invincible persona, founding the first of three hopeful competing leagues to adopt the name American Football League. Almost half a century later, the American Basketball Association would try the same thing with newfound stars and a flashy style of play, as would the USFL in the 1980s with Herschel Walker and Steve Young, not to mention Joe Namath of the most recent AFL.

George Halas was a man of many firsts: the NFL, the T-formation, and the perfection of the forward pass with a gutsy, innovative quarterback from Columbia named Sid Luckman. But in signing the collegiate star Grange, he called attention to the wealth of college talent awaiting the pro ranks. The NFL would gain steam in the 1930s and 1940s while pro basketball struggled with regional leagues that came and went by the decade.

Ironically, although basketball was invented intentionally as a collegiate sport, the original pros did not raid the college ranks for players as they do now. A number of factors contributed to the shift in focus as the decades passed, one of which was George Mikan, who put DePaul University and coach Ray Meyer on the map before doing the same for a fledgling NBA. A more complex cause can be traced to the demographic makeup of college teams, including but by no means limited to racial issues.

College attendance by anyone was obviously much less common in the 1920s than the 1990s, so there just was not that much basketball talent to go around. Besides, those persons receiving college degrees then could do much better sticking with their fields of chosen study (such as engineering, accounting, or teaching) than playing pro basketball. No basketball job was nearly as good as an entry-level business position on Wall Street or, for that matter, Main Street.

As colleges and universities themselves began to proliferate, so naturally did the basketball programs; and at the same time, basketball as a viable source of entertainment and collegiate rivalry gained momentum. As a result, college basketball developed value as an entertainment product, not only developing players in the process but also soaking up other potential players in greater numbers. This latter phenomenon would evolve into the opening of more and more university doors to minorities—notably black athletes—in all major intercollegiate sports, especially football and basketball. Without stirring unnecessary debate about whether affirmative action or supply and demand did more to promote the visibility of minority students, suffice it to say that competition did much to cause white America to embrace black athletes.

With pro leagues developing at the same time that colleges soaked up players, the forces of supply and demand caused all ranks to compete for talent. Initially the pro leagues were afraid to stir the wrath of collegiate America, so they refrained from raiding underclassmen. Had they not exercised restraint, the likes of Wilt Chamberlain and George Mikan may have surfaced in pro uniforms much earlier. But there was much more to the dynamics of basketball than the whims of the NBA or NCAA: players are people.

Players have rights as human beings, and this is still America; so, as Spencer Haywood's case demonstrated, there are greater forces at work. It is an antitrust violation for the NBA to freeze out players who have not used up their college eligibility. Not only is this an overt conspiracy by pro teams, it amounts to an implied (if not actual) conspiracy between the league and the NCAA to protect underclassmen. The word *protect* then becomes problematic, as the institutions argued for years that young athletes must be protected from the demons of pro sports, preserving the integrity, ethics, and college degrees of their young people. The argument lost steam with Spencer Haywood, who was already a pro when frozen out by the NBA on the grounds that other athletes his age had not used up their college eligibility.

Eventually a series of "hardship" rules were implemented by the NCAA allowing underclassmen to bolt for the pros, and today there are virtually no viable grounds to prevent any underclassmen from leaving college in favor of the NBA. But getting to this point was a power struggle of mammoth proportions in its own right, with the NCAA flexing its muscle against student athletes, coaches, and even its own member universities. Originally conceived to oversee the safety of college football players, the NCAA later became the tail wagging the dog, penalizing student athletes and fostering vendettas against some, notably UNLV coach Jerry Tarkanian.

The first public game of basketball seems to have been played on March 11, 1892, between James Naismith's students and their instructors, including Naismith himself and Amos Alonzo Stagg. The students won by the "underwhelming" score of 5–1. Since those innocent days, college basketball has come a long way, now a virtual proving ground for NBA players-in-the-making—but therein lies part of the problem.

Headquartered for much of its modern existence in Kansas City, Missouri, the NCAA developed as an enigmatic keeper of student athlete integrity almost at any cost, begging the question of whether the end justifies the means. Jerry Tarkanian would argue it does not.

Symbolizing what big-time athletics have become, as a rather well-paid coach at UNLV, Tarkanian was at one time the highest-paid public employee in the state of Nevada. This is not a particular indictment of either Tarkanian or Nevada—state employees do not generally make exorbitant salaries, and that includes governors. And no doubt major coaches at such public institutions as Michigan and Penn State make an incredibly good buck when sized up against state political leaders, school superintendents, and even the presidents of their own schools. Still, the notion of

"Tark the Shark" as the highest-paid in Nevada was a daunting pill to swallow if little else.

Moreover, Jerry Tarkanian is a human being, entitled to a certain level of fairness. Instead, he got a 26-year legal battle against the NCAA, including an action by Tarkanian for unfair prosecution. More than a quarter century of litigation was waged by countless lawyers, beginning as Tark arrived at UNLV in 1973. At first the issue involved alleged UNLV rule violations before his arrival, but the NCAA soon included Tarkanian himself as a target. After bouncing up and down the court system ad nauseam, including trips to the United States Supreme Court and at least three jaunts to the Supreme Court of Nevada, a Tarkanian suit against the NCAA was finally scheduled for trial on May 18, 1998, before a Las Vegas jury. On April 2, 1998, virtually on the eve of trial, the embattled Tark was vindicated by a $2.5 million settlement payment from the NCAA.

Tarkanian's skill and qualifications as a coach were remarkable. He had played basketball for Fresno State University, then after a stint coaching high school teams he led Riverside City College to a stunning 145–22 record. At Pasadena City College he did even better, going 67–4; and collectively, his junior college teams won four straight California junior college championships. Moving up as head coach for Long Beach State, Tark went 122–20 before moving on to the University of Nevada–Las Vegas, where in 1990 he won the NCAA championship by thumping Duke 103–73. The NCAA had threatened UNLV as early as 1978, strong-arming it to fire Tarkanian to avoid further NCAA penalties. By the time he was actually forced out many years later, Tark's UNLV teams had compiled a 503–102 record, and overall his Division I aggregate totals rested at 625–122, the highest ever.

Tarkanian almost beat the NCAA as long ago as 1988, narrowly losing in the United States Supreme Court by a 5 to 4 vote, including a scathing dissent by all four justices favoring Tarkanian's position: Justices White, Brennan, Marshall, and O'Connor. When the NCAA threatened UNLV, forcing it to dump its coach, Tarkanian fired back, suing the NCAA for due process violations.[2] Tarkanian's lawyers held that in forcing the hand of UNLV, a Nevada state institution, the NCAA violated due process with its kangaroo court approach to Tark's employment.

The Supreme Court ruled against Tarkanian, with five justices essentially concluding that "private" means "private" and that NCAA activity is not subject to due process scrutiny. The unusually strong dissent by four justices torched that idea, exposing it for what it was: form over substance. Aside from these procedural issues, the minority seems to have been appalled by the case and hearings against Tarkanian in the first place. The NCAA based its case upon unsworn innuendo; Tarkanian responded with affidavits and sworn testimony from real witnesses. The NCAA provided no witnesses for Tark's lawyers to cross-examine. In short, Tarkanian was railroaded.

Justice White, writing for the dissent, believed Tark should have won:

> The majority states in conclusion that "[I]t would be ironic indeed to conclude that the NCAA's imposition of sanctions against UNLV—sanctions that UNLV and its counsel, including the Attorney General of Nevada, steadfastly opposed during protracted adversary proceedings—is fairly attributable to the State of Nevada." I agree. Had UNLV refused to suspend Tarkanian, and the NCAA responded by imposing sanctions against UNLV, it would be hard indeed to find any state action that harmed Tarkanian. But that is not this case. Here, UNLV did suspend Tarkanian, and it did so because it embraced the NCAA rules of the hearings conducted by the NCAA concerning Tarkanian, as it had agreed that it would. Under these facts, I would find that the NCAA acted jointly with UNLV and therefore is a state actor.

Inspired by this strong dissent and other factors, Tarkanian fought back for 10 more years, suing the NCAA not for due process violations but other private sector issues founded upon fundamental fairness and, essentially, unfair prosecution. The Tark settlement was just one of many black eyes suffered by the NCAA over more recent years, chipping away at NCAA powers that were largely unbridled for decades. And then, also in the spring of 1998, the NCAA was hit with its most far-reaching setback ever.

Concurrent to the Tarkanian settlement before a Nevada court, the NCAA was slapped with a $67 million antitrust judgment in favor of NCAA assistant coaches whose compensation had been artificially controlled by a Sherman Act conspiracy to set—and limit—wages. A Kansas City federal jury found the NCAA rules and practices restricting the earnings of 1,900 assistant basketball coaches across the country were conspiratorial and illegal. By August of 1998, national news headlines reported talks of an NCAA breakup. Although a possibility, talk of the dismantling of the NCAA may be premature and certainly could not yet be regarded as likely. Still, it hangs over the NCAA like a foreboding cloud, casting a chilling shadow over NCAA authority.[3]

By no means have coaches and schools been the only victims of NCAA wrath. It often is deployed against students and, to be fair, often with good reason. There has been so much abuse of the collegiate system that it is impossible to condemn the NCAA for all the ills of intercollegiate sports. But trouble arises when the end begins to justify the means, when investigations become witch-hunts, when contempt for the underbelly of major college sports wrongfully inspires the NCAA to overreact when logic and constraint would do.

In the 1980s a pair of high-flying sports-agents-in-the-making amassed a stable of as many as 60 pro player clients, mostly by paying them thousands of dollars in under-the-table loans during their college careers. Norby Walters and Lloyd Bloom rose and fell as rapidly and dramatically as any sports agents possibly could, slipping cash to such collegiate standouts as Auburn star Brent Fullwood (Packers first-round pick in 1987), Rod Woodson (Steelers), Reggie Rogers (Lions), and many, many others, including basketball stars Derrick McKey and Brad Sellers. All payments were in flagrant violation of NCAA rules, so NCAA trepidation is quite understandable.

More recently, the agent for first-round running back Curtis

Enis was suspended by the NFL Players Association, the regulatory body for agent qualifications, for having bought Curtis a new suit in college. With colleges and universities the principal breeding ground for pro players in basketball and football, the temptation for agents to recruit players with cash and gifts is extraordinary, as is the genuine need by some players to take the money.

This intercollegiate farm system of pro player development is highly susceptible to abuses, undermining the integrity of college athletics. The NCAA clearly believed Tarkanian's program at UNLV was corrupt, and given that belief, its concerns were understandable. But the road to hell, as they say, is paved with good intentions—and suspending fundamental fairness, whether or not it comprised due process as a term of art, is seldom justified.

When the NCAA strays from safety issues, it frequently runs aground; and when it forays into the issue of student athlete eligibility, it often stumbles, sometimes even turning against the students it is supposed to protect. The problem is not new, of course, but how far back it goes is startling. Consider the following public remarks by William Faunce, the president of Brown University:

> We are living in a time when college athletics are honeycombed with falsehood, and when the professions of amateurism are usually hypocrisy. No college team ever meets another today with actual faith in the other's eligibility.

Those thoughts should generate little argument in today's world of intercollegiate sports—but considering that they were made in 1904, it is clear that college sports have been less than pristine for a long, long while. If that is not enough, try this excerpt from the *Atlantic Monthly*, November 1915:

> Roughly speaking, success in attaining the aims of athletics as education is inversely proportional to success in attaining the aims of athletics as business. Intercollegiate athletics today are for business. The question is pertinent whether schools and colleges should promote athletics as business.

The greatest source for strife in the world of amateur collegiate athletics is the inherent conflict between business and sport. Intercollegiate athletics has become a significant business at many, if not most, Division I schools, although the labor supplied by players is supposed to be strictly amateur. Amateurism is a noble objective for centers of higher education, but the laws of supply and demand cannot be broken by artificial rules or superficially good intentions. Economics will find a way. Money will seep into the pockets of coveted players, airplane tickets will magically appear, and sleek new cars will glide into otherwise innocent driveways, turning poor kids into virtual criminals.

Volumes have been written for the sole purpose of solving that conflict, and many volumes more will no doubt be published with little progress, so solving the problem may not be easy. Nonetheless, as a first step the fundamental premise of the collegiate sports business must be overhauled from the ground up, eliminating the intrinsic conflict in waging a for-profit business with nonprofit labor. Some argue that the NCAA should give up the ruse of amateurism and pay the players outright; others lobby for limited stipends or relaxed work rules; and many suggest that students should be students, so admission standards should be the same for all students, leaving the developmental farm system duties to those who can afford them: the pro teams. Baseball does it that way; hence, the public rarely hears of a paid-off college baseball player.

Each possible solution offers many pros and cons. For example, just raising academic standards might unduly prejudice minority members whose only hope at an education comes in the form of a college scholarship. On the other hand, perhaps minorities would be better served if the issue were handled more directly: if society desires to give minorities a break, then it should do so. But there is little logic in singling out football and basketball players, for vast legions of potential minority students are not athletes at all.

Either way, the fact remains that today's collegiate institutions have become the for-profit farm systems of the NBA, NFL, and various other pro and semipro leagues, generating a hostile playing field for student athletes forced to fight arbitrary admission and eligibility standards. For example, when the NCAA sanctions a university for past violations, it hurts the existing body of innocent student athletes. Does this seem like an honorable objective for an intercollegiate organization like the NCAA?

Bradley University star basketball player Hersey Hawkins did not think so, and neither did his teammates; they sued the NCAA in 1987 for equal protection and due process violations when Bradley was sanctioned by the NCAA due to the actions of players before them. They lost, but part of the problem could have been that Bradley was not a state institution. Hawkins went on to be a highly successful NBA standout, but his teammates suffered from the incident. Bryant Notree, a high school superstar basketball player, was forced to threaten suit when the NCAA changed the rules midstream. When Notree arrived at the University of Illinois to play ball, he came up a half-credit short, prompting the NCAA to rule him ineligible. Notree thought he had complied fully because of a consumer education course he took in high school during his junior year. At that time, the individual universities certified their own athletes—but after Notree was accepted by Illinois, the NCAA took control and disqualified certain courses. Suddenly Notree was out in the cold, unable to play Big Ten basketball even though he had followed all the rules.

To make matters worse for Notree, experts who were quoted publicly at the time believed Illinois did not appeal the ruling to the NCAA or support a legal action in court for fear of NCAA reprisals. Even though experts agreed that Illinois and/or Notree himself would win such an action as a breach of fundamental private sector fairness and due process, Illinois's position was reminiscent of the inherent NCAA power exposed by the Tarkanian case.[4] In Notree's case, the NCAA eventually relented, reinstating his eligibility. But others have not been so lucky, including Robert Parish who, before a stellar NBA career as center for the Boston Celtics, found himself on the wrong end of an NCAA eligibility issue.

In a twist of fate, another Illinois recruit was not so lucky. In 1996, the NCAA ruled that the minimum core high school course requirements were not met by basketball player Fess Hawkins.

The NCAA would not relent, so Hawkins left Illinois to attend West Arkansas Junior College. Hawkins obtained his associate degree and returned to Illinois where he played during the 1998 season.

In the early 1970s the NCAA operated under a standard then known as the 1.600 Rule, a formula designed to "predict" an incoming college student's likely grade-point average. The rule's name was simply derived from the minimum projected grade point necessary for athletic eligibility: 1.600 on a 4.00 scale. The requisite formula was a function of high school class rank, high school cumulative grade-point average, and a score on one of the two major college entrance exams, the ACT or SAT. Parish did not do well on the ACT portion of the predictor and therefore failed the 1.600 Rule, preventing his eligibility to play for Centenary College.[5] Parish then filed a federal lawsuit in Louisiana to enjoin the NCAA from applying the rule and, instead, to use his high school grades only.

Centenary had signed Parish to a full athletic scholarship on August 17, 1972, but by failing the 1.600 Rule standards he was ineligible to play, prompting his lawsuit. The actions of a private association such as the NCAA are subject to very limited scrutiny, the general rule being that these bodies are free to govern themselves with little to no judicial interference. In 1973, the court ruled against Parish, deferring to the inherently broad NCAA powers—a decision that would be less likely to occur today on the grounds that the now defunct 1.600 Rule would be deemed arbitrary and capricious, if not discriminatory. Most important, few courts today would give the NCAA a pass on the most interesting paradox of the case: by the time the court ruled against Parish a year later, he had actually maintained a higher average than the rule mandated. Thus, to follow an arbitrary rule designed at best to predict a student athlete's expected grade point in lieu of using the actual average available is ludicrous. In this day and age when the NCAA is no longer revered as the do-no-wrong messiah of intercollegiate competition, it is unlikely a federal judge would rubber stamp such an obvious injustice.

Even the judge in Parish's case recognized the "Hobson's choice" dilemma in balancing so many competing interests, from the careers of young athletes to the NCAA's right to govern to the ability of colleges to rule on the good standing of their own students. Nonetheless, he concluded—rightfully—that for equal protection issues to apply, the NCAA would have to be a government body, not a private institution. What the court failed to recognize, though, is an emerging body of law imposing private sector due process standards in lieu of strict Constitutional protection under such circumstances.

Win or lose, Parish demonstrated the absurd ends to which NCAA rules can be followed. Of course, if the NCAA were not a virtual farm system for the NBA, the issue might have been moot. If the NBA were run like baseball, there would be a minor league system to play in.[6] With the Spencer Haywood decision, the NBA can take underclassmen, expanding the farm system's flexibility and usefulness, and today even a handful of high school players are jumping straight to the big show of pro basketball. But overall the intercollegiate farm system flourishes, vesting corresponding power in the NCAA oversight of playmaster proportions, dictating the futures of students and universities alike, often arbitrarily.

More recently, the NCAA has pursued rule changes to allow student athletes to earn up to $2,000 per year from part-time jobs. Previously, student athletes were not allowed the privilege of working—putting them at a disadvantage to other students, at least where spending money was concerned (but not overall athletic scholarships, which are often quite generous, running up to $25,000 per year).

On a separate front, private entrepreneurs have announced plans to form a new pro league to accommodate hopeful players still developing for the NBA. Since only 44 percent of Division I male basketball players graduate anyway, this new Collegiate Professional Basketball League (CPBL) hopes to provide an alternative for talented players not otherwise qualified for, or interested in, college. This new CPBL hopes to field teams with corporate sponsors and qualified athletes up to 22 years old, paying the kids stipends of up to $17,000 per season. In some ways this duplicates the opportunity of the Continental Basketball Association, which has a history of breeding players who wind up in the NBA. But the twist is that in addition to compensation, the new league would encourage and even help kids stay in school if their pro careers do not pan out—and most will not. So the CPBL proposes offering scholarship money up to $20,000 per year for four years, a noble idea fraught with holes. Most kids who were ineligible for college in the first place and then fail in the pros as well are unlikely to enter, attend, and graduate college.

Whether the CPBL makes it or not, the league highlights much of what is wrong with the NCAA approach. Allowing student athletes up to $2,000 in part-time earnings may help some, but it will certainly not replace or discourage under-the-table cash from agents and boosters, which is more lucrative and less time consuming than a part-time job. For now, we are left with NCAA schools as the NBA farm system, and any meaningful change soon is highly unlikely.

ENDNOTES

1. In later years, Halas would not maintain a reputation as a big spender, inspiring Bears tight end and later coach Mike Ditka to once observe something to the effect that "Halas throws nickels around like manhole covers."
2. This is an incredibly complex legal issue. Constitutional due process applies only to state, local, or federal government action, and so it is not necessarily a restriction on private actors like the NCAA. However, a private actor can intertwine itself with a government body sufficiently to invoke jurisdiction indirectly.
3. It is hard to justify these restrictions as anything but conspiratorial, unfair, and illegal. With head coaches free to make high six-figure incomes (more in some cases), there is no rational purpose for a supposedly paternalistic organization to play a role in controlling university salary costs.
4. I was one of those experts quoted by the *Chicago Tribune* on October 21, 1994.

5. Actually Parish scored an "8" on the ACT, woefully poor, but not necessarily so reflective of his intelligence as of other issues such as education and cultural upbringing.

6. To some degree there is such an NBA system: the Continental Basketball Association (CBA), the official development league of the NBA. A modest league with teams from mostly small heartland cities (such as Columbus, Wichita Falls, Topeka, Rockford, and LaCrosse), the CBA has been around for over 50 years, spawning an impressive number of NBA journeymen on the way up, and harboring a few aging veterans on the way down.

THE ARCHITECTS OF FATE

PART II

7

THE MAGIC AND BIRD SHOW

History is a temporal beast, it appears— for as the future unfolds, it is the past that seems to change. Thus is the value of hindsight—sometimes overrated, sometimes underrated, but always more accurate than the present.

Some of the greatest players in NBA history were at one time in the grasp of teams that let them slip away due to neglect or perhaps just plain fate. Lakers icon Kareem Abdul-Jabbar began his career with the Milwaukee Bucks until he was shipped off for a bevy of journeyman-type players: Elmore Smith, Brian Winters, Dave Meyers, and Junior Bridgeman. Magic Johnson should have been drafted by the New Orleans Jazz in 1979, but the Jazz had already traded their number-one pick to the Lakers in 1978 for Gail Goodrich. And of course Wilt Chamberlain was a Warrior before he, too, wound up a Laker.

In 1956, Celtics owner Walter Brown and coach Red Auerbach wheeled, dealed, and wrested away Bill Russell from the St. Louis Hawks; in Boston, all Russell did was anchor a Celtics dynasty. And certainly one of the greatest foul-ups of all was Portland passing up Michael Jordan in the 1984 draft in favor of injury-prone center Sam Bowie. Actually, both Portland and Houston passed on Michael, but it is hard to criticize the Rockets, who chose Hakeem Olajuwon number one.

To set the cause
above renown,
To love the game
beyond the prize,
To honour, while you
strike him down,
The foe that comes
with fearless eyes.

—SIR HENRY
NEWBOLT

Various levels of fate, luck, and foresight have conspired to elevate and then re-elevate the NBA at numerous key points in its fragile history. In some ways those who made them happen can symbolize those "events": George Mikan, Chamberlain and Russell, Bird and Magic, and Michael Jordan.[1] All appeared on the scene at crucial times, taking the NBA to a new level and, in some cases, rescuing it from the negative vectors of fate. Mikan, of course, launched the era of the big man; Chamberlain and Russell took both the level of play and the league itself to a new stratosphere; Magic Johnson and Larry Bird rescued a lethargic, struggling league of the late 1970s; and Michael Jordan did his own magic, first maintaining the NBA torch beyond the eventual Bird and Johnson retirements, then torching the league for points, fame, and quantum leap dollars—earning every cent as he took the NBA to unimagined heights.

Although the 1970s sported its share of super players, the league began to struggle with the fame and money that often plague success. Allegations of drug use crept into the league, fan discontent and apathy took hold, and the NBA was forced to scramble. One of its two most productive moves was to install David Stern as commissioner, helping assure continuous growth and prosperity at least until the 1998 lockout. Another great accomplishment was more a function of luck, yet certainly all luck can be misused or just plain screwed up—so when the league landed Larry Bird and Magic Johnson in 1979, it was handed a key to the future that, fortunately, was not lost on the insightful Stern.

Both Magic and Bird proved to be stunning talents. Magic could play every position on the court, and even had a short stint at center for the Lakers when Abdul-Jabbar was injured. Both could shoot and score, and both regularly reeled off heart-stopping passes. Passes? Not until the era of Bird and Magic did an assist become a showstopper. Bird could do full-sprint no-look passes anywhere on the court—over his shoulder, behind his back, between his legs, and sometimes even between the defender's legs. Johnson perfected the no-look assist, and then developed the fake assist by pulling the string on the ball at the last minute to take it in himself, practically parting the surprised defender from his shoes. Johnson would continue to work his magic for a whole career, eventually setting NBA assist records for both a single game (24) and a whole season (989).

For the NBA, 1979 was a watershed year. The NCAA Final Four included a stubborn team from Penn; a strong DePaul team under coach Ray Meyer; Bird's Indiana State club; and Magic's Michigan State Spartans, led by veteran coach Jud Heathcote. In a head-to-head NCAA championship contest, the Spartans prevailed over Bird's Indiana State. After picking up the Final Four MVP honors, Johnson elected to leave school early and was drafted by the Los Angeles Lakers. Bird landed with Boston, and the rest is history—a lot of history.

With both a country-sounding name and hometown, Larry Joe Bird was a lanky 6′9″ symbol of middle America from Indiana's French Lick High School. Although known for his accomplishments at Indiana State, Bird actually spent time at Indiana University in Bloomington, scoring perhaps one of history's best "I-told-you-so"s with his departure. In three years at Indiana State (he sat out a year due to his transfer), Bird averaged 30.3 points per game on .533 shooting, picking up 1,247 rebounds along the way. Still technically a junior in 1978, Bird was drafted by Boston as the sixth pick of the first round.

Earvin Johnson, Jr., gained stardom at Michigan State University, where he played for two years until drafted by the Lakers as the very first pick of the 1979 draft. A product of Michigan all the way, Magic was born at Lansing on August 14, 1959, and first made his basketball mark in high school at Lansing.

Johnson was personable and articulate, perfecting his game on the hardwood and growing as an ambassador for the NBA off the court. Bird was much more quiet off the court, but both were fierce competitors in game situations. Although prolific scorers, neither would lead the league in scoring during any season, mostly because of their all-around team approach to the game with rebounding, scoring, and assists. They also had tough competition during their stay in the league from scoring leaders George Gervin (twice), Adrian Dantley (twice), Alex English, Bernard King, and Dominique Wilkins. Then, beginning in 1986–87, a human scoring buzz saw took over in the form of Michael Jordan, who led all comers with a 37.1 average. (Jordan would win the scoring title seven times in a row before his short-lived retirement during most of the two seasons from 1993 to 1995; then he would keep winning again through the 1997–98 season.)

Magic Johnson led the league in assists four out of five years from 1982 to 1987 (Isiah Thomas led in the middle with 13.9 assists per game for the 1984–85 season). Beginning in 1987, John Stockton took over with an impressive run of assists, and he was still piling them on in 1999. Oscar Robertson had a good run in the 1960s, winning the assist title six times in nine years. Bob Cousy took the league lead eight times in a row from 1952 to 1960, finally supplanted by Robertson in the 1960–61 season.

Understandably, perimeter players almost always won the assist title, notably point guards feeding the ball to post players and others. Magic, too, was a guard, although at 6'9" he was an imposing figure who played multiple positions. But one year the assist title would go to a center, and a dominating post player at that: Wilt Chamberlain. During his stint with the Lakers, Wilt scored much less than in his early years, instead focusing on rebounding and kicking the ball out to open perimeter players—especially in 1967–68, when he won the assist title. With that, the Lakers actually ran the court in reverse, with the point feeding Chamberlain and causing the defense to collapse, enabling others to shake free for a pass from the post. Sometimes Wilt would work a high post and fake the kick-out, turning and leaning in for a finger-roll basket, but during much of the 1960s and 1970s he became a prolific passer to the open man. In some ways his game sounds like that of Shaquille O'Neal, but Shaq still lacks the on-court savvy that made Wilt dangerous on every play, especially where assists and consistency are concerned.

Whether scoring points in quantity or not, Chamberlain was nonetheless a dependable shooter with his array of dunks, lay-ups, and finger rolls. No one in the NBA had ever shot over 50 percent from the field during the course of an entire season until Wilt arrived and shot 50.9 percent in 1960–61. By 1966–67, he shot a stunning 68.3 percent from the field; and the following year, when he won the assist title, Chamberlain still shot a remarkable 59.5 percent. The final year he took the shooting title was 1972-73 when he canned 72.7 percent of his shots during the course of the season.

Kevin McHale, Boston's lanky forward with a deceptive reach, led the league in field goal percentage for two years from 1986–88, no doubt helped along by a load of his own offensive rebounds plus some prolific passing by Larry Bird. Like Magic, Bird was a consummate all-around player. He led the league in free throw percentage four times from 1983 to 1990. Bird was MVP of the All-Star Game in 1982, a year before Dr. J won the honor. Listed at 6'9", the deceptively quick Bird could drive, shoot the three-pointer, dish off, or muscle for rebounds down low, and he was rewarded as the league MVP three straight years from 1983 to 1986. Michael Jordan and Magic Johnson would virtually share the title, trading off MVP honors over the next six years. With all his accolades, though, Magic did manage to come up short for the NBA Rookie of the Year award, losing out to his colleague and rival Larry Bird in 1979–80.

Bird was also MVP of the league championship finals twice, but Magic Johnson did it three times. With its string of superstars transcending different eras, it is not surprising the Boston Celtics have won the most total NBA titles: 16. With help from Mikan, Chamberlain, Abdul-Jabbar, and Magic, the Lakers are second with 11. The Chicago Bulls are third with six championships.[2]

The pre-Bird NBA of the 1970s certainly had its moments, sporting such diverse players as Pistol Pete Maravich, Walt Hazzard, Earl Monroe, Jerry Sloan, Dave Bing, Phil Jackson, and even Pat Riley. During the 1971–72 season, for example, Abdul-Jabbar led the league in scoring at a 34.8 clip, Boston's Havlicek third at 27.5, Spencer Haywood fourth with 26.2, and Jerry West seventh with 25.8.

The 1978–79 season, the year before the arrival of Magic and Bird, found the Seattle Supersonics winning the NBA championship under coach Lenny Wilkens. The Chicago Bulls finished last in their division at 31–51 and 17 games behind Kansas City. Artis Gilmore averaged 23.7 PPG as their center, racking up 156 blocked shots over the course of 82 games, and Reggie Theus, known now more as a broadcaster, was Chicago's flashy shooter. No team won more than 54 regular season games that year (the Washington Bullets at 54–28), and only three won at least 50 (Seattle, Phoenix, and Washington).

The pre-Bird Celtics were led by Bob McAdoo's 20.6 PPG average, and the 1978 Lakers were paced by Abdul-Jabbar's 23.8. Spencer Haywood led the Knicks at 17.8 after Bob McAdoo was sent to Boston midyear, and Julius Erving was going strong for Philadelphia at 23.1. Then, in 1979, Larry Bird shot to immediate stardom, leading the Celtics with a 21.3 scoring average while playing in all 82 games. His 370 assists were second on the team to Nate Archibald; he led the team in steals, and added an .836 free throw percentage for good measure.

The 1978–79 Celtics were dead last in their division, 25 games behind Washington with a dismal 29–53 record. With Bird, the 1979–80 Celtics skyrocketed to a 61–21 first-place finish, made the playoffs, and beat Houston four games straight in the Eastern Conference semifinals before they finally bowed to Philadelphia in the conference finals. The Lakers turnaround was less dramatic, but the ultimate results more spectacular with the assistance of Magic Johnson. Their pre-Magic record of 47–35 was good enough for third place in the Pacific Division. Already stocked with other capable stars, not the least of whom was Kareem Abdul-Jabbar,[3] the Lakers benefited from Magic's all-around game and leadership, upping their mark to a first-place 60–22. But Magic and the Lakers were not through, dominating the playoffs with a combined 12–4 run over Phoenix, Seattle, and Philadelphia to capture the 1980 NBA championship.

Let the rivalries begin. The very next season, Bird's Celtics tied Philadelphia for the best record in the NBA at 62–20, then swept the Bulls in the playoffs, outlasted Philadelphia 4–3 in the Eastern Conference finals, and beat Houston 4–2 for the NBA championship.[4] In 1981–82, both Boston (63–19) and Los Angeles finished first in their respective divisions. Boston made it through one round of the playoffs, succumbing to Philadelphia 4–3 in the conference finals, while L.A. marched straight to the championship with a 4–2 finals record over Philadelphia.

Led by the still dominant Julius Erving, Philadelphia was a perennial contender in those years, playing the spoiler against Bird or Johnson more than once. In 1981–82, Dr. J's 24.4 scoring average was good enough for fourth place in the league, ahead of Bird's 22.9 in tenth place. Magic checked in at 18.6, finishing out of the top twenty, although he was first in the league with steals and second in assists. Not to be totally outdone, Erving's 1982–83 Philadelphia team won it all, thumping the Lakers 4–0 in the finals.

But overall the NBA was hitting its stride in the early 1980s, spreading its wings as an entertainment dynamo sporting Johnson, Bird, Erving, and Abdul-Jabbar in a dazzling array of basketball talent. Showtime had arrived.

Other players would come and go, but Bird and Magic were a bastion of consistency. For example, in 1982–83 the Bulls' Reggie Theus arguably turned in as good a year as Bird individually. Reggie outscored Bird 23.8 (ninth best in the league) to 23.6 (eleventh). Bird had 148 steals, Reggie 143; Theus 484 assists, Bird 458; Bird shot free throws at an .840 clip with Reggie logging in at .801. Theus played in all 82 games that year, Bird in 79, although Theus was disqualified six times to Bird's zero. Bird outdid the smaller Theus for rebounds, though, by a whopping 870 to 300, but Reggie made almost 100 more free throws than Bird.

The 1982–83 Philadelphia champions were in the hunt from the start, streaking to a stunning 65–17 regular-season record, good for a nine-game lead over second-place Boston. The Lakers won their division by five games over Phoenix and met the powerful 76ers in the finals only to be drubbed by Dr. J's team in a four-game sweep. Moses Malone led Philadelphia that year with a 24.5 scoring average, while Erving was second on the team at 21.4.

Finally, Bird and Johnson met head-on in the 1984 NBA Championship Finals, a relentless seven-game war. Win or lose, both teams scored over 100 points every game. The Lakers marched into Boston and stole a six-point win 115–109 in Game 1. But the series was hard fought all the way. Two games went into overtime with the Celtics winning both, a 124–121 victory at home and a crucial 129-125 road win at Los Angeles. Both teams held serve over the last three games, Boston holding on at home for a 111–102 Game 7 triumph.

Bird and Magic had turned in particularly good efforts during that 1984 season. Bird led his team in rebounds, garnering one more than his imposing center Robert Parish, and his 24.2 scoring average was seventh best in the league (Utah's Dantley was first at 30.6) while Bird led the NBA in free throw shooting at .888. Magic only turned in a 17.6 scoring mark (second to Abdul-Jabbar on his own team, who had 21.5), but he fed everyone else on the team to the tune of 875 assists, leading the NBA with a 13.1 assists per game average. Those assists were 2 per game ahead of second-place finishers Isiah Thomas (Detroit) and Norm Nixon (San Diego), who came in at 11.1 each. Magic also logged 2.24 steals per game, fifth best in the league.

In 1985 both the Lakers (62 wins) and Celtics (63) won over 60 games, taking their respective division titles and plowing through the playoffs to meet again in the championship series. The Lakers took Phoenix, Portland, and Denver by a combined 11 games to 2, and Boston eliminated Cleveland, Detroit, and Philadelphia 11–4. In the finals Boston roared to a 34-point home victory to take Game 1 148–114, but the shell-shocked Lakers fought back with a 109–102 road victory in Game 2. Going home for Game 3, the Lakers stomped Boston by 25 points, then let Game 4 slip away by 2. In Game 5 Los Angeles held serve, setting up Game 6 back in Beantown, where Magic's Lakers surprised Bird's troops with an 11-point win to take the series 4–2.

The 1984–85 season would prove to be a turning point, although it was not entirely obvious at the time. Bird exploded for a 28.7 per game scoring average, good for second in the league behind the Knicks' Bernard King (32.9). Bird was also eighth in rebounding (10.5 per game), second in three-point field goals (.427—a remarkable feat for a 6′9″ forward) and fifth in league free throws at .882. Magic turned in his usual consistent performance with a second-place finish in assists (12.6 behind Thomas's

13.9), ninth in field goal percentage (.561), and, of course, capturing the 1985 NBA championship.

But something else happened in that 1984–85 year that would change the NBA forever. The league then maintained eight official categories of individual statistics: points, field goals, assists, rebounds, free throws, steals, blocked shots, and three-point field goal percentage. That year a skinny, tongue-wagging kid with bright eyes and a sparkling future crept into the NBA top 10 finishers in two of those categories: points and steals.

ENDNOTES

1. There certainly have been other great players, even many who made historic imprints on the game, including Oscar Robertson, Kareem Abdul-Jabbar, and Hakeem Olajuwon. But none of them changed the game itself both on and off the court.
2. If 1999 is any indication, the once dominant Bulls will not be padding their total anytime soon.
3. Other notable names on the roster included the likes of Norm Nixon and Spencer Haywood, rounded out by Jamaal Wilkes, Michael Cooper, Jim Chones, and Don Ford.
4. Houston had squeaked into the playoffs with a mediocre regular season mark of 40–42, surprising the Lakers in a short three-game series in the first round, then outlasting both San Antonio and Kansas City to the championship series.

8

A CHANGING OF THE GUARD

Just as the Chamberlain–Russell match-ups launched the NBA to credibility as an entertainment dynamo, the Magic-Bird show elevated the league to yet a new level of stardom. In 1986 Boston was in the finals again, capturing still another championship, this time 4–2 over Houston. That particular title run included a first-round three-game sweep of the Chicago Bulls and featured a rousing 135–131 Boston home victory in double overtime. It also provided a glimpse of basketball to come, for Michael Jordan lit up the Celtics with 63 points, the most ever in an NBA playoff game—2 more than Elgin Baylor's 61 and 7 better than Wilt Chamberlain's third-place performance of 56.

Be not afraid of greatness: some men are born great, some achieve greatness, and some have greatness thrust upon them.

— WILLIAM SHAKESPEARE

Jordan was the new kid on the block, capable of great individual efforts but not quite ready to capture the essence of greatness itself. While he flashed glimpses of the grandeur he would later radiate on the hardwood, Jordan was relegated to the NBA roster of neophytes (though a very, very good one) still paying their basketball dues.

The following year once again found the Lakers atop the NBA with a 4–3 finals victory over a tough, defense-minded Detroit team just beginning to spread its own wings as an NBA contender. Detroit had beaten the Celtics 4–2 in the Eastern Conference finals and fought valiantly against a strong Lakers team in a series of trademark defensive struggles. In five of the seven games at least one team failed to break 100 points, and the high score of the series was logged by Detroit when it won Game 4 at home 111–86.

Many NBA changes were afoot by that 1987–88 season. Erving was gone from Philadelphia, and the 76ers were gone from the playoffs altogether with a 36–46 record, 21 games behind division-leading Boston. Michael Jordan again topped the league in scoring with a 35.0 average, Bird was good for a strong third place at 29.9, and Boston teammate Kevin McHale logged in at 22.6, good for eleventh best in scoring and first in field goal percentage at .604. Magic was absent from the top 20 scoring list, but he was still a major force with 11.9 assists per game, second to John Stockton's 13.8. Magic won the championship, too, but Bird had a better individual year in scoring (29.9), free throws (.916), and three-point shots (.414). That same season Dennis Rodman, wearing a Pistons uniform, turned up in an odd category of individual performances—no, not rebounding (he was not in the top 10) but, rather, in field goal shooting. In 1987–88, Rodman shot 398 for 709, good for sixth best in the NBA at .561.

Jordan continued to shine defensively, leading the league in steals with a remarkable 3.16 per game. He also had 131 blocked shots, an impressive number for a guard. By contrast, Magic blocked only 13 that year and had 114 total steals to Jordan's 259. And of course Magic's scoring average of 19.6 PPG was just over half of MJ's 35.0. How did Bird do? He logged 125 steals and 57 blocked shots, hauling down 703 rebounds to exactly 449 for each of Jordan and Johnson.

Although Magic demonstrated less-than-spectacular individual statistics, he still was a powerhouse competitor, winning the championship ring and leading his team on and off the floor. The Lakers under coach Pat Riley had the best record in the NBA that year at 62–20, five more victories than second-place Boston.[1]

Eventually the Magic-Bird era would come to a close, but it did not go quietly—and, contrary to the collective public memory, it was not supplanted by Jordan and the Bulls. A roughneck bunch of competitors out of Detroit would not be denied a place in the sun, and they energetically followed coach Chuck Daly to the promised land not once, but twice in those intervening years.

With not one player averaging over 19 points per game, the 1989 Pistons were an enigma. Seven other NBA teams had two players over 19 that year, and three more teams had three players each: Dallas (Aguirre, Blackman, and Dantley); the Lakers (Magic, Worthy, and Scott);[2] and Phoenix (Chambers and the two Johnsons, Eddie and Kevin). But the Pistons had no fewer than seven players averaging double figures, all bunched together from Bill Laimbeer's 13.7 PPG to Mark Aguirre's 18.9. Isiah Thomas scored a more-than-respectable 18.2 in 80 games played and added 8.3 assists per game, good for ninth best in the NBA. An emerging Dennis Rodman, who flourished under the "players' coach" Daly, was close to double figures with 9.0 PPG, but he *led the league* in shooting at a .595 clip. The pesky Rodman also began to find his niche in rebounding, logging 772 while playing in all 82 games.

During Detroit's 1988–89 season the whole team had not one player among the NBA leaders in scoring, free throws, steals, blocked shots, or three-pointers—yet they led the league in regular season victories (63–19) and won the NBA title with a 4–0 thrashing of Magic's Lakers in the finals. How could that be? To begin, they were second in the league in team defense, allowing only 100.8 points per game, just behind Utah's 99.7. They also led the league in team free throw percentage at .785 and were nearly unbeatable at home with 37 wins, best in the NBA. The Pistons were also stocked with talented veterans and role players, including a very effective John Salley, Rick Mahorn, and James Edwards—not to mention a very underrated Joe Dumars, who averaged 17.2 per game. They also had wily coach Chuck Daly, one of only two coaches (along with Phil Jackson) to command the respect of the irascible Rodman.

Perhaps most of all, those Detroit teams won with attitude, hustle, and sheer intimidation. Cocky and physical, the Pistons changed how other teams played, frustrating them with a relentless in-your-face defensive style designed to bring out the worst in opponents. It did, and it worked.

But the Pistons were not without competition. The year before, an emerging Bulls team finally fought its way beyond the first round of the playoffs with a 3–2 series win over a frustrated Cleveland team forced to witness the maturing heroics of Michael Jordan. But those 1987–88 Bulls ran into a Detroit buzz saw in the Eastern Conference semifinals, falling to the Pistons 4–1. Punishing the Bulls with two consecutive blowouts on the road in Chicago for Games 3 and 4, the Pistons at once humiliated the Bulls and set the stage for a bitter rivalry.

In 1988–89 Jordan's Bulls were mired in fifth place, a full 16 games behind league-leading Detroit. But their respectable 47–35 mark was good enough to qualify for the playoffs, where once again they met Cleveland for a five-game first-round series. The Bulls stole home-court advantage with a Game 1 victory at Cleveland, but both teams held serve for the next two. Cleveland took a Game 4 war in Chicago in overtime, 108–104, setting up a Game 5 thriller in Cleveland. Faced with a do-or-die challenge, the Bulls scrounged a 101–100 last-second victory on the shoulders of Jordan's ending nail-in-the-coffin bucket remembered in the annals of Bulls lore simply as "the shot."

Again the Bulls had asserted themselves, moving forward to take on a tough Knicks team in New York for the semifinals. Their confidence growing, Chicago wrested home-court advantage once again with an opening overtime victory. The Knicks held on for Game 2, but Chicago won two in a row at home, holding the Knicks to only 88 and 93 points. The Knicks won again at home, trailing the Bulls by a game at 3–2 with the Game 6 stage set for Chicago.

By 1989 the Knicks' identity as a physical force was much entrenched behind the likes of Patrick Ewing, Charles Oakley, and Rod Strickland. The Bulls were finding an identity, too, settling into their triangle motion offense that produced five players averaging in double figures, including, of course, Jordan's league-leading 32.5. Ironically, as Jordan's average slipped ever so slightly, the team began to go deeper into the playoffs with a balanced cast of role players beginning to take shape: Scottie Pippen, Bill Cartwright (the former Knick, a quid pro quo for former Bull, Charles Oakley), the emotional power forward Horace Grant, and the quiet three-point sharpshooter Craig Hodges. With an eclectic supporting cast of Will Perdue, the priceless John Paxson at point, the disappointing 7-footer Brad Sellers, plus Dave Corzine, Jack Haley, and Ed Nealy, the Bulls defense checked in at fifth best in the league, holding opponents to a 105 scoring average.

The Knicks, down 3–2 on the road against a confident Chicago and relentless Jordan, were ripe for the taking. The Bulls did not disappoint the home crowd, engineering a two-point squeaker to take Game 6 113–111 and the series 4–2. For the second year in a row they would confront the brute-force Pistons in a deep playoff round, this time for the conference finals.

Meanwhile, the once-mighty Boston Celtics were fading. They finished third in their division, 10 games out, with a 42–40 record. Age and injuries were catching up to Larry Bird, who played in only six games all year, averaging less than 20 points in those with McHale and Parish picking up the slack. Still, Boston sneaked into the playoffs only to be dismantled by the mighty Pistons 3–0 in a short series, succumbing in Game 3 at home by 15 points.

The Lakers were faring much better. Their 57 regular season wins were good enough for the Pacific Division title by two games over a balanced, high-scoring Phoenix team that lead the NBA in offense at 118.6 PPG. With Abdul-Jabbar fading in scoring and rebounds, Magic carried the team on his shoulders. Johnson was forced to score, and he came through with a 22.5 average, good for fifteenth best in the league, a superlative achievement given that he still logged 988 assists while directing the team from the point, not to mention 607 rebounds and 138 steals along the way. Magic's assists were second in the league again (12.8 to Stockton's 13.6), but in 1988–89 another name would slip onto the list at the tenth spot: Michael Jordan. Still, Magic was "the man," nailing 988 total assists to Jordan's 650 on the year.

Magic's Lakers exploded into the playoffs, first lambasting a weak Portland team three games straight, then stunning a good Seattle group 4–0. Armed with home-court advantage, the surging Lakers awaited the Phoenix Suns, who had only needed five games to eliminate a decent Golden State team.

Phoenix was an interesting team. Not spectacular, not formidable—just interesting. It had won 55 games to finish only two behind the division-leading Lakers; and with five players in double figures, three of whom logged over 20 PPG,[3] the Suns could light up the scoreboard, which they did, leading the league in team scoring. Their downfall was defense. Mired in sixteenth place in total defense, the Suns gave up an average of 110.9 PPG. They had no players among the league leaders in steals or rebounds, although center Mark West did manage 2.28 blocks per game, good for seventh best in the NBA. On the other side, Eddie Johnson hit three-pointers at a .413 rate, sixth best in the league, and his teammate Kevin Johnson was sixth best in free throws at .882.

When Phoenix matched up against the Lakers in the 1989 Western Conference finals, it bared its Achilles heel right away. Scoring an impressive 119 points on the road against the Lakers, the Suns' offense held true in Game 1—but the defense caved in, allowing Magic's Lakers 127. As they had proven all year, the Lakers were much more balanced as a team, fifth best in the league in scoring, eighth best on points allowed. Although the two teams were close in total victories during the regular season, each winning 35 out of 41 home contests, Phoenix telegraphed another potential flaw especially when pitted against playoff caliber teams: at 20–21, the Suns actually had a losing road record during the regular season.

Both weaknesses would be exposed by the formidable Lakers in short order. Not only did L.A. take the first two home games of the series, it exploited the Suns defense in Phoenix with two straight road wins, embarrassing the Suns 4–0 in the conference finals. With an 11–0 playoff run, the Lakers were more than ready for the finals against either Jordan's Bulls or Isiah Thomas's chip-on-the-shoulder Pistons.

When the Lakers dislodged Phoenix in the fourth game on May 28, 1989, the Bulls-Pistons Eastern Conference finals matchup was only three games old. Armed with a 4–2 triumph over the Knicks, the Bulls marched into Detroit to steal Game 1 with defense, winning 94–88. Detroit held on to take Game 2 at home 100–91, but Chicago eked out a two-point home win to lead the series 2–1.

The Detroit-Chicago war was a push-comes-to-shove battle of relentless defense. The Bulls ranked fifth in league defense that year, allowing only 105 points per contest, and Detroit was second at 100.8. Indicative of its aggressive style, Detroit was an NBA second in total fouls committed, ranking a dubious first in total player ejections during the year with 28. With team personalities inverse to the Phoenix Suns, neither Detroit nor Chicago managed to score heavily all season. The Pistons were sixteenth best at 106.6 points, the Bulls alongside in seventeenth place with 106.4. Except for Jordan, neither team had a player in the top 20 in scoring, although Thomas was ninth in assists with Jordan right behind in tenth place. Detroit's Laimbeer was among the league leaders in rebounds, while Jordan was third in steals.

With the Lakers already in the finals and Detroit down 1–2, the Pistons met the Bulls in Chicago for a crucial Game 4. Showing a level of maturity and poise not yet mastered by its opponent, Detroit held the Bulls to just 80 points to tie the series 2–2. Back home, the Pistons would take the Bulls by nine to go up 3–2. Armed with the upper hand and a better overall road record, the cocky Pistons returned to Chicago for another nine-point win, besting the outmatched Bulls 4–2. In those six games the Chicago offense failed to break 100 points even once, and Detroit managed to do so only twice, with just an even 100 at home in Game 2 and 103 in Game 6.

On June 6, 1989 (D-Day in perhaps more than one sense), the magic, style, and experience of the Lakers was pitted against the streetfighters of Detroit, a series at least as remarkable for what did not happen as it was for what did. What did *not* happen was the Lakers playing like the 11–1 playoff Lakers. They surprised everyone, including themselves, by failing to win one single game against the surly Pistons.

The home team in any key NBA series is normally expected to win Game 1. When it does, the opposing team has two chances to assert itself either by stealing home-court advantage with a Game 2 win, or at least returning home to hold serve in Game 3. Detroit took the Lakers comfortably in Game 1 at home, 109–97.

Although the Lakers fought hard in Game 2, they still came up short by three points. Game 3, as it often does, proved the turning point. With a home victory the Lakers could have avoided a three-game deficit and incumbent panic, looking forward to another home game to even the series. Instead, the Detroit offense scored the most points of its 1989 playoff run with a 114–110 defeat of L.A., and the handwriting was clearly on the wall. The Lakers could not muster a face-saving win, rolling over 105–97 to suffer a stunning four-game sweep.

The Pistons were atop the NBA, if not the world, and they approached the 1989–90 season with confidence. The team's 59 total victories that year were tied for second in the NBA, but four major problems loomed on the horizon. Larry Bird was back for Boston; the Lakers won the most regular season games with 63; the Jordan Bulls would win 36 home games to finish just four behind the Pistons in the Central Division; and a stubborn Portland club would tie Detroit for total victories at 59.[4]

That season proved a remarkable year for individual performances. Tom Chambers had a 60-point game against Seattle, and an unstoppable Karl Malone poured in 61 against Seattle. Two months later, on March 28, 1990, Michael Jordan rocked Cleveland with 69. The Suns' Kevin Johnson hit an eye-popping 23 out of 24 free throws against the Jazz, just 12 days after Jordan had canned 21 of 23 at the expense of Cleveland, contributing to MJ's 69 total. Hakeem Olajuwon hauled down 25 rebounds twice, and Bill Laimbeer grabbed 23 twice, but neither could match the 27 snared by one James Donaldson of Dallas in a triple overtime game with Portland. Dennis Rodman managed 20 boards once for Detroit, still unable to compete with teammate Laimbeer, who sucked down 20 or more four times.

It was also a year when Larry Bird would reassert himself, leading Boston in scoring at a 24.3 pace to tie for eighth place in the NBA, hitting a season-high 50 points, snaring in 712 boards to go with a team-high 562 assists. Perhaps embarrassed by the 1989 finals, Magic Johnson would re-emerge with a vengeance, leading a balanced Lakers attack that featured six players in double figures. Magic was also second in the league in assists (11.5) and seventh in free throws (.890). Still balanced and dangerous, the Lakers would finish the regular season with the sixth-best offense and seventh-best defense in the NBA. Detroit's defense would finish first, but Chicago would slip to a respectable but disappointing twelfth. Boston would finish one notch ahead of the Bulls in both team offense (eighth) and defense (eleventh) behind Bird, McHale, Reggie Lewis, and Robert Parish.

The Boston Big three (Bird, McHale, and Parish) were good enough to dig out 52 wins and a second-place division finish, with the help of rising star Reggie Lewis. But even though all three averaged over 20 points through a five-game playoff series against the Knicks, the aging Celtics would fall to New York 3–2. Their age made them especially vulnerable on defense as the Knicks hit them with staggering point totals of 128 in Game 2, 135 in Game 4, and 121 in Game 5. Still, the Celtics firepower and determination were impressive, for even the Knicks' 128 was not good enough against an atomic point explosion when Bird & Company rang up 157 to win Game 2 at home. But the Knicks outlasted the Celtics, spelling the beginning of the final end, the last of an era, the ultimate changing of the guard as the 1990s emerged.

Fate contributed to the Celtics demise, robbing Boston of two top draft choices from 1986 and 1987. Powerful Len Bias of Maryland was taken by the Celtics in 1986, only to die suddenly two days after the draft with traces of cocaine reportedly in his system. Then, after asserting himself as a legitimate NBA star, 1987 first-rounder Reggie Lewis died in a pickup game under disputed circumstances. Whether drugs were involved or just a fateful heart condition caught up to him, Lewis's sudden death cast a pall over the Celtics' future as Bird, McHale, and Parish neared their Waterloo.

The Knicks were rewarded with a date against the champion Pistons, who had already eliminated Indiana 3–0. Unfortunately for New York, both the Detroit defense and offense showed up. The Knicks could muster only 77 points while the Pistons racked up 112 to take Game 1 in Detroit by a convincing 35. The Knicks fared better in Game 2, losing by only seven before returning to the Big Apple for the all-important third game of the series.

The New York Knicks were—and are—a proud franchise, anchored by great athletes and tradition. Patrick Ewing played in all 82 regular season games in 1989–90, averaging an impressive 28.6 PPG. Patrick carried those Knicks on his shoulders that year, squeezing 45 victories out of a physical team short on firepower and surprisingly weak on defense, given the likes of Ewing and Oakley. As a team they ranked twelfth in offense at 108.3 points per game, and defensively they were fifteenth, giving up 106.9 per contest but still scratching out a +1.4 in average point differential.

Even with Gerald Wilkins, Mark Jackson, and Mo Cheeks on the court, the Knicks would have struggled—no, suffered—without Ewing. Patrick showed up among NBA leaders in four different individual categories; the rest of the team produced not one top 10 player in any key offensive or defensive category. Patrick was third in league scoring behind Jordan and Malone; he was sixth in field goal percentage (.551); fifth in rebounds (10.9 avg.); and second to Olajuwon in blocked shots, averaging nearly 4 (3.99) blocks per contest, besting such notorious 7-foot blockers as Manute Bol, Mark Eaton, and Rik Smits.

So Patrick Ewing loaded the Knicks onto his back and marched into Game 3 against the Detroit juggernaut. The Knicks did what they absolutely had to do, mustering an eight-point win at home to take Game 3 and narrow their deficit to 2–1. But that was their last hurrah against Isiah and the boys, as Detroit would recover to take both Game 4 in New York and the fifth game back home, ousting Ewing's Knickerbockers 4–1 to set up a grudge showdown with Jordan's Bulls for the Eastern Conference title.

Those Chicago Bulls were nothing if not a peculiar bunch. The team had suffered a string of awful number-one draft picks from 1966 to 1983, drafting mostly bust-outs plus a few journeymen. Only 1978 pick Reggie Theus became a genuine NBA star for the Bulls in those years, although good Bulls teams had been constructed with a patchwork variety of trades and non-first-rounders, such as the early 1970s clubs with Chet Walker, Bob Love, Norm Van Lier, and Jerry Sloan.

Then, of course, in 1984 they backed into—I mean drafted—one Michael Jeffrey Jordan, ending a string of such non-household names as Dave Schellhase, Larry Cannon, Kennedy McIntosh, Tate Armstrong, Quintin Dailey, and Sidney Green.[5] Occasionally they drafted a decent name out of college, but those players either went bust or did not play for the Bulls, ranging from Maurice Lucas on one end of the spectrum to Scott May on the other. After Jordan they made some good picks and trades, landing both Scottie Pippen and Horace Grant in 1987, elevating the Jordan Bulls to new potential heights. But they still managed to draft poorly, even though the prechampionship Bulls were not dredging the bottom of the draft barrel. They took Keith Lee[6] from Memphis State in 1985, Ohio State's Brad Sellers the following year, and Will Perdue in 1988 (not so bad, especially since they would later trade him to the Spurs for Dennis Rodman, one of the keys to their second string of successes after Jordan's short retirement).

In 1989 they took Jeff Sanders from Georgia Southern, point guard B.J. Armstrong out of Iowa, plus Oklahoma's Stacey King. The 6'11" King was a dynamo at Oklahoma, but never really got on track in the pros. Jeff Sanders failed to contribute, but B.J. became a better-than-average point guard, contributing significantly to the first string of championships. By 1989, the emerging Bulls included Jordan, Pippen, Bill Cartwright (from the Knicks for Oakley), John Paxson, Stacey King, three-point leader Craig Hodges, B.J., Perdue, Jack Haley, Ed Nealy, and Jeff Sanders. Five Bulls scored in double figures for the 1989–90 season: Jordan (33.6), Pippen (16.5), Grant (13.4), Cartwright (11.4), and Paxson (10.0).

Steadily improving, the Bulls had finally compiled a very good 55–27 record, finishing second to the mighty Pistons, only four games back. The Bulls were ninth in total offense and twelfth in defense with a decent +3.3–scoring differential. They also had Michael and a growing disdain for the rough-and-tumble Pistons, so the 1990 conference finals matchup was destined for intradivisional warfare.

Like the Knicks, the Bulls were forced to open in Detroit; and as New York had just done before them, Chicago scored only 77 points on the road, losing by 9. Detroit took Game 2 by 9 points again, sending the Bulls home down 0–2. Again like the Knicks, the Jordan Bulls rose to the occasion, outlasting Detroit in Game 3 by 5 points, 107–102. Unlike their New York counterparts, however, the Bulls held off Detroit at home for a second win by 7, evening the series 2–2. The tired metaphor of two slugging heavyweight fighters came to mind, and the analogy failed to disappoint.

Back in Detroit for Game 5, the irascible Pistons fought back, thumping the Bulls by 14 points. In Chicago again, the Bulls returned the favor, making an 18-point statement of their own to take Game 6 109–91, again tying the series 3–3 and raising the ire of the Pistons club for a dramatic Game 7 in Detroit. On June 3, 1990, the Pistons showed who was still boss, holding the tired and bruised Chicagoans to a playoff-low 74 points. The Bulls finally succumbed to Detroit by 19 points.

The 1990 championship series against Portland was much less dramatic. The Trail Blazers had outlasted Dallas, San Antonio, and Phoenix (who had taken the Lakers 4–1) to gain a shot at the Pistons, a dubious honor. After losing Game 1 in Detroit, Portland surprised the Pistons in overtime 106–105. Detroit took the loss unkindly, responding with three straight wins to take their second NBA championship in a row.

Detroit again held the title, but the NBA guard had already changed. Few then knew it—perhaps only Michael Jordan himself and a handful of believers—but the Chicago Bulls, who just had gone the distance with the unstoppable Pistons, were on the verge of greatness. Reminiscent of the fictional Rocky (who himself was patterned after a real fighter or fighters[7]), the Bulls proved to themselves they could go toe to toe with Detroit, faring better than any opponent had managed in two years of playoffs.

Nothing could have been worse for Detroit, or more fateful for the Bulls and the rest of the NBA, than a confident Jordan and an inspired sleeping giant in Chicago. With that, the era of Jordan the playmaster was already under way, positioning itself for an adorned place in the annals of NBA lore.

ENDNOTES

1. The Lakers stars were formidable, featuring Abdul-Jabbar alongside James Worthy, Byron Scott, and, of course, Magic Johnson. The role players were on their game, too, including Michael Cooper, A. C. Green, Kurt Rambis, and Mychal Thompson. Indeed, the Lakers had seven players in double scoring figures, an impressive scoring balance attributable in large part to Magic's prowess at the point.

2. Abdul-Jabbar logged in at only 10.1 in 72 games, clearly approaching the twilight of his stellar career.

3. Tom Chambers (25.7, ninth best in the league, even ahead of Olajuwon at 24.8 and Ewing's 22.7); Eddie Johnson (21.5, nineteenth best overall); and Kevin "KJ" Johnson (20.4), who also dished out 991 assists for a third-place 12.2 average behind Stockton and Magic.

4. With names like Drexler, Porter, Duckworth, Kersey, and Petrovic, the Trail Blazers were ready to make a statement.

5. Bulls GM Jerry Krause did not draft Jordan; he did draft or trade for every player thereafter, beginning in 1985.

6. Keith Lee was the eleventh pick; Karl Malone was still available until Utah picked him thirteenth. The Bulls then traded Lee and Ennis Whatley for the draft rights to Charles Oakley and Calvin Duncan. Oakley was a good, even necessary, power forward for the Bulls, but Karl Malone he was not.

7. Muhammad Ali outlasted Chuck Wepner with a TKO in 15 rounds on March 24, 1975, then won a 15-round decision over Joe Bugner on July 1, 1975, with one or both events reportedly inspiring Sylvester Stallone's Rocky story.

9

THE JORDAN LEAP

Michael Jordan was the product of a 1984 NBA draft that supplied an historic roster of rookies and eventual stars that may have changed the modern pro basketball era like none other.

One man with courage makes a majority.

—ROBERT KENNEDY

The 1990s version of Michael was a sports evolution of Darwinian proportion. As MJ aged and the competition grew younger and stronger, Michael reinvented himself, constantly working and pushing the envelope to new outer limits of basketball played with such intelligence and cunning that it was almost cruel in its implementation. The slasher Jordan developed a jump shot, a three-pointer, and a masterful fadeaway nearly impossible to block, retaining enough above-the-rim acumen to rock an entire league back on its collective heels.

MJ the rookie was a raw but energized third pick out of North Carolina as an underclassman. Houston took Olajuwon first, a highly justifiable move. Still, Houston already had 7′4″ Ralph Sampson from the 1983 draft, a skinny but reasonably mobile center, and one could argue that a trade to Portland (who took 7-foot underachiever Sam Bowie) or Chicago (who wanted Bowie) could have sent Jordan to Houston instead of the Bulls. In hindsight, Houston probably would have agreed—and apparently did agree many years later when it acquired an aging but still effective Clyde Drexler. Clyde the Glide was a big, fast guard with some of Jordan's moves, style, and leadership and who, when finally paired with the dominant center Olajuwon, did fill the missing championship link by bringing the second of two titles to the Rockets during the two-season era of Jordan's interim retirement.

But Sampson stayed put at the time, Bowie landed on the Blazers, and Sam Perkins, also of North Carolina, was picked just behind Jordan in the fourth spot and turned in a terrific NBA career. With the training of coach Dean Smith, his own good head for the game, and more quickness than a number of centers, Perkins was the real thing. Sometimes listed at 6'9", Sam lacked dominating size—but on the other hand, he sported an uncanny three-point shot that gave fits to opposing centers unaccustomed to perimeter play.

Even with Hakeem, Jordan, and Perkins under wraps, the 1984 draft was just warming up. In the fifth slot came Charles Barkley from Auburn, the venerable bad boy power forward—one of the few players, it seems, who could actually get into the head of Dennis Rodman instead of the other way around. Armed with 20-20 hindsight, no team in the league today would pass up a chance at a youthful Barkley, who, even with a spate of injuries and Father Time gaining from behind, was invariably a fiercely effective competitor. Always powerful, Barkley was especially rotund out of college, as reflected by one of his early nicknames: the Round Mound of Rebound. Listed at 6'6", he was also deceptively short for a power forward, especially since many players and other inside observers will attest he is closer to 6'4".[1]

Had the 1984 teams been armed both with hindsight and rational behavior, the draft would have started off with Hakeem at number one and Jordan (for Sampson) right behind—both landing in Houston. Barkley would have been picked third by Chicago, followed by the actual sixteenth pick going fourth to the Mavericks instead: John Stockton. A Hall of Fame–caliber point guard, Stockton devoted his long career to singlehandedly rewriting the point guard record books, specifically including almost every assist mark imaginable—not to mention running offenses and slashing to the basket with cold eyes, cool nerves, a nasty attitude, and killer instinct, most notably as the floor general to Karl Malone and a stellar Utah Jazz franchise. Although Kevin Willis, Alvin Robertson, Michael Cage, and Vern Fleming were still available, and regardless of the alleged "needs" of any respective team, it would and should have behooved any team to take the best available among Olajuwon, Jordan, Barkley, Stockton, and Perkins.

The "filling of needs" argument, in fact, seems to be the bane of NBA drafts, shooting team after team in the foot based upon a false premise that should be nearly extinct in an era of free agency. The 1984 Portland Trail Blazers "needed" a center because they already had Clyde Drexler from the prior year, not to mention the very capable 2-guard Jim Paxson (brother to John, who would help the Bulls win their first championships). But which Blazers trio would have provided more value to the overall Portland franchise: Jordan-Drexler-Paxson or Bowie-Drexler-Paxson? The former provided enormous trade bait to nail a proven star center if that is what the Blazers wanted, comprised enough firepower to impress an all-star team, and had the star qualities of a basketball entertainment juggernaut.

If a basketball team is in position to draft a genuine superstar franchise player—be it Chamberlain or Russell, or even Ewing or Barkley—history argues it should. If it can land Larry Bird or Magic Johnson, hindsight verifies that it should not be swayed by the internal need for a power forward, especially a mediocre one. Draft Bird and figure it out later. Dump your other 3-spot; trade Bird for what you really want; or do nothing—no alternative is worse than passing up a Jordan, Bird, or Johnson.[2] The proof is in the pudding: two teams passed up Jordan, four teams took a pass on Barkley, and fifteen teams missed out on Stockton.

Even the Bulls were highly vulnerable to a mistake in priorities. The 1983–84 team felt deficient at center and really desired Bowie. The Bulls of the very early 1980s had 7'2" Artis Gilmore at center, who, in 1980–81 for example, led the league in field goal percentage with a sizzling .670 from the floor, ranked eighth in rebounding, and was fifth in blocked shots. But by the 1983–84 campaign, Gilmore was gone and the Bulls were struggling behind slow-footed Dave Corzine, a less-than-athletic journeyman, as the regular center. The Bulls were a very weak team in those days, making do with Orlando Woolridge, David Greenwood, and Ronnie Lester behind their one legitimate star, Reggie Theus. The temptation for a big 7-footer, from basketball mecca Kentucky no less, was difficult to resist.

Of course, in the end the Bulls did resist, with then GM Rod Thorn proclaiming the rookie Jordan a very good but not over-powering offensive player, and "not the kind of guy who will sin-glehandedly turn around a franchise." Based upon all the information available at the time, Thorn and the Bulls were not overtly wrong. The NBA had traditionally built teams from the big man 5-spot on down, a legacy born with the dominance of George Mikan, then confirmed by Chamberlain, Russell, and Abdul-Jabbar.[3] Therein lies the true greatness of the athlete Jordan: for he not only turned around the Bulls, he changed how the NBA game is played, taking it from a plodding, predictable low-post exercise to a quicker, unpredictable game driven by ball handlers and shooters.

To a degree, Bird and Magic were catalysts, even missing links, to that evolutionary process. Both were big, yet size was not their only strength—flashy, determined quickness was their true forte, opening the door for Jordan & Company in 1984. Although Michael did not turn the Bulls around completely right away, the stage was set very quickly. The 1983 pre-Jordan club was mired in fifth place in the Central Division with a dismal 27–55 mark, a full 23 games behind first-place Milwaukee. In MJ's rookie year the Bulls improved by 11 games to 38–44, good for third place but still 21 games behind Milwaukee.

Although Jordan naturally led the Bulls in scoring that year (28.2 PPG, good for third in the NBA), the breadth of his individ-ual impact is staggering. He led the team in steals with 196, almost three times the steals logged by any other teammate. Jordan was also first in team assists (481) and rebounding (534), outdueling even the centers and power forwards with a full 99 boards more than second-place Orlando Woolridge. Just for good measure, the super rookie Jordan was also second on the team in blocked shots with 69.

The turnaround was derailed during Jordan's sophomore year in the pros because he missed 64 games with a stress fracture in his foot. The Bulls record responded accordingly, sinking to 30–52, this time 27 games behind Milwaukee. But an injury-free Jordan surged in 1986–87, playing in all 82 games and leading the NBA in scoring at a 37.1 PPG clip, a full 8.1 points better than Dominique Wilkins. The Bulls improved by 10 games to 40–42, sneaking into the playoffs, where they were taken to school by a three-game Celtics sweep in the first round despite one game that featured a superhuman 63 points from MJ. Still, the losses were disappointing, costing Bulls coach Stan Albeck his job in favor of Doug Collins and the transcendental assistant Phil Jackson. But the Jordan factor was for real, and the march toward destiny had begun.

In 1989 and 1990 the Bulls took a run at the playoffs, stalling badly when faced with the tenacious bad boys of Detroit. But the relentless Bulls, fueled by Michael Jordan, did not give up, entering the 1990–91 season with renewed determination. Finally Chicago broke through with a stable lineup that gelled all year. Michael, Scottie, B. J. Armstrong, and John Paxson each played in all 82 games, with Horace Grant and Bill Cartwright logging 78 and 79, respectively, as the Bulls notched an impressive 61-win season and first place in the Central Division. Although Chicago finished a full 11 games ahead of nemesis Detroit, the playoffs were another matter and, sooner or later, the road to the finals would likely pass through the Motor City.

Although they had only three players average in double figures (Jordan, Pippen, and Grant), the Bulls' balanced scoring attack was good for seventh best in the NBA. But their team identity was shaping up as defense, partly inspired by the impenetrable Pistons defense that always seemed to manhandle the Bulls at crunch time. The Bulls finished fourth in defense that year, yielding only 101 points per contest, with the best point differential in the league at +9.0. Trouble was, Detroit finished first in team defense, giving up a remarkably stubborn 96.8 points a game. Yes, the road to the finals would indeed run through Detroit.

The lumps Detroit routinely pounded on Chicago exposed a number of Bulls weaknesses. The most glaring of those shortcomings was the lack of a tough-guy enforcer underneath to complement the fierce elbows of center Cartwright and the finesse game of power forward Horace Grant. One day they would more than satisfy those needs with Dennis Rodman, one of the original Detroit bad boys acquired via San Antonio, and Ron Harper, a 6'6" guard who could score and play great defense. But in the fall of 1990 they had to settle for Cliff Levingston, an upbeat journeyman who played over his head to contribute valuable minutes, and guard Dennis Hopson, a big name originally drafted by the Nets ahead of Pippen who would be remarkably uninspired as a Bull. Jordan campaigned for a former North Carolina alum, Walter Davis. The Bulls would not oblige, effectively snubbing the disappointed Jordan. But they did come up with a 6'2" three-point wizard in Craig Hodges, a product of the Chicago area, who contributed a 44–115 effort from downtown that year.

Although Jordan led the league in scoring by 2.5 PPG over second-place Karl Malone, the Bulls had few players among league leaders in most categories. Jordan himself ranked third in steals with 2.72 per game, and Pippen fifth at 2.35, but only John Paxson cracked the top 10 in anything else—good for tenth place in field goal shooting (.548). Paxson was a solid point guard who lacked exceptional speed but played big, especially in big games. In fact, he was the only guard among league-leading shooters, a difficult spot, given the number of outside shots the guards must take, including three-pointers. Indeed, Paxson shot a whopping .438 from long range, but his 42–96 did not qualify for league recognition, which required a minimum of 50 shots made. Had Paxson made at least 50 baskets from three-point land, his .438 would have ranked second in the league ahead of such luminaries as Trent Tucker, Jeff Hornacek, Scott Skiles, Danny Ainge, Hersey Hawkins, and Glen Rice.

Maybe the Bulls became winners *because* they lacked a number of individual superstar efforts, requiring them to play well together as a team. Indeed, their vaunted triangle offense was a throwback to motion basketball that kept NBA defenses honest—and tired. As the Bulls swung the ball with crisp precision, each man on offense was forced to react, sometimes deploying a triple-post motion offense in which almost every player had to play almost every position at some point. With athletic ball handlers like Jordan and Pippen—a finesse power forward—and the technically perfect Paxson, the triangle was tailor made for these Bulls. Of course it never hurt to have a superstar effort when needed, and Mr. Jordan was not one to disappoint—so in the end these Bulls rallied behind MJ all season.

All but one, perhaps. As unique as the triangle was, Bulls coach Doug Collins, the former Olympian and 76ers guard, struggled to keep Jordan in the offense, continually dissuading him from taking too many shots. Assistant Phil Jackson shared the team concept philosophy, a habit he learned as one of Red Holzman's Knicks in the early 1970s. But Jackson in those years was second banana, and his quiet, cerebral approach was clearly dominated by the unbridled emotions of Collins, who would run up and down the court, yelling both instructions and encouragement all game long, working up a noticeable sweat rivaling that of his drenched starters.

Although intelligent and fiercely competitive, Collins's emotions ran amuck, so the tension between him and MJ mounted. According to one account by Chicago sportswriter Sam Smith, during the 1990 playoffs against Detroit a recalcitrant Jordan intentionally took only eight shots just to show up Collins. But Doug failed to see the forest for the trees of Jordan's success. MJ's competitive drive was a compulsion, so one has to take the good with the bad and adapt—partly conceding to the superstar, partly digging in to be firm where necessary, but being careful to pick the right battles and retain the appropriate respect. But Collins could not, so he would not last long enough to share the Bulls' first title.

And so it was Phil Jackson who led the Bulls toward glory in 1991, a playoff run that began with a bang as the Bulls hosted New York in the first round. On April 25, 1991, the Chicago Bulls served notice, thumping the Ewing-Oakley-Jackson-Starks Knicks by 41 points in a 126–85 dismantling of the New Yorkers. Although less dramatic, the Bulls won Games 2 and 3 easily, advancing to a series against Philadelphia that Chicago took 4–1. Meanwhile, the Detroit bad boys outlasted Atlanta 3–2 and then handled Boston 4–2 en route to a conference finals showdown with the Bulls in waiting.

Between the bad blood and defensive prowess of both teams, everyone expected a Detroit-Chicago war. A battle broke out all right, but it was more like Waterloo. Chicago took Game 1 at home by 11, holding the Pistons to 83 points. The Bulls held onto an 8-point win for a 2–0 lead going to Detroit where, on May 25, 1991, the Pistons dug in to lose by only six at home. Down 3–0, Detroit was mentally, if not physically, defeated already. The young, hungry Bulls coasted to a 21-point demolition on the road, embarrassing Detroit with a 4–0 sweep. The devastation did not sit well with the proud Pistons, who stormed off the court in a display of arrogant unity—ironically, all except Dennis Rodman, himself a Bull-in-waiting, although virtually no one would have guessed it then.

In the Western Conference it was Magic Johnson's Lakers making their mark, stopping Houston 3–0 before handling Golden State 4–1. With Abdul-Jabbar no longer around, this was truly Magic's team. The Lakers were a formidable group, including James Worthy, Byron Scott, Sam Perkins, Vlade Divac, A. C. Green, and Elden Campbell. Five players averaged in double figures, and as a team they ranked an impressive NBA second in total defense, allowing just 99.6 points per game. And Magic himself had a great individual year, ranking a league fifth in free throws at .906, and second in assists with 12.5 per contest to complement his 19.4 scoring average.

When the Lakers took Portland 4–2 to gain a share of the finals, the Jordan vs. Magic hype was understandable, although team defense was probably more important to the overall outcome. On June 2 the Lakers took the court in Chicago against the Bulls for Game 1, stunning Chicago with a two-point road victory and a 1–0 series lead. Was this the end of the Bulls playoff run? Was Chicago destined to make the finals but no more?

Jordan's Bulls answered with a resounding "no" as they manhandled the Lakers by 21 in Game 2. Still, tied at just 1–1, the series was there to be had for either team as the Bulls headed for L.A. Game 3 on the road was crucial, and Chicago came through with a 104–96 overtime win—so when the Bulls took Game 4 on the road by 15, the handwriting was on the wall. Back in Chicago for the fifth game, the Bulls held on for a 108–101 victory and a rendezvous with destiny. The Jordan Bulls were finally alone on top, where they would stay for as long as Michael remained.

With the Detroit monkey finally off their backs to complement the 4–1 finals spanking of the proud Lakers, the Bulls added the only missing ingredient to their mounting team resume: confidence. Armed with a deserved swagger missing from prior years, the 1991–92 club attacked the playoffs with a vengeance, demolishing Miami in the first round, a three-game sweep that included Chicago victories by margins of 19, 30, and 5 points. In round two, however, the Bulls got a glimpse of their new nemesis, the rough-and-tumble New York Knicks. Patrick Ewing's Knickerbockers marched into Chicago and stole Game 1 94–89. The Bulls held on to take Game 2, then returned the favor by capturing Game 3 in New York 94–86; but they could not put the Knicks away, and they eventually returned to Chicago tied 3–3 for the pivotal Game 7. With their backs against the wall in a one-game sudden death showdown, Jordan's Bulls stormed over a tired New York club by 29 points, wrapping up Game 7 with a daunting playoff statement.

The young Bulls also would lose a home game to the pesky Cavaliers in round three, but Cleveland succumbed 4–2 without mounting a serious threat to the determined Bulls, who would meet a strong Portland franchise for the championship. Led by Clyde Drexler, Terry Porter, Jerome Kersey, Kevin Duckworth, Cliff Robinson, and Danny Ainge, the Blazers sported six double-figure scorers in the playoffs. But Drexler was clearly the team leader, averaging 26.3 PPG in the 1992 playoffs, including impressive victories over the Lakers (3–1), Phoenix (4–1), and Utah (4–2). Developing a deserved reputation as closers, the Bulls would take Game 6 and the championship with the greatest come-from-behind fourth-quarter surge in NBA Finals history. Down at home by 17 points in the third quarter and trailing by 15 to start the fourth, the Bulls clamped down defensively and hit the Blazers with a 14–2 run to start the final period. Holding Portland to just 14 total fourth-quarter points, the Bulls lit the Blazers up for 33 to notch a 97–93 home court championship-clinching victory.

In the six Portland games, Jordan emerged as an unstoppable superstar, logging respective team-high scores of 39, 39, 26, 32, 46, and 33 for a Finals average of 35.8, a stellar six-game performance that included 10 steals, 39 assists, and a sparkling free throw mark of .891. MJ's counterpart Clyde Drexler carried Portland as far as he could, averaging 24.8 PPG and nearly leading his team in rebounds with 47—but Michael and the Bulls were too overpowering. In Game 1 Pippen had added 24 points to the cause; in Game 2 he and John Paxson scored 16 each. In Game 3 it was Pippen and Horace Grant contributing 18 apiece, and Game 4 saw Pippen complement Jordan's 32 with 17 of his own. Scottie added 24 to Michael's 46 in Game 5, notching 26 more in the final contest for a series average of 20.8, well ahead of anyone countered by the Blazers.

With back-to-back titles under their burgeoning belt, the Chicago Bulls had matched Detroit's run in the late 1980s, but their sights were already set on more—much more. In each of its first three championship runs, Chicago encountered an NBA superstar in the finals—indeed, one of the top 50 all-time, first in Magic Johnson, then Clyde Drexler. But neither had more pride than the fiercely competitive Charles Barkley, who led his Phoenix Suns into the 1992–93 playoffs with almost a do-or-die resolve.

Meeting last season's finalist Lakers in the first round, the Suns had their work cut out for them, especially when L.A. stole Game 1 on the road at Phoenix by four points. It became downright bleak when the Lakers held on to win the second game in a row in Phoenix, this time by a margin of five. Down 2–0, the Suns headed for Los Angeles and a hostile Forum crowd. Lo and behold, Phoenix returned the favor, stealing Game 3 by five in enemy territory. Two days later, the Suns surprised L.A. with a second straight win, this time by a more formidable 15 points as they held the Lakers to just 86 at home, setting the stage for the decisive fifth game back in Phoenix.

Could the Suns win three in a row after dropping the first two? Could L.A. avoid self-destruction by holding on for a third win after dropping two straight? The answers were not easy in coming. The visiting Lakers took Barkley's Suns into overtime before bowing 112–104, propelling Phoenix into the semifinals against San Antonio. In the interim, the Bulls took Atlanta to school with three double-digit wins, then swept Cleveland 4–0 to set up the conference finals with the nasty Knicks.

The home team won each of the first five games in the Suns-Spurs series. Game 6 was in San Antonio, where Phoenix eked out a 2-point road win to take the series 4–2. The Bulls were on the road in New York, losing both games to return home 0–2. Chicago made a statement in Game 3 with a 20-point thrashing of the hated Knicks, followed by a 10-point win in Game 4. Once again in New York, the Bulls fought to a decisive 3-point road win to go up 3–2, with the next game at home in the Windy City. Back in the friendly confines, Chicago cruised to a 96–88 victory to take the series 4–2, setting up a return to the NBA Finals and a chance for the elusive threepeat. Michael would face Barkley for the title, as the Suns outlasted a very good Seattle club 4–3 in the semifinals, a high-scoring series in which at least one team scored over 100 points in every game, with Seattle breaking 120 once and the Suns twice.

Barkley's piercing eyes telegraphed his intense resolve. By this time his profound friendship with MJ was widely known, but it could not stand in the way of true competitors—and it did not.

The Suns notched a pair of single-digit losses in Chicago, falling behind 0–2 just as they did against L.A. The superstars showed up for Chicago, Jordan logging 31 and Scottie adding 27 in Game 1. Horace Grant stepped up for Chicago in the second game, but MJ stole the Bulls show with a resounding 42 while the proud Barkley carried Phoenix on his back, matching MJ's 42 in the same game. Eighty-four points by Barkley and Jordan, two superstars slugging it out on the hardwood.

Could lightning strike twice, with Phoenix on the road again down 0–2? In Chicago, the Suns unleashed a powerful offensive Game 3 attack. Eight Suns scored in the game, seven of them in double figures—including 28 by Dan Majerle, who nailed six three-pointers; 25 points from Kevin "KJ" Johnson; and 24 from Barkley himself, who was also a one-man wrecking crew under the boards, hoarding a game-high 19 rebounds. The Bulls did not roll over, however, logging 44 points from Michael and 26 more from Scottie. But this time Phoenix just had too much firepower, prevailing 129–121 in a triple overtime thriller that chewed up 3 hours and 20 minutes before it was over. In that marathon, KJ logged a superhuman 62 minutes, Majerle 59, and Barkley 53—a stellar feat almost matched by B. J. Armstrong (58), Jordan (57), and Pippen (56).

Barkley and the Suns dropped Game 4 in Chicago to go down 1–3, but refused to crumble, taking Game 5 on the road by 10 despite 41 from the relentless Jordan. The Suns had just taken two of three on the road against the defending champion Bulls, finally going home 2–3 with a legitimate shot at pulling out the championship. The Suns fought valiantly at home, but eventually were felled by the narrowest of margins—one solitary point—in a 99–98 loss to the threepeat world champion Bulls. No one will ever know for sure, but had the Bulls' slim margin in Game 6 gone just one point the other way, could the Suns have rallied to steal the title? Perhaps. But Jordan the legend has taught history one thing above all else: MJ the playmaster does not go down easy, if at all. Ever.

ENDNOTES

1. Perhaps partially haunted by the 1984 draft, Houston later acquired an aging Barkley for added power during the second installment of the Jordan championship era.

2. There is less support for such an approach to football. College superstars are not always pro football superstars, or even stars—just look at the Heisman list. Also, clear-cut superstars cannot turn a football team around as readily as a basketball team because basketball players (a) obviously play offense and defense, (b) individually comprise 20 percent of the lineup at any given time, (c) can touch the ball on almost every play, maximizing their individual opportunities, and (d) can be effective by scoring or passing, a phenomenon absent on almost every play in football.

3. Perhaps the broken pattern has been confirmed by Shaquille O'Neal. One of the quickest, strongest centers in history, he is unable to consistently carry a franchise on his back in an era of ball handlers and sophisticated team defenses. The 1999 playoffs were a case in point, as the Lakers were swept in four.

10

THE RISING TIDE

Is Michael Jordan a complex individual? How about Phil Jackson? Karl Malone, Charles Barkley, Dennis Rodman? Or are these icons of sport profoundly *un*complicated, simple in their approach to life, hiding little about their true inner spirits?

The cream rises if you put forth the effort.

—MICHAEL JORDAN
(QUOTING HIS LATE
FATHER)

Sometimes the simple things in sports, as in life, are the most difficult to dissect. Golf, for example, is easy to analyze: keep your head down, do not swing too hard, fulcrum your shoulders, and follow through. Golf is so simple it supplies no opponent other than oneself. Yet that is the greatest opponent of all, for in the mirror we see our own demons when others do not.

As important as Phil Jackson's approach to basketball is, his approach to basketball *players* may be more telling. Even the irascible Dennis Rodman once quipped, "He's the coolest cat I ever played for." With six championship rings, he certainly deserves the respect of his players, but for some reason Jackson does not receive overall praise commensurate with his accomplishments. Some supposed pundits believe he did little more than ride Jordan to six rings, but he also coached the Jordan-less Bulls to within one shot of the 1994 conference finals in a heart-pounding loss to the Knicks, who eventually took Houston to seven games in the NBA Finals. Indeed, the 1993–94 season may have been one of Jackson's best coaching performances as he guided those Bulls to a 55–27 mark, a .671 winning percentage—good for second place in the Central Division, just 2 games behind Atlanta, 8 games ahead of third-place Cleveland, and a full 35 games in front of both Milwaukee and Detroit. That team had Pippen and Grant, but not Jordan of course. Bill Cartwright played in only 42 games; Steve Kerr and B. J. Armstrong in all 82; Kukoc in 75. This was the year they acquired Luc Longley from Minnesota—a solid addition overall, but his best contributions were in later years. This team looked more like the Clippers or Mavericks than a world champion, so 55 wins had to be a testament to the coaching they received not only that year, but in the prior years under Jackson as well.

Success was not a stranger to the Bulls coach. Phil was also Coach of the Year in the CBA before his arrival in the "big leagues." He would later recount one element in his formula for team success: Jackson always played all his players—maybe not in every game, but every player got playing time during important situations, not just garbage time. This kept the lesser players from developing hostile attitudes, a sense of futility, or low self-esteem. They all had to contribute, they were forced to step up during the season. Direct result? No cancerous attitude problems at the end of the bench or in the locker room. Indirect result? Winning teams.

Look at the 1990s Bulls. The pre-Jackson team could not win, even with Michael Jordan. After Phil took over, role players sparked the team to victory on numerous occasions, including Steve Kerr's key shot over Utah in the 1998 finals, crucial shots by Kukoc and John Paxson, especially Paxson's contribution in the championship win over the Suns. With a policy of inclusion, not exclusion, all the players had a feeling of respect for themselves and each other. And they certainly had the respect of their coach, who, among other things, gained a reputation for personally selecting books for his players to read on long road trips—in particular, the arduous West Coast jaunt each season.

Are these habits born of a deep-rooted complex personality, or are they just a common sense display of empathy and respect? Contemporary athletes receive money, fame, material possession, women—everything, it appears, with one possible exception: honesty. They are pampered, revered, lied to, and even used by admirers afraid to upset them, afraid of their scorn or wrath. Few dare tell them the truth—so few that when simple honesty shows up in the form of Phil Jackson, the vestige of truth becomes ingenious.

Phil Jackson is not the only honest man in basketball, but he and a few others do stand out from the crowd. In an era when the respect of players is waning, Jackson is a beacon of humanity, always taking the time to learn what makes others tick to motivate with respect, not fear or intolerance.

Michael Jordan, too, is a complex individual driven by simple truths: he has always been a compulsive competitor and winner, a human being with a big ego but an even bigger smile, earning the respect of players and fans alike. When he abruptly left the NBA just before the 1993–94 season, the true reasons had to be deeply important. Was it due to the tragic death of his father? And that begs the follow-up question: Was his father's homicide a random act or was there deeper meaning? Did MJ's then mounting profile as a gambler enter the picture in any way? Was NBA commissioner David Stern backed into a corner, forced to confront some sort of suspension over those gambling episodes? (And could that be why there is such animosity between David Stern and MJ's agent David Falk?) Or did Michael just suddenly have an uncontrollable passion for baseball as he says? The last explanation seems hollow in the non-sports world, but championship athletes do listen to a different drummer, and so Michael's professed motives cannot be dismissed. After all, who would have predicted that Muhammad Ali would have risked the pinnacle of his fame and success when he took a stand against the federal government? Ours is not to reason why, but one thing is for sure—the basketball world was much different in MJ's absence, a daunting truth that will resurface one day soon, if it hasn't already.

Those Jordan-less Bulls of 1993–94 had four players average in double figures. Most NBA teams that year had more: Phoenix (five); Philadelphia (seven); Seattle (six); Washington (five); Minnesota (six); Detroit (six); and even the lowly L.A. Clippers (six). In fact, that Bulls team ranked twenty-third in the league in team offense.

So how did they do it? Defense. They were not deep in household names, but they could play team defense, ranking third in the NBA, allowing just 94.9 points per game. Pippen was a league second in steals to complement his eighth place in scoring at 22.0 points a game. They generated just enough offense from Pippen, Kukoc, and the three-point shooting of guards Armstrong (second in the league) and Kerr (fourth) to go deep into the playoffs.

The Bulls took Cleveland in three straight, although they needed overtime for the third win. They lost to the Knicks in seven games, including a 1-point Game 5 loss in New York that broke their backs. Although the game featured a controversial foul, it was still a loss. The Bulls held serve at home, but succumbed in New York for a 10-point Game 7 loss. The championship run was over.

Meanwhile, the Houston Rockets were making a statement, taking Portland in four games, outlasting Phoenix in seven, and thumping Utah in the conference finals 4–1. The Rockets were a balanced offensive team with five players averaging in double figures, plus one more at 9.9 PPG (Robert Horry) and another at 9.3 (Mario Elie), including Hakeem Olajuwon's 27.3 average, good for third in the league behind David Robinson (29.8) and Shaquille O'Neal (29.3). Hakeem, of course, was a one-man tornado, ranking ninth in NBA field goal percentage, fourth in rebounds, and second in blocked shots en route to a 58–24 team mark (.707), the second-most wins in the NBA behind Seattle's 63.

As the alleged best team of 1993–94, the Sonics had six players average more than 12 points per game: Shawn Kemp, Gary Payton, Detlef Schrempf, Ricky Pierce, Kendall Gill, and Sam Perkins. With two big men shooting threes from outside, they were a difficult club to defend: Schrempf nailed 22 of 68 (.324) and Perkins 99 of 270 (.367). Another big man, Kemp, was fifth in league field goal percentage (.538). On defense, Seattle was quick and athletic, placing 2 players in the top 10 for steals, including Nate McMillan in first and Gary Payton at seventh. Overall, Seattle was the fifth team in offense and sixth in defense, a dangerously balanced combination that produced a +9.0 scoring differential, tops in the league.

With home-court advantage and a 36–5 regular season home record, Seattle was poised to challenge for the title. But the championship was not to be theirs, for the Sonics were caught napping in the first round by Denver 3–2, including overtime Nuggets wins in Game 4 at home and Game 5 in Seattle. It was a bitter pill for Seattle, a team that would be snakebit in the playoffs more than once. (Denver could not make it past Utah, losing the next round in seven games.)

When the Knicks and Rockets finally met in the 1994 finals, it was destined to be a defensive battle. With such physical players as Oakley, Ewing, Starks, and Anthony Mason, the Knicks ranked an NBA best in team defense, matching up well against the fifth-place Rockets. With Patrick Ewing on the heels of Olajuwon in points scored, rebounds, and blocked shots, a low-post war was in the making.

Although each team would win one game on the road, the home-court advantage was a deciding factor, Houston winning the last two on home court to take the title. But a strange series it was, with neither team scoring more than 93 points in any game. New York's average score for the seven games was 86.8; Houston's was even lower at 86.1, even though the Rockets won the series itself. Pretty or not, one thing was for sure: the Chicago run was officially over, and Olajuwon's Rockets were the new world champions.

The following season would find Orlando, San Antonio, Utah, Phoenix, New York, Indiana, and Seattle seriously in the hunt all year. The once-invincible Bulls faded further, checking in with a 47–35 regular season mark that included a *losing* road mark of 19–22. The chameleon of the league turned out to be the Magic. With Shaq logging 29.3 PPG to lead a supporting cast of Penny Hardaway, Nick Anderson, Dennis Scott, Horace Grant, and Brian Shaw, Orlando led the NBA in scoring at 110.9 PPG. Most impressive of all was Orlando's nearly invincible home mark of 39–2.

But the Magic were an enigma that year, actually posting a losing record on the road: 18–23. They also failed to play much defense, ranking well down the NBA pack at nineteenth place. Unable to win at home or play top defense, the Magic had not one but two Achilles' heels, a foreboding sign for the playoffs.

In addition to Orlando, the top-scoring teams in 1994–95 were Phoenix, Seattle, San Antonio, Utah, Golden State, the Lakers, and Houston. The Rockets were also something of an enigma. Fresh off a world title, they struggled all year, managing only third place in the Midwest Division at 47–35. But this was the year they picked up Clyde Drexler midseason from a disenchanted Portland franchise. Clyde would play 35 games for Houston, averaging 21.4 PPG as a member of the Rockets, complementing Olajuwon, Vernon Maxwell, Otis Thorpe (who only played in 36 games), Kenny Smith, Robert Horry, Sam Cassell, and Mario Elie. But Houston also had trouble with defense, ranking a mediocre fourteenth leaguewide; although dangerous, they were not viewed as a serious threat as the regular season unfolded.

The top defensive team in the NBA was Cleveland, which played a painfully slow, deliberate game and, accordingly, gave up only 89.8 PPG all year. Next came New York, Atlanta, Indiana, Chicago, Charlotte, and Utah. Phoenix, the second highest-scoring team, was next to last in team defense, essentially neutralizing its own offensive output.

The Bulls showed interesting balance, logging a somewhat respectable twelfth place in scoring to go with their outstanding team defense that was good enough for fifth place. Chicago had only three players average in double figures all year, exposing their lack of deep talent. But they did get a lift from the spectacular return of Michael Jordan, who emerged from retirement to lay 55 points on the Knicks in spectacular fashion. Jordan would play the final 17 games of the season, but was noticeably rusty as the playoffs began.

What prompted Michael's return may be as much of a conundrum as his retirement. In any event, he had a tailor-made excuse in the form of the baseball strike. Michael had strongly professed his basketball retirement was necessary to play baseball—and if baseball were letting him down, his return to the NBA was nothing more than a natural progression of logic. Cynics would call it luck—an excuse to get back where he belonged in the first place. Either way, MJ was back with a vengeance for the playoffs.

Orlando bested a mediocre Boston entry in the first playoff round, serving notice with a resounding 47-point demolition at home in the first game, 124–77. Still, the Magic telegraphed another weakness—lack of a killer mentality—for they allowed Boston to beat them at home 99–92 in the second game (only Orlando's third home defeat all year). Meanwhile, Indiana took out Atlanta in three; New York bested Cleveland in four; and the pesky Bulls surprised the Hornets in Charlotte, taking that series in four also.

In the Western Conference, San Antonio and Phoenix swept Denver and Portland, respectively. Spurs expectations were particularly high in 1994. Led by David Robinson, Doc Rivers, Sean Elliott, J. R. Reid, and an increasingly volatile Dennis Rodman, the Spurs logged a league-best 62 regular season wins, including a 33–8 home mark. Ranked fourth in the NBA in offense and twelfth in defense, San Antonio had the balance and experience necessary for a serious playoff run. In the second round they took the Lakers in six, including two overtime games, both home victories.

Houston, quiet most of the year, finally woke up to beat Utah in five during round one, then went the distance again to outlast Phoenix in seven, a high-scoring affair that included four games where both teams scored over 100—including Game 1 to Phoenix 130–108 and Game 7 to Houston 115–114. The Rockets won by the skins of their teeth, but they were notching series wins nonetheless, each time inching closer to the Finals.

Led by a still out-of-sync Jordan, the Bulls took on powerful Orlando in the Eastern Conference semifinals. Although they lost Game 1 in Orlando, the Bulls sucked it up to beat the odds in Game 2, overcoming the league's best home team of 1994. The Bulls could not hold serve, however, losing Game 3 at home 110–101. Eventually tied at two wins apiece, the Bulls and Magic returned to Orlando, where the Magic strength took over, finally wearing down the tired Bulls as Nick Anderson stole the ball from Michael Jordan in a crucial crunch time situation. MJ's own magic had run into the real Magic, and Orlando won. The Bulls were out, of course, but history suggests this embarrassing defeat may have contributed heavily to the historic Chicago season to follow.

In the West, Dennis Rodman self-destructed, distracting himself and the Spurs as Houston bested San Antonio 4–2, another series that would make a contribution to history. The Spurs were emotionally finished with the seemingly uncontrollable Rodman, setting into motion one of the most productive trades in Chicago Bulls history.

When Houston took on Orlando in the finals, they faced a team with a superior regular season record and a nearly immovable object in Shaquille O'Neal. When Houston took Game 1 at Orlando 120–118 in overtime, the Rockets exposed yet another Orlando weakness: immaturity. Even with a number of veteran players, Orlando for some reason was prone to distractions, an immature quality that would also contribute to historic changes in the NBA. When a motivated Houston beat the Magic in Orlando for Game 2 as well, the series was all but over. Although Orlando gave it a valiant try, they came up 3 points short in Houston to drop Game 3, then lost Game 4 by 12. The Rockets had swept the mighty Magic to capture their second straight NBA title, capping off a strange playoff series that would inspire front office playmasters to change the NBA landscape forever.

Unable to win with Shaq, the Magic would eventually go through a metamorphosis that, among other things, would ship O'Neal off to the Lakers.[1] But that would be little compared to the gutsy move pulled off by the Chicago Bulls, who shocked much of the sports world by trading Will Perdue for the man-child Dennis Rodman. Perdue was a white journeyman center, a 7-footer who played well enough at times, but generally soft. Rodman was his antithesis. Noticeably black, not especially tall at about 6'6", barely coachable but displaying enormous heart, emotion, and an uncanny ability to play above his head as well as the rim, Dennis Rodman would either spark the Bulls inside game or tear the team apart completely.

Chicago was desperate to bolster its inside muscle, especially in rebounding and tough play, and desperate teams do desperate things. Rodman had turned into the league's best rebounder and, although he had shown scoring ability in Detroit, he had no emotional need to score heavily, thus complementing what Chicago already had in Jordan and Pippen. The issue was whether Rodman could be controlled. Conventional wisdom said no, but there was little that was conventional about Jordan, Jackson, and Rodman himself. If the in-your-head Phil Jackson could not control the head case Rodman, then perhaps MJ could. If both failed, then probably the Bulls would fail—but then again, failure was not normally in the repertoire of either Jackson or Jordan.

With overt tattoos, obnoxious hair, and a very weird approach to the game (if not life), Rodman provided an emotional spark to the Bulls on both defense and offense. Above all else, Dennis displayed a remarkable knowledge of the pro game, always making the right pass, driving defenses crazy with one or two pinpoint outlet passes to burn napping defenses each game. And his rebounding was second to none, complementing the finesse of his superstar teammates to perfection.

For some reason Rodman's peculiarities were the right kind of distraction for the all-business, almost corporate Bulls team. From cross-dressing to ever-changing kaleidoscope hair, Rodman kept the team from taking itself too seriously, ironically allowing the Bulls to make a serious run at history. Although there were a few meltdowns along the way, such as the head-butt of referee Ted Bernhardt, Rodman showed up to play, leading the league in rebounding 14.9 to David Robinson's second-place 12.2.

With renewed vigor in Jordan and with Rodman cleaning the boards with abandon, the rejuvenated Bulls marched through the league with a devastating swagger. Jordan led the NBA in scoring again, Steve Kerr was second in the league in three-point shooting, and Jordan was a league third in steals. Pippen added 19.4 PPG to go with a well-rounded complement of assists, rebounds, and steals while his role-playing teammates performed to perfection.

On and off the court, 1995–96 was an important year in the evolution of the NBA. Not only did Jordan return to the Bulls, but Magic Johnson returned to the Lakers and then left again. Magic had retired after announcing his status as HIV-positive—a chilling sign of the times in America and in particular the NBA, where player indiscretions were beginning to run rampant, sexually and otherwise. Magic had been gone over four years but was doing extremely well and decided to give it another try. Noticeably out of shape, Magic struggled to find rhythm and respect over a span of 32 games. He averaged almost 15 points and 7 assists over that run, but still the "magic" was gone.

On a different front, after going nearly 50 years without a player attacking an official, the NBA saw two such incidents in the course of one month during this watershed season. First, Rodman was fined and suspended for the head-butt incident, then Nick Van Exel of the Lakers attacked referee Ronnie Garretson during a game in Denver, costing him $188,000 in fines and lost earnings during his seven-game suspension. The league brass refused to officially acknowledge the mounting trend, but it was apparent that the NBA was becoming more physical and, necessarily, more violent. Further, player egos were escalating while their emotional fuses shortened, probably due in part to burgeoning salaries and fame, unfortunate side effects of success.

Still, the biggest story of the year was on the court as the Bulls shattered the regular season record for victories with a spectacular 72-win season. At one point an undefeated home record looked possible, but Chicago faltered, losing two for a final 39–2 home mark. Given the leaguewide difficulty in winning away from home, the Bulls' road record of 33–8 was probably most impressive of all. By contrast, Seattle, a 64-game winner that year, logged "only" a 26–16 road mark, and 60-game winner Orlando could muster only 23–18 away from home. Utah, at 55–27 overall, was just 21–20 on the road, and 52–30 Indiana actually had a losing record in away games (20–21). As remarkable as the 72-win season was overall, the 33 road wins should be a very longstanding mark on its own.

But the playoffs were still another thing, a risky punctuation mark to a phenomenal season, for it would all be for naught if the powerful Bulls were to stumble in the postseason. Jordan had been embarrassed the year before in Orlando, and humiliating MJ is never a good idea. The division winners that year were the Rodman-less Spurs under coach Bob Hill, George Karl's Seattle club, Orlando under Brian Hill (who would later suffer a player revolt that got him fired), and, of course, Chicago with its monster regular season wins. Other teams seriously in the title hunt included Utah, Houston, New York, Miami, the Lakers, Indiana, and Cleveland.

In his first full year after the short-lived retirement, Jordan performed particularly well. He led the league in scoring again (30.4 PPG to Olajuwon's 26.9); had the highest one-game total of the year (53); was a league third in steals; and shot a respectable .495 from the field and .834 from the free throw line. Most of all, he led the Bulls, who by this time included Pippen, Kukoc (13.2 PPG), Longley, Kerr (second in NBA three-point shooting), Ron Harper, Rodman, and Bill Wennington. The rest of the bench role players included two more former Pistons (aging center James Edwards and forward John Salley), Dickey Simpkins, guard Randy Brown, and rookie forward Jason Caffey. Caffey, who saw action in 57 games, showed promise—but was playfully labeled by Jordan as the "black hole" because a ball passed to Caffey allegedly never came back again. Still, Caffey was strong, quick, aggressive, and unafraid to attack the basket, so he found a niche on the team.

In an uncanny display of muscle and balance, the Bulls of 1995–96 were a league first in team scoring and second in team defense, choking opponents on both ends of the court. Rodman fit in as the year wore on, showing extraordinary speed and endurance, never looking tired during or after any game. And he seemed to pick up the triangle offense without a hitch, gelling with Jordan and Pippen from the get-go and even goading the quiet Kukoc into more aggressive play.

In the end, it took the Bulls only 11 games to log the 10 victories necessary to reach the finals, losing just one contest to the Knicks at New York in overtime (a series that saw Jordan average 36 PPG at the Garden). In the Western Conference, Seattle took Sacramento in four, swept Houston, and survived Karl Malone's Utah club 4–3 to reach the finals. Also ranking high in both team defense and offense, the Sonics had the second-best record in the league and were poised for a run at the title. Led by the powerful but sometimes troubled Shawn Kemp, who averaged a double

double over the entire year (19.6 PPG and 11.4 RPG), Seattle benefited from a stellar cast of Gary Payton, Detlef Schrempf, Hersey Hawkins, and Sam Perkins.

When the finals began on June 5, Seattle ran into a Chicago buzz saw, dropping Game 1 on the road by 17 points. The Bulls held serve in the second game by 4 points, then traveled to Seattle for a three-game road set. In Game 3 at Seattle they thumped the Sonics again, this time by 22 points, leading most pundits to declare the series effectively over. But the Bulls fell victim to their own press clippings, losing to the Sonics by 21 points in the fourth game. Even that failed to awaken Chicago, for the Bulls lost again in Game 5, setting up a sixth game back home. Down only 3–2, the Sonics were gaining both confidence and momentum, so the Bulls dug deep to quash the uprising, taking Game 6 87–75 and the title 4–2.

The Bulls played 100 regulation games that storybook year, winning 72 in the regular season plus 15 more in the playoffs, losing a total of only 13 in the process: 87–13 overall. Like all records, this one may very well be broken, but it may be the equivalent to Bob Beamon's celebrated long jump—a quantum leap over sports history, destined to stand a long, long while.

ENDNOTES

1. Although Shaq would play for Orlando again in 1995–96, the team's playoff failures spelled the beginning of the end for Shaq's Magic era and contributed to a season of dissension before his ouster to Los Angeles.

11

MEDIA MADNESS

Drama stirs the soul, and sporting events serve up live drama on an electronic silver platter called television. Although attending these events in person is uniquely exciting, with all the pomp, circumstance, and bombarding sideline entertainment—especially at NBA games—television captures the pure drama better. Resonant announcers call the play by play, and color commentators provide insight into the game, the players, and even the emotions. The omnipresent camera captures fear, determination, puzzlement, and agony in the eyes of coaches, players, and fans, beaming an intense stream of entertainment directly to the American soul, sometimes propelled emphatically by giant screens and gut-stirring surround sound that delivers an NBA dunk straight to the solar plexus.

The illusion engages our emotions. The suspense engages our intellect. The identification engages our spirit.

—LEONARD KOPPETT

So effective is the television medium that it sometimes becomes a part of the game, as with instant replay or commercial timeouts. But most of all it has changed the sports landscape forever by providing the incumbent decadence of fame and fortune at the expense of pure sport, transforming the essence of uncontaminated competition to what big-time sports really are: entertainment. As the medium transmits, finances, and controls sports contests, television sometimes *becomes* the event, blurring the line between entertainment and manipulation, fueling controversy and sweeping changes. Indeed, after the record Bulls run of 1995–96, a yearlong exercise in sports drama climaxing with an emphatic playoff statement, the NBA changed. Not overnight, really; not overtly or with the obvious drama of a double overtime win; but change it did, lining pockets and fueling egos, setting the stage for the latest idioms of contemporary sports folly: strikes and lock-outs, grievances and unfair labor practices.

One of the first changes surfaced in the June draft, when a record 17 underclassmen were selected. Then over 150 players hit the free agent market at once, all looking for money and the respect it allegedly brings.[1] The players wanted big money fast, but the owners were in the fray, too, searching for the reward and ego gratification of overnight success—in other words, the playmaster owners, consciously or not, embarked upon a perpetual hunt for the next Michael Jordan. (But as noted before, the next MJ may not even be a basketball player. Still, the owners press on, almost "looking for Mr. Goodbar" in their never-ending quest for money and greatness.)

While some basketball experts pondered the meaning of the new NBA with its underclassmen and free agent pool, others reflected upon the Bulls' great 72-win year, speculating about whether this was the greatest team of all time, stirring debate, and fanning the flames of innocent controversy. Clearly this was a phenomenal Bulls team, but what about the 1987 Lakers with Kareem and Magic? The 1986 Celtics of Bird, McHale, and Parish? Chamberlain's 76ers or Lakers teams? Or how about Bill Russell's Celtics?

Since all speculation is really just a cheap shot at history, wholly unprovable of course, it does not add much to historical fact. Still, in the interest of perspective, it is important to situate the present in the context of history, giving insight to the evolution of sport in general and, in the present case, the NBA. The first rule to such musings: time alone changes the landscape. For example, boxing's great 1920s heavyweight champion Jack Dempsey, at 5′10″ or so and 190 pounds soaking wet, would not fare well against Joe Louis, George Foreman, or Muhammad Ali. Any of those three would have overwhelmed Dempsey with size, speed, and strength. By the same token, can one translate that logic to team sports to compare, for instance, the 1996 Bulls to the Celtics of old?

Greatness is a function of fate, timing, and perspective. Compared to the rest of the league, the Russell Celtics may have had a lock on greatness; then again, the whole NBA is deeper and tougher in the 1990s, so perhaps the Bulls' accomplishments were more challenging and therefore greater in the context of NBA history. The different, more volatile issue becomes whether the old Celtics, for example, were indeed better than the contemporary Bulls—forget arguing about the strength of schedule or whatever else, just ask the one fundamental question: if those two teams could meet head to head right now, what would happen? Simply put, the Bulls would win—probably big. Why?

Both teams sport impressive credentials. Russell's Celtics won the title 11 of 13 years; Jordan won 6 in 6 full seasons of the 1990s. But the best season-long point differential those Celtics could muster was +9.2; the Bulls' best was +12.8 during the 72-win season, and they also exceeded +10 points twice more in the championship years. Defensively, the Russell Celtics never held opponents to an average of under 100 points for a season; the Bulls did it five times in six title runs, including a stingy opponent average of 89.6 in 1997–98.

A further key is to compare apples to apples—how do the players stack up against each other? In 1960–61 there were eight teams in the NBA,[2] each playing a 79-game season. The Celtics that year featured Bob Cousy, Billy Sharman, K. C. Jones, Sam Jones, Tommy Heinsohn, Gene Guarilia, Jim Loscutoff, Gene Conley, and Hall of Fame center Bill Russell. The greatness of Russell in his time is not to be denied or even questioned; but the truth is that he was around 6′9″ and not so powerfully built as today's NBA stars. We know for a fact how well Russell did defending Chamberlain, but how would the Celtics star do one-on-one against, say, Scottie Pippen? Scottie is only 2 inches shorter, but is lightning-fast with powerful weight-trained shoulders. Pippen can handle the ball like a gazelle, shake and bake and drive the lane, or pull up for deadly threes. And Pip can steal the ball from anyone, especially a big man like Russell.

Some say the old teams played a less diluted schedule, with only 8 to 12 NBA teams pounding lumps on each other. Less diluted compared to what? There is so much more basketball talent today playing sophisticated ball at all levels that there still is more to go around, even with more teams. Indeed, today the players are plucked from Russia, Croatia, Greece—you name it—not to mention the powerful college teams of big guards and quick centers playing highly competitive ball at nearly every Division I level.

Forget the Bulls for the moment. Take instead two of the mediocre playoff teams from the Bulls' record year of 1995–96: Houston and Miami, both of which finished third in their respective divisions. Those Rockets were big, strong, fast, and deep. If Russell could stay with Olajuwon—a rather big if—then who would have matched up against Drexler? Drexler, like Pippen, is only a couple of inches shorter than Russell, yet his powerful, quick body is a basketball machine. Was Billy Sharman or Bob Cousy going to stop him? And if those two doubled Clyde, who would take on Sam Cassell or Robert Horry?

Now look at the Miami Heat, a team that finished two games over .500 that year, good for the very last playoff spot in the Eastern Conference. Again, if Russell and Alonzo Mourning could neutralize each other, who would take on Tim Hardaway, Rex Chapman, Walt Williams, or Chris Gatling?

Today's stars are bigger, faster, stronger, and more athletic as a group, a conclusion supported not just by the stars, but by the breadth and depth of the journeyman players. The contemporary journeymen and bench players reflect an enormous talent pool. What 1960 Celtics guard would have stopped Toni Kukoc, a 6′11″ guard/forward who can pass, dribble, drive, and shoot—and is a foot taller than his typical counterparts of the era? What would be the 1960 answer to J. R. Reid, Horace Grant, Chuck Person, Antoine Carr, Felton Spencer, John Starks, Dan Majerle, Dee Brown?[3] Take the 1995–96 Washington Bullets, a nonplayoff team that finished four games under .500. Could the 1960 Celtics really beat a team consisting of Chris Webber, Juwan Howard, Calbert Cheaney, Gheorghe Muresan, Rasheed Wallace, Brent Price, Tim Legler,[4] and Jim McIlvaine? Gheorghe is a full 10 inches taller than Russell. Although Russell was no doubt quicker, what would he have done with Muresan? And then what about Webber and

Howard, both probably stronger and quicker that almost anyone of Russell's day?[5]

Today's track stars, who probably are not even our best athletes (the best are likely in the NFL or NBA), are quantifiably and undeniably better: stronger, faster, higher jumpers with greater endurance. Not only are all the important records from the 1960s gone forever, they are routinely broken or challenged by college and sometimes even high school stars. Think about it: Russell, Chamberlain, and Oscar Robertson stood so far above the other players precisely because they were ahead of their time. They are the stars who could survive in today's NBA, so they were truly all-world in their day and, thus, the proof may be in the pudding from this angle: only the superstars from 40 years ago could even survive in today's NBA.

Now analyze the issue from yet another perspective: could Wilt Chamberlain have set his quantum leap records in the 1990s NBA? Not even close. Against what players would he score 100 points: Shaq, Malone, Mourning, or Kemp; or over double teams by, say, Rodman and Pippen, Ewing and Oakley, or Howard and Webber? The past was great, it truly was; but the past is also over, it truly is. There is no shame in progress. Contemporary journeyman track athletes could run rings around Roger Bannister, but that does not diminish Bannister's accomplishments. The truth is, every contemporary NBA team has a Bill Russell or better—but that certainly does not mean Russell was not among the greatest of his day. In fact, Russell and the rest blazed the trail for today, for without the likes of Chamberlain, West, Barry, Baylor, Hayes, Robertson, and Russell, the NBA that ultimately did evolve would likely not exist at all.

The NBA certainly did not change overnight, but change it did, on and off the court. The evolutionary process has been at work for 50 years, but has accelerated in the last decade or so with those 72 Chicago victories calling attention to the metamorphosis. Did those wins come against a diluted talent pool? No. Did they come in the face of Chamberlain and Russell? They did not, but they did emerge at the expense of Olajuwon, Ewing, Mourning, Kemp, Malone, Shaq, Barkley, Robinson, Mutombo, Baker,

Hill, Howard, Webber—not to mention Muresan, Hardaway, KJ, Stoudamire, Kidd, Stockton, Rice, Payton, and Drexler. And of course everyone else had to face the Bulls themselves: Jordan, Pippen, Rodman, Kukoc, Harper, Longley, and last but not least, coach Phil Jackson himself—not a pleasant thought for the rest of the league.

Yes, today's NBA is full of Russells, if not Chamberlains—not the Wilt of yesteryear playing almost in a 6′4″-and-under league, but today's Chamberlains all playing and neutralizing each other. If the monstrous Ewing, Shaq, and Malone cannot dominate today's league as Chamberlain did, does that mean they are no good, or that the rest of the league is head and shoulders better than in Wilt's day? The answer should be obvious, but in case it is not, then turn the tables one more time. Put today's Michael Jordan on Wilt's old Lakers—how would he do against the rest of the league, the Celtics included? Or transport Mourning, an inch taller and about three generations stronger than Russell. Pippen? Unstoppable in 1960. Kukoc?[6] Ewing? Shaq? O'Neal would have been better than Chamberlain in another era, for Shaq is bigger, faster, stronger, more athletic, and can jump. (Neither could shoot free throws; Wilt was almost as bad as Shaq is.) Wilt was strong for his day, but he had neither the shoulders of Malone nor the outside shot of Ewing. He did have the temperament of Mourning, it appears, and the rebounding ability of Mutombo if not Rodman, but he was slow afoot and could not handle the ball a lick. Although very tough, Russell was not as strong and probably not as mean, and he was not known as an offensive superstar. Put the 6′9″ Russell on today's Knicks and 7′1″ Patrick Ewing on the old Celtics, and which team gets better? Or how about Olajuwon for Chamberlain himself? Again, Wilt was strong but slow and could not handle the ball; so imagine the agile Hakeem transported to an era of 5′11″ guards and 6′5″ power forwards, none of whom was as powerful as Barkley, Pippen, or perhaps even the muscular, broad-shouldered Jordan.

And with all that, the 1990s Bulls were great for yet one more reason. The whole was worth more than the sum of the parts. The players and coach were perfect for each other, elevating the whole team to new heights. Would Pippen be as good in a different style of play? (He did not fare so well with Houston in 1999.) Rodman? Kukoc? This is the essence of the new NBA on the court—today's winning basketball is fast, tough, rough, innovative, and—very important—is played above the rim with defenses spread by fast athletes and a beguiling three-point line. That is the essence of contemporary pro ball, the variety played by today's winners such as the Rockets, Jazz, Knicks, Lakers, and others, most notably the Bulls: defense, innovation, athleticism, and years of player seasoning against stringent competition from seven or eight years of age.

Even with those 72 wins, the Bulls themselves were by no means through, driven to repeat title after title—even to repeat the three-peat, logging six titles before the great playmaster lockout of 1998–99. And off the court, those 72 wins symbolized all the NBA had become, including its role as an entertainment juggernaut built upon conflict and drama, tailor made for the greatest catalyst to the growth of big-time sports in America: television.

All the drama, speculation, and fun of sports now comes full circle—television, a modern-day money machine raising sports awareness and interest, elevating team values and player salaries alike. Television fuels ours fantasies and stirs the heart of a nation hooked on vicarious sports "participation" via thousands of hours of telecasts beamed directly to bar stools and family room sofas. There it "engages our spirit," as sports journalist Leonard Koppett might put it, the live drama stirring something in our souls, perhaps waking some primal corner of the collective subconscious, arriving at what we recognize as entertainment.

Indeed, what better television drama can there be if not a fist-clenching, tooth-gnashing, come-from-behind live victory? Whether basketball, football, baseball, or boxing, good television captures the essence of human conquest or, as they have said over the airwaves for decades now, the "agony of defeat." Even more to the point, fans see their teams as extensions of themselves, a conclusion supported by Edward Hirt, assistant professor of psy-

chology at Indiana University, who has researched the sports identification phenomena. Says Hirt, "team success is personal success,
and team failure is personal failure."

Michigan fans wear a swagger—no doubt for many reasons,
including academics, but much of it is derived from Michigan's storied sports history. When Wisconsin goes to the Rose Bowl, a
whole state beams; when the Packers win, it is almost a referendum on the quality of Wisconsin life and those who live there. The
Bears did that for Chicago for many decades, a responsibility
assigned more recently to the Bulls.

Free agency put a crimp in the notion, but did not kill it. Still,
when players seldom changed teams, the personal identification
became even stronger. Joe Namath was a Jet, a New Yorker. Ernie
Banks a Cub, always. Dick Butkus a Bear. Mays a Giant. Even the
lesser players on a team were household names, contributing to the
myth of one giant sports family. Now there is even franchise free
agency, a more serious threat to the sports illusion and, possibly,
fan loyalty and the incessant lure of television. When the Browns
left Cleveland, they broke the hearts and spirit of a community, as
did the Colts many years before when they exited Baltimore.

But it is not only the vacating teams that are a problem. When
a new team comes to town there is usually (but not always) a rush
of excitement, after which the team must stand on its own. New
teams have a built-in disadvantage: no storied fan history or fan
base. If a new team rides into town and flops, there is no longstanding history to keep fans in the stands. Chicago Bears teams,
for example, can endure many painful seasons before losing the
fans, for being a Bears fan is something of a religion, handed down
from generation to generation. It does not wane easily. But what
about new teams in Tennessee, Baltimore, Charlotte, or Jack-
sonville? There is increased business risk to owners, the league,
and the television networks because no one can measure the
breadth or depth of untested fan support. In short, the world of
sports grows a little more unstable with each franchise move.

Nationally, the demand-pull of fans craving more and more
sports programming has created a channel-surfing frenzy, spawning dozens of cable channels providing sports competition: ESPN,

ESPN2, Fox, TNT, ESPN Classic, WTBS and other superstations, and many more. And since American business abhors a vacuum, exploitation of this fan frenzy has manifested itself with a new phenomenon of contemporary sports simplistically described as *sports marketing*. Be it participating in a newly devised event such as Chicago's outdoor Bulls 3-on-3 tournament, watching a skins game golf event, or buying an autographed bat or jersey, there is hardly a home in the country that sports marketing has not touched.

Perhaps it started with selling bubble gum baseball cards to eager Little Leaguers, which in turn spawned the notion of players signing those cards, then autographing bats, helmets, caps, and jerseys. Events sprung up around sports marketing concepts such as all-star games and home run contests, after which television began to simply create events like the old Bobby Riggs vs. Billie Jean King tennis match, the longstanding world's strongest man competition, or today's skins games of golf.

As it happens, the first televised sporting event was a college baseball game between Columbia and Yale on May 17, 1939. The electronic media had little influence over the world of sports for the following decade, but in the 1950s brought the drama of George Halas's National Football League to the collective American sofa. In 1951 the old Dumont network televised five NFL games plus the league championship. CBS jumped into the sports fray by the middle of the decade with a $1.8 million annual TV package. In a strategic corporate move intended to identify itself with sports, a move that has lasted over 40 years and counting, Gillette inked a then-whopping $8.5 million sports programming deal with ABC in 1959.

At the time of the early NFL deals, however, the league itself did not control the television rights of individual teams on a collective basis. The whole process evolved *ad hoc*, more or less, with each team negotiating its own package—a decided advantage to big-market teams in New York and Chicago. Eyeing an opportunity to strengthen the league, its youthful commissioner Pete Rozelle encouraged the teams to package their television deals to both maximize overall value and to spread the wealth, strengthening the league as a whole. Immediately Rozelle and the NFL entered into a lucrative two-year TV deal with CBS, inspiring, among other things, an immediate antitrust lawsuit accusing the NFL teams of conspiring to restrain trade in violation of the federal Sherman Act.

Undaunted, Rozelle turned to Congress for help. In one of the most sweeping playmaster moves of the 1960s, Rozelle and the NFL owners persuaded Congress to pass the Sports Broadcasting Act of 1961, the sole purpose of which was to blatantly exempt the packaging of sports league television rights from antitrust scrutiny and control. With federal protection firmly in place, the stage was set for an explosion of NFL growth and profits in the 1960s and beyond. CBS paid the NFL $4.65 million to televise football for each of the 1962 and 1963 seasons, but by 1964 the money machine began to accelerate, with CBS winning a bid to pay $14 million for the NFL television rights. Even more remarkably, the fledgling American Football League[7] cut a then-staggering $36 million five-year deal with NBC. A decade later the three networks chipped in a collective $186 million in football deals, and by 1992 the multiyear totals exceeded $2 *billion*, almost 500 times what it was 30 years before.

By then the television cart was clearly pulling the horse. Tv money, protected by the Sports Broadcasting Act, first began to fuel the NFL, then served to redefine the NFL. By the mid-1960s the AFL and NFL had finally punched each other out with bidding wars for players like Joe Namath and John Brodie, so the two leagues discussed and finally agreed to a merger deal. Still fearful of antitrust action, however, Rozelle turned again to federal legislation for help. Congress then amended the Sports Broadcasting Act to specifically exempt the NFL–AFL merger from antitrust violation, greasing the way for a combined football league and television bonanza.

The modern-era playmasters had arrived, manipulating television, money, and even Congress not only to fatten wallets but to change the structure of the leagues themselves. How could this be? Did Rozelle own Congress, or was he just a good ol' boy dazzling Congress with the glamour of big-time football? A little of both, apparently.

As it happened, the NFL dangled the promise of a new expansion franchise for New Orleans, Louisiana, the state of powerful Congressional committee chairs Senator Russell Long and Representative Hale Boggs. Like magic, the NFL–AFL merger was anointed, and the New Orleans Saints football team was born.

The explosive media growth of football did not immediately catch on with basketball. Only five NBA games were broadcast on network television as recently as 1982, and for two years before that CBS failed to carry live the final game of the championship finals, opting instead for a tape delay telecast.[8] When the NBA attempted to emulate the NFL approach to packaged television deals, it ran into strong resistance in home markets that had popular teams and a big television base. Chicago's television superstation, WGN, owned by the powerful Tribune conglomerate, would eventually acquire a unique lock on the Bulls market. But the NBA believed the interests of the league outweighed those of local markets, so in 1979 the league board of governors had adopted a resolution granting the league an exclusive right to negotiate all cable television deals. In 1980 the board went on to reduce the number of games available for local cable broadcast to 41, half the regular season total.

By 1990 the NBA signed a $150 million per year deal with NBC and increased its leaguewide TNT cable contract from $27 million to $69 million a season. The rising tide lifted all NBA boats, for the net television revenue after expenses was then divided equally among all the clubs. Push came to shove in Chicago, however, because the biggest television draw was shaping up as Michael Jordan and the Bulls. By this time the league restricted local superstations to 25 games per year, and WGN picked up the entire package of available Bulls rights in 1989. The Bulls exposure grew dramatically, for WGN's cable breadth reached 30 percent of America and a national average of 650,000 viewers, not much below the national ratings of TNT at the time.

Then the NBA attempted to further reduce the number of games available to WGN from 25 to 20, prompting a lawsuit by both the Bulls and WGN alleging an antitrust conspiracy in restraint of trade. The litigation endured years of hearings and appeals, and was eventually settled by a WGN-NBA compromise. The case was over but the point remained: television money had become the life source of professional sports, coveted by superstations, owners, and now the players and their unions, setting the stage for the sports-world version of Armageddon: labor wars.

ENDNOTES

1. After the first $25 million or so, the player issue becomes respect, not financial security. Egos propel salaries as much as economics, with each star in a given sport jockeying for the most lucrative slot in the pecking order of value. Money at that point is no longer a medium of exchange, it is a method of keeping score—not a surprising result, given the innate nature of sports contests in the first place.
2. Only one, Los Angeles, was west of St. Louis, and there was no franchise in Chicago at all.
3. Dee is a quick 6′1″ guard with strong sinewy legs and long arms who in his rookie year won the NBA Slam Dunk Contest with his eyes literally closed. Ever see Cousy or Sharman dunk a ball—let alone over the top of someone like Russell? Point guard Kevin Johnson, at 6′2″, actually dunked one over Olajuwon once—what would KJ do against a less mobile Russell, let alone a slower, diminutive Billy Sharman?
4. Objectively speaking, the seemingly nondescript Tim Legler, who worked hard just to find a spot in the NBA, would at his peak probably perform better than the great Bob Cousy in a head-to-head battle. At 6′4″, Legler is nearly half a foot taller, shoots the lights out from three-point range, and is quick and tough enough to defend today's physical guards and small forwards. Nothing against Cousy at all, but today's NBA player is a quantum leap from the past. A player like Legler has had intense training and competition from the early grammar school years, sporting a very sophisticated high school varsity and college resume—and in Legler's case, a couple of tough years in the CBA for seasoning. Not to mention that at 210 pounds, the stronger Legler probably outweighed Cousy by at least 30 pounds.
5. Try watching ESPN Classic for an eye-opening journey to the past. Teams from the 1960s and even 1970s did not play much above the rim, and the athletes were noticeably more frail, from the guards to the centers. Even players with size, such as Oscar Robertson, did not have the powerful, massive shoulders of today's weight-trained stars. Just look at Karl Malone, who is as tall as Russell, but twice as wide and obviously more powerful without losing a step. Is Karl slower than Russell? No way; don't kid yourself for a second.

6. Kukoc would have been an interesting study in 1960. He might have challenged Chamberlain's scoring records. Who could have guarded him? The 1960 guards were short and/or frail, and even the centers were not as big—and none was as fast. Sure, Wilt was 7'1" but would he have stopped Tony's outside shot? How about Russell at 6'9", a defensive-minded center who infrequently strayed from the paint?

7. The AFL was the predecessor of today's AFC conference. As one of the few new sports leagues to successfully challenge an established league, the AFL benefited greatly from the television money machine. After the AFL and NFL merged, the still newer USFL was formed in 1981 to accomplish the same thing but failed miserably, its owners (like Donald Trump) outspending television revenues by an outrageous clip, sinking into insolvency and suing the NFL for antitrust violations supposedly for monopolizing the television market. The USFL lost, fading quickly into oblivion.

8. This emphasizes the true value of Magic Johnson and Larry Bird, both of whom arrived when the NBA was in the doldrums, after which they almost singlehandedly turned the league around.

12

THE GLASS CEILING

Cynthia Cooper.

It is premature and largely unfair to suggest the WNBA Houston Comets star could be a female "Michael Jordan," but still there are favorable comparisons. Yet the greatest aspect of Cynthia's basketball career is not Cynthia's wonderful athletic achievements but, rather, the fact that she has the opportunity to play—not succeed necessarily, just to play.

According to *Basketball News* and just about everyone else who sees her, Cynthia Cooper is likely the world's best female basketball player. Like her male counterpart in Mr. Jordan, Ms. Cooper has led her Houston Comets team to the top, winning the league MVP along the way. But very much unlike MJ, Cynthia became an overnight success 20 years in the making. Suddenly, at 35 years young, she exploded onto the professional basketball scene with the advent of the WNBA—but where had she been all these years?

Looking for opportunity, it appears. Cooper helped lead her USC Trojans team to the NCAA Final Four three times, capturing the title twice in 1983 and 1984, and then she disappeared. To Spain.

In her first year overseas Cooper *averaged* 45 points per contest on the Sergovia team. She then moved up to the tougher Italian league, where she devoured the competition for 10 years, averag-

No person shall, on the basis of sex, be excluded from participation in, be denied the benefit of, or be subjected to discrimination under any education program or activity receiving federal financial assistance.

—FEDERAL TITLE IX
[ENACTED 1972]

ing a Jordan-esque 30.4 PPG over her last 8 seasons there.[1] When the WNBA was launched in 1997, Cynthia was a premier player but not expected to be the star of the league. The deserving Sheryl Swoopes offered the highest expectations, as did rising stars Lisa Leslie and Rebecca Lobo. Undaunted, Cooper took Houston and the league by storm, suddenly appearing from apparent obscurity as a legitimate American superstar, becoming, among other things, the first WNBA player to reach the 1,000-point plateau.

But gender, backward mores, and stagnant laws betrayed the Coopers of the world—or at least those in the United States—for most of American history. Although the first girls high school basketball game ever played in the state of Illinois, for example, occurred on December 18, 1896, just five years after Naismith invented the sport, basketball did not surface as a credible women's sport until the late 1960s—and even then its acceptance was tenuous at best. Women's basketball did not really emerge as a serious major sport until the 1980s as NCAA teams from UCLA, USC, Tennessee, UConn, and others took root, generating intense rivalries and fan enthusiasm.

Today we have the glitz and glamour of the WNBA, complete with television contracts, endorsements, and on the court a game of surprising speed and motion. Even the WNBA has a long way to go, but it has already snared a place in the history of the NBA. As basketball began to proliferate on television as a commercial product, it was inevitable that money would lure a product extension of sorts into the realm of professional women's basketball. But the genesis of women's basketball today was not the NBA or even the NCAA; it grew from a federal mandate for gender equality in education, including sports opportunities.[2]

When the federal Title IX law was enacted in 1972, it inspired alarmists everywhere. Predicting the swift demise of high school and college football for men, the naysayers feared rigid equality standards would either require equal spending for women's sports or the dismantling of the expensive but high-profile men's football programs. Indeed, Senator John Tower, in a less-than-inspirational fit of backward progressive thinking, proposed a 1974 amendment to Title IX to specifically exempt all NCAA programs from Title IX coverage. Congress rejected the changes. Nearly 30 years later it is clear that the girls were not the demise of NCAA football, but it is equally apparent that increased funding, opportunity, and interest have spurred an explosion of women's sports in America from middle schools to now the pro ranks.

Before 1972 virtually half of America's youth were denied meaningful participation in credible interscholastic sports programs. For the most part the girls were relegated to intramural volleyball or badminton, plus a peculiar sport called girls basketball that was hamstrung by a bizarre web of female rules, including, for example, six-person teams and restrictions on which players could even cross the midcourt line.

But even with Title IX legislation, old mores, habits, and discrimination died hard. The most common ploy has been the safety argument: girls cannot play "for their own good," a spurious notion cloaked with "good" intentions that were and are transparently fake. Parents, administrators, and even doctors fell into the "we know what's best" abyss of backward thinking, but many courts took Title IX seriously, piercing the veil of transparent intentions to give the girls an initial boost but, most of all, just to assure them an equal playing field.

Much of the early controversy stemmed from girls playing on boys teams, a concept that virtually begged the safety issue to surface. Thirty years ago the "glass ceiling" on female sports made no pretenses at invisibility—the lid was a cast iron vault, publicly holding the ladies in check. But even with all the incumbent obstacles, an occasional female athlete would surface with sufficient abilities or determination to singlehandedly assault "the system."

In 1977, 16-year-old Donna Hoover, a Colorado high school athlete, aspired to play varsity soccer. Her school, however, maintained no girls soccer team, although it did have a boys soccer team. Further, the Colorado High School Activities Association had invoked a rule prohibiting coed soccer teams on safety grounds, a somewhat dubious distinction given that there was no similar rule for Colorado baseball (or cross country, either, but a cross country safety argument would hardly seem remotely logical, let alone necessary or compelling).

The local medical community supported Hoover's school, citing the possibility of injury to her health or safety—but possibilities of injury are not always sufficiently compelling to override individual rights protected by federal law. Still, they demonstrate the cultural inertia that all disenfranchised citizens must tackle over time. "For your own good" sooner or later surfaces as a justification for many, if not most, discriminatory acts; certainly it has been invoked to support black people riding in the back of the bus or eating in separate public restaurants. Hoover, like many others before her and since, refused to take no for an answer.

Citing her new rights under Title IX, Donna Hoover filed suit in federal district court to enjoin her exclusion from the soccer team. As often happens in the genesis of a groundbreaking case, the establishment ran for cover. The doctors wanted no part of any responsibility or liability in qualifying her for the boys team. If an injury did occur, due to her gender or not, would someone be liable for letting her play? With the doctors already voting no, the state authorities and school administrators doubly ran for cover, fearing even more liability for letting her play in the face of contrary "expert" opinion. So what was left but an appeal to a federal judge, the first person up the legal food chain with no fear of liability. Result? A logical analysis and balancing of the issues at hand.

As it happens, the state athletic association betrayed its own argument. Purporting to act as the protectorate of the frail or disadvantaged, the association imposed stringent rules for girls in interscholastic athletics predicated upon size, weight, condition, and skill. However, there were no such rules for any of the boys. The frailest of boys were free to compete against the fastest, largest, and strongest of boys—yet no girl could participate on a boys team, even if no girls team was available, regardless of her size, weight, condition, or skill. This not only violated the letter of the law, it flew squarely in the face of Congressional intent designed to prevent gender as being the only criteria for discrimination in any federally (or state) funded educational program, including school sports programs. Donna Hoover won, enjoining the state and school from denying her the right to participate in varsity soccer.

Donna Hoover's gender discrimination case was not the only one; there have been thousands since, most receiving little fanfare. But not until 1997 did the United States Supreme Court lay to rest lingering issues regarding the fairness of entire sports programs at the high school and college levels.

In 1991, Brown University, an Ivy League bastion of quality and tradition, stepped into a quagmire of Title IX litigation when it attempted a number of sports program cutbacks to save money on its athletic budget. The university elected to drop four varsity sports, two women's teams (volleyball and gymnastics) and two men's teams (water polo and golf). The annual savings on the women's teams was calculated at approximately $61,000, the men's teams about $17,000.

These cost-inspired moves were implemented exactly 20 years after Brown University had merged with the all-female Pembroke College. Attempting to accommodate its new female contingency, Brown established 14 women's varsity teams over the ensuing six years. By 1991 Brown fielded 16 men's teams and 15 for the women, but because of the football factor the 328 varsity women comprised only 37 percent of all varsity slots available. At the time, the female student body proportion had grown to 48 percent. In other words, even though women comprised nearly half the total number of student population, female athletes aggregated just over one-third of the total student athletes. The move, however, affected 37 men and 23 women, leaving the ratios about the same after the cuts.

Many female students affected by the cuts brought suit in federal court to enjoin the reduction by Brown University, igniting a six-year firestorm of litigation over Brown's Title IX compliance. The lead named plaintiff for the women was one Amy Cohen, who found herself fighting an entire establishment, not to mention Amy's own university, which was decidedly against her. By the time the case went to trial in 1993, the ratios had worsened slightly for female varsity athletes at Brown. Women then comprised 51 percent of all students at Brown, but female varsity athletes were only 38 percent of the total varsity population.

In a sweeping precedent supported by its comprehensive written opinion, the United States Court of Appeals upheld a federal district court injunction favoring Amy and the other affected women. However, instead of dismantling the football program or turning the athletic department upside-down, the court entered a reasoned analysis and order reflecting the reality of the situation while taking seriously the spirit, intent, and letter of the Title IX legislation. In blazing a trail for other universities and courts to follow, the Cohen court found three distinct ways an intercollegiate institution can comply with the law.

First, if the ratio of female athletes to males equals the female proportion of the overall student body, the university will be deemed in compliance. Or, second, if the students of one sex are underrepresented, then the institution must demonstrate a "history and continuing practice of program expansion which is demonstrably responsive to the developing interest and abilities of the members of that sex." Third, if the institution fails to qualify under either of the first two tests, the university can still comply if it can demonstrate that all the athletic needs of its female student population are being met. In other words, the ratios will not be held against the school if in fact all the women desiring intercollegiate sports programs are being accommodated. However, if one such student athlete files suit, it is prima facie evidence that the needs of at least one are not being met, and so the school would logically be left with one of the first two options.

Undaunted, Brown University continued to fight Amy Cohen and her companion student athletes, taking the case to the United States Supreme Court.[3] A plethora of friend-of-the-court briefs were filed supporting Brown's position against Ms. Cohen, even from members of Congress, suggesting a lingering widespread fear of Title IX. Undaunted, Amy Cohen fought on, and when the Supreme Court refused to hear the Brown case, it let the Court of Appeals decision stand as law. Amy and her teammates had won.

Title IX has posed no material threat to major football programs; rather, it has inspired a nation of female athletes to push forward, excelling at every level from middle school[4] to the Olympic team. As recently as the 1960s, female Olympic teams were woeful, even embarrassing, in many sports. But since 1972, female proficiency has soared in every conceivable area. From gymnastics to speed skating, basketball to ice hockey, United States female athletes are no longer the joke of world athletics. Swimming, diving, track and field, soccer, skiing, and even snow-boarding have all captured the collective hearts of American girls, spawning world-class athletes in nearly every major sport.

Ironically, the NBA was by no means the first to embrace professional female basketball. Although a few teams cropped up in the 1980s they were ahead of their time and never really took hold. Then in 1996 the female American Basketball League was launched by Gary Cavalli, a former assistant athletic director at Stanford, along with funding from Phoenix Insurance and others. According to Cavalli, the league was formed "to keep American basketball players at home, to give them an alternative to playing only in Europe." Regardless of its original purpose, the ABL got the drop on the NBA, beating it to the women's basketball punch by a full season.

Indeed, the ABL might have aced the eventual WNBA by a much longer margin but for the NBA's nimble commissioner, David Stern, who scrambled to put the WNBA on the map fast. There was only one viable way to launch an entire league in a hurry, and Stern found it. He politicked, cajoled, and jawboned a handful of NBA owners into launching adjunct female teams utilizing their own management structure and stadium facilities—a concept that could only work by playing women's basketball off season in the summer.

And so Stern's WNBA was born. Utilizing NBA television muscle, the WNBA was quick to gain visibility if not acceptance. Still, the ABL had no intention of quitting. It paid its players better and gave them year-round health insurance and related benefits, plus it offered the dignity of playing during the regular basketball season. Its stars were many, including four-time Olympian Teresa Edwards and one-time NCAA Player of the Year Saudia Roundtree, not to mention Yolanda Griffith, Jennifer Rizzotti, and Kara Wolters.

While it was pioneering a viable women's professional product, the ABL also experimented with a different kind of league owner-ship. Unlike the NFL or NBA itself, the ABL was not a consortium of individual teams separately owned. Rather, it was one single entity that owned all the teams and all the players. Why? Control.

The whole league was formed as one giant for-profit venture, allowing it to maintain both business and legal control. As a single entity, the ABL was essentially immune from antitrust laws because as a one-owner structure its individual teams were legally incapable of "conspiring" with each other in restraint of trade. When each team is individually owned, the separate owners must be mindful of antitrust conspiracy laws when they talk to each other, implement mutually beneficial programs, or otherwise cooperate for the common benefit of the league.[5]

But eventually the ABL folded. In its third season it began to spread its wings into core NBA cities like Chicago, in addition to its benchmark teams at New England (near UConn) and Columbus. Attendance in Chicago was good, but other teams like Philadelphia struggled. The ABL may have been partially betrayed by its single-entity structure, because rather than just go out of business the poor-market teams actually dragged the good ones down. The league attempted to stem the financial tides by selling off team operating rights in individual cities, a program that looked something like franchising. But the "owners" under the plan would never really own anything tangible—they just had the right to operate an individual team, but if the league were to go bust, all would be lost. The new structure failed to generate enough interest to save the league.

Although CBS committed to a pair of playoff games and Fox agreed to show several games of interest during the course of the year, the ABL was never able to land a major television package. Without meaningful TV, the league lost revenue, visibility, and credibility. In the midst of its third season, the ABL finally went broke.[6] It had valiantly put women's professional basketball on the American map, but it could not generate sufficient attendance, television exposure, and revenue quickly enough to outlast the WNBA.

Perhaps the beginning of the end had come when ABL league MVP Nikki McCray jumped the ABL for the WNBA. Even though the ABL began with more on-court talent than the WNBA, there was concern whether it could hold onto the players indefinitely. To do so would have required big money commitments, and that prospect grew more dubious without more television and bigger attendance figures.

The WNBA survived the first major women's professional basketball war. If it can sustain its growth, attendance, and television exposure with an outstanding product, the NBA may be able to retain its hold on female basketball indefinitely. Succeeding at its first major product line extension bodes well for future NBA endeavors.

ENDNOTES

1. It appears the records for the first two seasons of the Italian League are lost or otherwise missing.
2. Technically referred to as Title IX of the Education Amendments (20 U.S.C. Section 1681), the text of Title IX is uncomplicated: "No person . . . shall, on the basis of sex, be excluded from participation in, be denied the benefits of, or be subjected to discrimination under any education program or activity receiving federal financial assistance."
3. Although Brown intended to save a precious $61,000 per year on the terminated women's programs, one wonders how much it spent on legal fees when it attempted to put Amy and her friends in their place—$500,000? A million dollars? Six-year, high-profile legal battles up and down the federal system to the Supreme Court are not cheap.
4. One price paid by the younger girls is the loss of no-cut sports at the middle school level. Where only 8 to 12 girls may have tried basketball at a given school, now 18 to 20 try out, necessitating the cruelest act in all of sports: team cuts.
5. If IBM cooperates with Apple or Dell or Gateway to restrain competition, that is an antitrust violation. When IBM's own internal divisions share information and cooperate companywide, that is not a conspiracy because they are all under one ownership unit.
6. I was asked to assemble an investor group to participate in the purchase of the Chicago Condors operating rights in conjunction with team general manager Allison Hodges. The group was assembled, but elected not to make the investment.

13

THE SALARY CAP CONSPIRACY

The NBA salary cap and related issues fueled an historic six-month league lockout and labor war that came to a head in early January of 1999. The NBA had never lost a single game due to labor strife, then suddenly the entire 1998–99 season was spiraling down a slippery slope toward basketball Armageddon. Why?

A nickel ain't worth a dime anymore.

— YOGI BERRA

Salary caps themselves are nothing new. The pre-1950 Basketball Association of America (BAA), one of the precursors of the contemporary NBA, had at one time a team cap limit of $55,000 per year. But with the television money machine fueling accelerated NBA growth, the cap issue has ballooned into a war over the spoils of basketball entertainment, deteriorating trust and eroding cooperation at a rapid rate.

Ironically, though, the modern NBA salary cap was not a product of wealth or greed. It surfaced in 1983 as a partial solution to the woeful financial state of the entire league, a time when two-thirds of all NBA teams were losing money. Struggling for maturity, the adolescent NBA of the 1970s found itself embroiled in image problems due, in part, to a surfacing drug culture and public perception of a league that embraced too many junkies and thugs. It was a time of public apathy: even the championship finals could barely find room on national television, and those telecasts were often tape delayed. There were racial undertones, too, with some of white America slow to accept the emergence of black NBA stars at the perceived "expense" of white players like Cousy, Havlicek, Maravich, and others. For example, a glimpse at the 1969–70 champion Knicks team photo reveals six white players and seven African Americans, not to mention a white coach (Red Holzman), team president, chairman, general manager, and chief team scout. Although the black members were certainly great players (like Walt Frazier, Cazzie Russell, and Willis Reed), the white members were major contributors, too: Dave DeBusschere, Bill Bradley, and Mike Riordan. Although injured that particular year, Phil Jackson was normally a significant contributor as well.

Five years later the world champion Golden State Warriors had only two white players: Jeff Mullins and team captain Rick Barry. The team also had black ownership and black coaches, including head coach Al Attles. It was a commendable, groundbreaking scenario, demonstrating an acceptance of minorities at all levels in the league. Coincidentally, and unfortunately, the black emergence coincided with NBA drug problems, skewing perceptions of a skeptical fan base and, in particular, the television audience.

The 1979–80 champion Lakers trotted out three whites, none being household names: Brad Holland, Mark Landsberger, and Marty Byrnes. But the African American players were spectacular, including Abdul-Jabbar, Spencer Haywood, Jamaal Wilkes, Michael Cooper, and Norm Nixon. Still, the most significant element of that 1979–80 championship team was a spirited young phenomenon so wonderful that only the term "magic" could apply—one Earvin Johnson.

The arrival of Magic and Celtics star Larry Bird did more for the NBA than any other single occurrence at that time. They were good for the league and good for each other, appearing at the right time to capture a growing multiracial sports audience. In that regard it was helpful that Bird was white, but it was just as significant that the charismatic Johnson was black, for Magic endeared himself to all basketball fans, whittling away misperceptions about race in the NBA and setting the stage for both a black and white America to soon embrace an African American star like none ever before: Michael Jeffrey Jordan, whose 1984 arrival spawned a universal acceptance transcending races even more than the legendary Ali had once done and the popular Joe Louis before him.

But notwithstanding the valuable inroads of Magic and Bird, change was not immediate and certainly did not translate into big dollars for the league right away. So in 1983 NBA commissioner Larry O'Brien negotiated an innovative salary cap concept designed to both control costs and assure players a constant share of the revenue pie, assuring economic stability and labor peace for the better part of 15 years.

O'Brien's cap provided partial relief for the struggling league, but the most innovative portion of the commissioner's program was the guaranteed share of league revenues, then pegged at 53 percent. With that formula in place, the rising tide could be assured of lifting all boats, establishing a harmonious relationship with the players union. The union had reservations about the cap, of course, but could harbor few legitimate complaints over the mandatory revenue sharing, and so a negotiated peace was at hand.

The initial NBA team cap for the 1984–85 season was set at $3.6 million per team. By 1997–98, the last full season before the labor lockout, the rising economic tides had elevated the cap to approximately $32 million per team. Yet in that same year Michael Jordan's playing salary exceeded the cap all by itself—a remarkable condition for numerous reasons, but especially noteworthy because of the salary cap implications.

Although several changes were implemented as a result of the lockout, the salary limit has always been something of a "soft" cap—meaning, simply, it contained numerous exceptions in a convoluted web of negotiated or court-mandated[1] compromises. The most famous exception has been labeled the Larry Bird Rule, so christened for Boston's ability to keep Bird on the payroll in an era of cutthroat free agency. (Later it should have been rechristened the Michael Jordan Rule, for he benefited like no other before him.)

By 1986–87 the cap had risen 25 percent to $4.5 million as league revenues continued to grow. Still, in practice the cap created problems for individual teams and players, especially free agent veterans who desired to stick with their respective teams.

Often a player's own team was bumping up against the cap limitations and could not legally "afford" a raise commensurate with market value; therefore, the veteran could be paid his true worth only by shopping around, effectively subsidizing instability for teams, players, and the league as a whole.

But even turning players into free agent nomads failed to solve the issue because most team payrolls soon developed cap problems, preventing many teams from signing other veterans. By 1987 push came to courtroom shoving when journeyman Junior Bridgeman filed an antitrust action against the NBA over the salary cap issues. In its most simplistic form, the leaguewide cap is necessarily a "conspiracy in restraint of trade," subjecting it to antitrust scrutiny. On the other hand, Bridgeman's case had problems because some conspiracies are necessary, especially in sports, and so the courts have developed a "rule of reason" approach balancing the positives and negatives of team cooperation in the context of professional sports. It is not unprecedented for employers to fix salaries in the first place, and certainly sports teams, although competitors, must necessarily cooperate to create and operate a league to enable the players to play each other.[2]

Bridgeman himself was a journeyman on the decline. In 70 games played over the 1982–83 season he averaged 14.4 PPG for the Milwaukee Bucks, third on the team. The following year he played in 81 games for the Bucks with a 15.1 average, again third best. In 1984–85 Bridgeman scored 13.9 over a span of 80 games, this time for the Los Angeles Clippers, fourth on a team that sported six players in double figures. By the next year, however, he could muster only 58 games for the Clippers with a noticeable decline in scoring at 8.8 PPG. In 1986–87 he was back on the Bucks, playing in just 34 games with a 5.1 average and a season-high game of only 12 points. He did not play the following year.

The Bridgeman suit did set the stage for a league compromise implemented in 1988, however. The so-called veteran exception, the one later dubbed the Larry Bird Rule, evolved from that compromise, allowing teams to exceed the cap to re-sign their own veteran free agents. This allowed the star players to maximize their market value, but it had a chilling effect upon both free agency and the salary levels of lesser players.

The first problem was that in many cases only a veteran's own club could afford to sign him under the cap. Other teams were forced to make roster moves and otherwise try to manipulate under the cap, a process that grew more difficult over the years. Second, as teams scrambled to save dollars for big-money signings of free agents—their own or otherwise—they could not avoid squeezing the rank-and-file players. Eventually the NBA evolved into an unusual economic beast with teams comprised of high-paid superstars and a bench full of low-paid journeymen and role players. The championship Bulls teams began to look that way, especially with Jordan's salary leading the way. The bench included good, dependable role players who meshed beautifully under coach Phil Jackson. And every couple of years those players changed, but the new ones continued to produce.

In 1989, for example, the prechampionship Bulls listed Craig Hodges, Will Perdue, and Ed Nealy. By 1992 they effectively utilized Cliff Levingston, Scott Williams, Bobby Hansen, and Stacey King. When the second threepeat came around in 1995–96, the Bulls had Steve Kerr, Bill Wennington, Jud Buechler, Dickey Simpkins, James Edwards, Jason Caffey, Randy Brown, and John Salley, all complementing Jordan, Pippen, Harper, Kukoc, Longley, and, of course, Rodman.

The role players came and went, but the cornerstones were Michael and Scottie, while Phil Jackson was a transcendental glue holding the disparate juggernaut together. Rodman, though, was unique for a number of reasons, one of which was that he was a superstar role player. Rodman proved a remarkable talent and probably was directly responsible for at least one of the titles if not more. The Bulls had made a bold move in acquiring Rodman the tough guy and rebounder, but they also got Rodman's hustle, disarming quirkiness, speed, agility, superior conditioning, capable offense when needed, and uncanny savvy for the game. So, with all that, was indeed Rodman the true genius of Bulls GM Jerry Krause, who finally signed him? Or was he ultimately the gift of

Phil Jackson, Zen's only known contribution to the coaching world? Or does credit belong with the charisma of Jordan, who perhaps willed Rodman into reality long enough to be effective? Maybe it was all three or a combination, but two things are nearly certain: few teams, if any, would have taken a chance on Dennis, and only the Bulls could have pulled it off anyway.[3]

So, yes, Rodman did fill a role on a team of role players, few of whom would have been there without a host of team salary cap exemptions. But meanwhile subtle tremors brewed within the players union, for superstar money was crowding out available funds for the rest of the players. At the same time, the owners were annoyed with each other, for every time a team signed a free agent for big money, a new standard was set that had to be beat by the next superstar, all of which spiraled league salaries out of control.

And so the story goes, owners and players fighting it out over egos and money. But their actions are not wholly deserving of public contempt, for these hostile conditions are the nature of the animal, a beast unique to the world of big-time sports. Owners are entrepreneurs, and as such they are fierce competitors driven to succeed at every level to the point where they, too, lose sight of the economics, preferring to use money as a means of keeping score. Of course, this sounds exactly like many athletes who also have an emotional need to compete. Jordan's teammates and colleagues alike confess he is among the most tenacious competitors they have ever witnessed, on and off the court—be it baseball, basketball, golf, or, at least at one time several years ago, gambling.

The sports industry is therefore an anomaly, conceivably the only business in which the employees are at least as competitive as the owners. When there was a huge disparity in the economics, such as when Mickey Mantle played for the Yankees, the owner power overcame the spirit of the players. But with multimillion-dollar pro athletes working for multimillionaire owners, the balance of power has shifted—not wholly in the players' favor, but enough to make a big difference in the conduct of sports as a business.

There were no strikes or lockouts in 1920 or 1940, or even 1960—not because sports were more pure than today (a common supposition), but because all the power was one-sided, forcing an appearance of purity. It was no fun for Mantle to be locked up as a Yankee and paid whatever the owner felt like doling out.[4] Neither was it palatable for St. Louis Cardinal Curt Flood to be traded and told where to go and how much to make, but at least by Flood's era in the 1960s and 1970s players could afford powerful representation, enough to file lawsuits as Flood himself did.[5]

This is not to say more recent players achieved full control, but their leverage did increase over time both collectively as a union and individually as superstars with superagents squeezed top-dollar contracts out of reeling owners. Even so, the league was by no means defeated or helpless, even with multiyear player contracts flirting with the $100 million range. But clearly the NBA was losing grip.

When Minnesota drafted untested rookie Kevin Garnett straight from high school (and then later inked a record $126 million deal),[6] Garnett made more than headlines—he caught the profound attention of NBA owners, who finally recognized what they had become: out of control. No one—perhaps not even the owners themselves—can point for sure to the genesis of the 1998 labor strife and owner resolve; but a good bet would be the day of Garnett's contract, an economic missile that sent shockwaves straight through league playmaster wallets in the early fall of 1997.

The playmaster owners and league officials forged a plan of attack with surprising acuity and solidarity. Commissioner David Stern was anointed with power and the requisite authority to proceed, and there was very little evidence of owner misgivings in the press. Stern ran the show, and the impending labor battle was his to win or lose.

The owners benefited from a glimpse of hindsight, too, for the 1994 baseball strike showed the true level of player vulnerability. That year the baseball owners ultimately lost some of their leverage by engaging in an unfair labor practice after the striking players were themselves on the economic ropes, but still the NBA owners witnessed the weakness of a sports union comprised of both superstars and journeymen, each group having its own agenda. The vast majority of rank-and-file players live in a world much different from that of the stars. Not only do they make less money (much less), they have less influence over what team they are on or where they live. In short, the journeymen need money and stability while the superstars really need more of neither. Ironically, though, those same superstars need the role players both on and off the court, depending on them for assists, rebounds, and, when necessary, union votes.

Armed with the inspiration of Garnett's contract and the guidance of the contemporary baseball strike experience, the owners aptly exploited the two-tier union structure with a preemptive labor lockout, squeezing those same role players whose union support is crucial by sheer numbers alone. The resultant basketball carnage is now legendary, but all the effects will not be digested for perhaps three or four years (it took baseball that long to dust off its own labor stigma). Still, hindsight suggests a great economic toll not only in the form of lost salaries and league revenue, but also in the spillover to other factions of the sports entertainment and marketing business. NBC, which was to televise two lucrative games on Christmas Day plus the All-Star Game around midseason, reportedly lost up to $24 million for those two days alone. Some sources estimate total NBA game losses around $1 million per home date per team, much of that suffered in the form of stadium concessions and food sales, ancillary businesses that were deeply hurt by the lockout.

The City of Philadelphia reportedly estimated a loss of $35 million due to cancellation of the All-Star Game, and as of mid-December New York City was guessing losses of $70 million by the first of the year. Meanwhile the players were racking up losses, too. The superstars lost more in nominal terms, of course, but the journeymen losses hurt more. A player at the NBA minimum salary was losing around $3,500 per game, important money if one has a family, little savings, and no substitute job. Even million-dollar players lack ample resources for an extended labor stoppage, losing about $12,000 per game over the course of an entire regular season.

The internal money pressure continued to boil for 191 straight days when finally the union could keep peace and order no longer.

Players began negotiating in the press, a mistake noticeably absent on the owners' side, carving gaps between union factions. Published reports quoted Shaquille O'Neal as "going to New York to knock out Ewing and Zo." He was referring to both the Knicks' Patrick Ewing and Miami's Alonzo Mourning, both staunch union supporters. Finally, by January 5, 1999, union chief Billy Hunter could hold the dike no longer, caving in with a call to David Stern. Hoping to avoid mutiny and save dignity for the union, Hunter was not only ready to talk, he was willing to make concessions.

The very next day a tentative resolution was announced. David Stern was indeed gracious in victory, but he could afford to be. Among other things, his grand sports league had just become the first to cap not just team salaries, but individual salaries across the board at various levels depending upon years of service in the league. The cap on individual players was placed at $14 million each, but only for those players with at least 10 years in the league. Working backward, the ceiling for players in the 7- to 9-year range became $11 million each, and $9 million for players with 6 years or less.

If the top players were net losers, the lesser members improved their lot at the low end of the scale. Rookie minimums took a small jump from $242,000 per year to $287,500, while rank-and-file veterans benefited from minimums of $350,000 for second-year players up to $1 million for 10-year veterans. It was the prospect of these increases that ultimately caved the union, for the majority of players were about to benefit significantly, and in labor law there is power in sheer numbers.

With labor costs under control, the NBA hastily worked to salvage a 1999 season that would unfold as a year of uncertainty, change, and one last shockwave instigated by the wily veteran Michael Jeffrey Jordan: the second (and last?) retirement of the one and only. After toying with the media and owners, Jordan delivered upon earlier predictions of his retirement. With Jackson gone, Pippen on the way out, and Rodman just plain "way-out," Jordan probably made the right choice. The 1999 Bulls would never field a supporting cast good enough to capture a fourth consecutive title (and their seventh overall), and the handwriting was clearly on the wall for all to see.

Even at the championship rally in Chicago's Grant Park after the 1998 title, there was public talk about that season's "last dance." Phil Jackson actually announced it on stage; Jordan was on record that he would never play for a coach other than Phil. When the Zenmaster Jackson was shown the door and Iowa State's Tim Floyd anointed, the message should have been clear: essentially Jordan was fired. It was a graceful means to escape the spiraling Jordan salary and rebuild the team in GM Krause's image—or at least his subjective perception thereof. With Jordan gone, there would be no Bulls player left not personally found, picked, or approved by the id of Krause, who, at last, could make a run at the ultimate feat of Boston's multiple dynasties.

And do not forget the Bulls' investors. Jordan's presence built the league and helped take the Bulls' team value from under $20 million in the early 1980s to the range of $200 million to $300 million by 1998. But during the second Chicago threepeat of the 1990s, the Bulls organization propped up the league with Jordan's quantum leap one-year salaries. It was the least they could do, by the way—but still the ultimate burden fell on the investors, and so Jordan may have worn out his economic welcome. In 1999, the team will make significant money with a sold-out United Center arena, a young band of bright-eyed but cheap pups on the court, and no Jordan.

However, the organization's great challenge now is to rebuild quickly, for the paying fans will not continue to support a loser—or worse, a comedy show—for more than about a season and a half. By the year 2000, Mr. Krause will have to implement a rational plan to land exciting, winning players. To his credit, he has laid it all on the line: if Krause fails, he and his pressure tactics on Jordan and Jackson will have blown up in his face; if he succeeds, the credit will be all his and, in that event, perhaps history will yield the credit he yearns for. Genius or goat, the risk of the Bulls future belongs to Jerry Krause.

ENDNOTES

1. Rookie player Leon Wood almost immediately challenged the NBA, alleging that the cap as used in conjunction with the player draft was an illegal horizontal conspiracy among clubs in restraint of trade. When Wood, a gold medal Olympian, was drafted by Philadelphia in 1984, the 76ers were already over the allowed cap and therefore under the rules could pay newly drafted rookies only $75,000 on a one-year deal. A federal appeals court agreed with Wood, so the league had to address the rookie element of the system, tinkering with special rookie provisions and eventual free agency. (Wood, by the way, later became an NBA referee.)

2. Bridgeman had another problem: the labor exemption protects most sports leagues from antitrust scrutiny because the courts will not recognize employer conspiracies where a player union is in place as a collective bargaining unit.

3. The 1999 Lakers gave it a try, but the unpredictable Rodman lost focus if not interest and was cut mid-season.

4. Published accounts suggest that at one negotiating session, the owner confronted Mantle with an illicit sexual affair he was having, remarkably enhancing the team leverage.

5. Flood sued Major League Baseball for antitrust conspiracy, hoping to overturn baseball's absurd antitrust exemption created by the federal baseball Supreme Court case of 1922. He lost, but at that point he and union chief Marvin Miller switched gears, electing to gain power under federal labor laws instead of antitrust protection, setting the precedent for powerful sports labor unions.

6. Garnett turned out to be a terrific young man as well as a superlative player with a big smile and even bigger NBA future, probably earning his keep, but his unprecedented contract was unnerving to the league as a whole.

PLAYMASTERS ON TRIAL

PART III

14

SECRET GAMES

The only truly even playing field is in the game of natural laws: science. Gravity is gravity for everyone; no one can manipulate Newton's law, prejudice it, or even suspend it. But games are creatures of artificial restrictions. Rules. And rules must be devised, interpreted, and enforced by human beings, fallible mortals influenced by a plague of emotions, from greed and envy to anger and fear. Inject human emotion into the game of life and one gets the real world, but at least everyone potentially plays on the same dog-eat-dog footing. But to play sports and keep the endeavor from reverting into a *Lord of the Flies* free-for-all, human rules, interpretation, and enforcement are crucial. Everything has a price, and the cost of organized competition is human error and manipulation.

Cheating. Manipulating games is nothing new, of course, but when do clever behind-the-scenes machinations go too far? When legendary Packers coach Vince Lombardi took his cerebral pregame tour of the gridiron, noting soft spots, divots, standing water, and mud, he was skillfully—and fairly—searching for a competitive advantage. But if the Detroit Pistons really tightened the visitors' first-half rim to keep defensive games close as they were accused by various Bulls players of the late '80s and early '90s, was this an unfair manipulation? How about the dingy, cramped, dark, cold, and wet locker rooms meant for Celtics vis-

O, what a tangled web we weave When first we practice to deceive!

—Sir Walter Scott

itors in the old Boston Garden? Was that an unfair disadvantage to other teams or just an unfortunate quirk of fate?

How about Pat Riley's Miami Heat, alleged to have produced a 10-psi game ball at home even though the league attempts to mandate 7 to 9 pounds per square inch? The greater pressure would tend to reward the inside game and hinder outside shooters with exaggerated unfriendly bounces off the rim, also producing very long, predictable rebounds. Could this be one reason that recent Heat teams were so prodigious at home and so very ordinary on the road?

Moreover—could—or does—the league itself manipulate games? In recent years NBA home teams seem to win a statistically inordinate number of home games, with even mediocre teams[1] sometimes managing to win 60-plus percent of their home-court contests to just 39 percent or less on the road. Is this disparity adequately explained by the traditional "party line" reasoning about home-court advantage: no travel, friendly fans, and familiar court environment? Or is all this home-court hyperbole a not-so-subtle ruse to keep home team stadiums filled with hopeful fans? Perhaps we will never know. Maybe no one knows, for the subtleties could be cognitively unintentional, somewhat subconscious influences due to the emotions of home teams and their crowds.

If one were to manipulate a home-court contest, where would the greatest potential influence lie? Probably referees, which is one reason the league and others are so nervous about gamblers. Point spreads and home wagers generate fan interest, attendance, and ratings, but they also produce potential risks of outside or inside influence. Point shaving scandals are nothing new to sports in general and basketball in particular, especially at the college level, including Northwestern University and Arizona State in the 1990s, not to mention a number of mostly Eastern schools in a notorious public scandal from the 1950s. Although gambling is a part of baseball lore from the 1919 Black Sox to Pete Rose, it has not crept into the modern NBA so far as history has revealed to date.[2] Perhaps this is because contemporary players are paid so well that gambling would hardly influence their incomes in the same material way that it could bolster a college player or, for that matter, the lesser-paid Black Sox baseball players from 80 years ago.

But referees are potential targets. They do *not* enjoy multimillion-dollar contracts and they *do* have great influence over subjective and seemingly objective components of NBA games. At least one concerned IRS agent, Tom Moriarty, has publicly commented on the unique potential for problems in connection with the 1998 incident over NBA refs failing to report cashed-in travel vouchers as income.

Officials logically and necessarily influence league games (after all, that is why they are there), but suggesting they do so intentionally is a long stretch. Still, the question is legitimate in view of the potential stakes involved. The Chicago Bulls championship teams of the 1990s hardly had reason to complain much about anything, but they still had their problems with certain referees. Bulls fans loath Hue Hollins, who once cost Chicago a crucial playoff game in New York with a last-second foul call on Scottie Pippen during Jordan's first "retirement" year and who, more or less, seemed to "have it in" for Scottie and the Bulls in later years. Such appearances could be attributable to fan paranoia rather than any hidden agendas or conspiracies, but there are some statistics that do suggest personal referee biases—hardly a surprising discovery in any field of human endeavor, but still interesting in the context of basketball history and the potential influence of NBA playmasters.

The *Chicago Sun-Times* ran an impressive full page spread in May of 1998 dissecting the statistical relationship between Bulls wins and losses when compared to individual referees working the games. In 1998, the final year of Chicago's championship run, the Bulls were undefeated (33–0) when any one of six different officials was on the court: Michael Smith, Bill Oakes, Bernie Fryer, Bill Spooner, Derrick Stafford, or Tom Washington. Of course there is little statistical intrigue in the Bulls winning in 1998 or any of the six championship years of the '90s. They did plenty of that regardless of the officials or the opposing players.

But given all that winning, it is telling to study the officials on the court during Bulls *losses*. In 1998 alone, MJ & Company actually had *losing* records when any one of these four different officials took the court: Monty McCutchen, Ron Olesiak, Leon Wood[3], and Luis Grillo. Chicago was one game under .500 when any of those officials worked the floor. Where was Hue Hollins? Not one of the worst, but close. The Bulls were an even 2–2 in Hollins's games during the 1998 regular season. Curiously, though, in three playoff years Hollins was one of only two NBA officials to work more than one Bulls loss, during which time Chicago was 5–2 before Hollins in postseason play. (They were 8–3 in games worked by Joey Crawford.)

Does all this mean the officials were cheating or gambling? No. Does it suggest there could be some bias? Yes, there could be, and perhaps some officials are more susceptible to home crowds or noisy fans. But does it confirm that the potential for manipulation exists, either by gamblers or by other playmasters? Definitely.

Home-court advantage is so widely accepted that it has actually become an American cliché creeping into business, politics, and law as obvious advantages of the "home court" influence strategic planning and important litigation. The notion is so much a part of basketball that referee intervention is not only accepted, it is *expected* by players, coaches, and fans. Not only do coaches and home crowds work the officials with the express intent of influencing calls, they actually expect results and sometimes get them. Bobby Knight, Pat Riley, Jerry Sloan, George Karl, Phil Jackson, and others have all found ways to work the refs and influence the games, mostly by winning the referees over regarding three-second calls, holding, illegal defenses, and the like. Sometimes a coach is able to coax a makeup call, the universally accepted means of atoning for blown calls when an official who realizes it can give the next "gray area" decision to the victimized team.

That is the essence of home-court advantage: the discretionary gray area, almost all of which is dictated by the officials. But still, the officials do not control everything. The home playing field, whether in basketball, football, or another sport, has certain inherent advantages: the players do not have to travel, the home crowd is boisterous and supportive, and the actual nuances of the court and home decibel levels are familiar. It also allows for weird home-court tricks, from tinkering with the rims to turning up the heat in the visitors' locker room to setting off the fire alarm in the away team's hotel during the middle of the night.[4]

The old Chicago Stadium was famous for its raucous acoustics, and the original Boston Garden was infamous for "hidden" dead spots, cracks, and gaps on the parquet floor. The savvy Celtics were used to them, reports coach and player K. C. Jones, but visiting teams were mystified.

But in the realm of immediate, effective power to influence games, the officials and the players themselves are in a position to render the most influence. According to a report in the *Chicago Tribune* on June 3, 1998, the players are keenly aware of each ref's strengths and weaknesses, quoting one-time Laker Michael Cooper, who accused one unidentified official of being particularly vulnerable to home crowd influence.

The home-court advantage is decidedly real. Only five teams have won the title without it in the last 19 years, and every one of those clubs had already won the championship at least once. But is any part of the home-court advantage discretionary, intentional, or reversible? Perhaps. In basketball the officials have a profound effect upon nearly every facet of the game, from calling fouls, zone defenses, traveling, and three-second violations. How they call a game influences a player's drives, shooting percentages, rebounds, fouls, and even turnovers.

Although one element is curiously unaffected by the whims of referees—free throw percentages, at home and on the road—the home-court advantage is statistically linked to winning percentages and point totals. In 1997–98, every single NBA team had a better win–loss record at home than on the road. The Hornets and Pistons were 13 games better at home, the Bulls 12 better, the Jazz 10, for example. And even inferior teams enjoyed an advantage, although Toronto was just 2 games better at home than on the road.

Further, only four NBA teams scored more points in away games than at home (Pacers, Clippers, Timberwolves, and Raptors), but that was by an average margin of less than one point per contest. Yet in the one area where officials had absolutely no control over the outcome—free throw percentages—the entire league average revealed no statistical difference![5] For the entire 1997–98 season, all home teams shot a combined average of .7391 (73.91 percent) from the charity stripe and road teams shot an aggregate .7352 (73.52 percent), a meaningless statistical difference of .0039.[6] Take the officials out of the picture, therefore, and the results are statistically equal regardless of rims, home-court noise, and even crowd free throw distractions with signs, balloons, and waving arms. (One classic video clip shows Larry Bird about to shoot a free throw when a fan directly in his line of vision suddenly unveils his large poster of a bikini-clad female bombshell. Bird noticed, grinned, and made the shot.)

Not only were all home and away percentages statistically equal, 11 NBA teams actually shot free throws better on the road than at home (some significantly better, such as Atlanta—77.5 percent vs. 73.7 percent; and Milwaukee—78.6 percent vs. 74.9 percent). Eight of those teams shot field goals better at home, and three shot better in away games, meaning that teams shooting the better free throws were not just better shooting teams on the road in general. Regardless of how the component parts are examined, it is remarkable, even stunning, that home and away free throws have no difference leaguewide. The one activity left entirely to the players without intervention by coaches or officials is dead equal, even in the face of hostile fans, noisy arenas, and erratic travel schedules.

So what is the point? Home teams win. Sometimes they win because of the home field or supportive home crowd, sometimes it is because the home crowd influences the officials in addition to inspiring the players. Does the league want home teams to win? Absolutely. Fans like to see their team win, and even the worst teams manage to win games at home. Consider the 1998 New Jersey Nets (one of the teams that shot free throws better on the road), a middle-tier club with a record of 43–39. Those Nets were mired in mediocrity, but they were world-beaters at home with a 26–15 mark and a winning percentage of .634. The Houston Rockets had a strangely inverted year in 1998 with a home mark of 24–17 and a mirror image away record of 17–24.

The 1998 Celtics won twice as many games at home (24) as away (12), even though they were en route to a dismal overall record of 36–46. The Hornets were an anomaly, logging a splendid home record of 32–9 only to be net losers (19–22) on the road. Even the 1998 Bulls had their problems outside Chicago. They lost only 4 games all year in the United Center, dropping four times as many (16) on the road, where they logged a good but mortal mark of 25–16 outside the Windy City. The Pistons were 9 games over .500 at home, mustering an anemic 12 total victories away from the "Palace." But the biggest beneficiaries were fans of horrible teams such as the Mavericks. Dallas dropped a whopping 62 games on the year, but still managed to win 13 times at home, giving local fans at least a glimmer of hope with a motley group that somehow won almost a third of its home contests. So whether impacted by the home crowd, the human emotions of officials, the comfort of the players, or any conspiracy theory one might reasonably muster, NBA teams, even bad ones, win a disproportionate number of home games.

But on the court at crunch time, the issue of gamesmanship is hardly open for debate. Players and coaches do whatever is legally necessary to win—and then some. During Chicago's heyday, great care was given to manipulating the man-to-man defense rule. Dan Bernstein, a cerebral young sports reporter and anchor on Chicago's WSCR sports talk radio, publicly reported his own glimpse of a board in the Bulls locker room showing a typical "x" and "o" diagram unabashedly labeled "barely legal." When the Bulls played the Jazz in the finals for Chicago's last championship in 1998, there was a great deal of debate over Scottie Pippen's defensive role as a "free safety"—roaming the court causing havoc, yet staying a step ahead of the illegal out-and-out zone.

When coaches work the refs, when the defense takes an intentional delay of game call on a crucial inbounds play, or when a team calls timeout to "ice" an opposing free throw shooter, the game is being manipulated. Either by rule or custom, those machinations are widely accepted. But if someone makes a crank call to the stadium and falsely reports a family emergency to one of the players, have not the bounds of "fair cheating" been blatantly crossed? That happened to Michael Jordan when the Bulls played the T-Wolves in Minneapolis in 1998. Jordan missed part of the game as the second half opened, not to mention his composure.

The hoax worked, perhaps, as the Timberwolves beat the Bulls for the first time in team history, notching a 99–95 win.

But NBA players will attest that Jordan was not without his own tricks. He normally kept his cool, but Jordan could intimidate opposing players with his piercing eyes or a raised "don't do that again" eyebrow. Jordan was even known to slap his own leg if cornered and in trouble, creating an audible illusion he had been fouled. And of course MJ was well known for his patented traveling moves to the basket, not to mention his savvy catlike "pushoffs" like the one he apparently pulled to win the 1998 finals against Utah.

Sports shenanigans are no doubt as old as sports history itself, generating genuine concern as the modern era unfolded. Educators as early as 1904 complained that college sports teams were laced with ringers paid under the table. In 1927 over 105,000 raucous fans packed Chicago's Soldier Field to watch a ferocious Jack Dempsey attempt to regain the heavyweight boxing title from Gene Tunney. A determined Dempsey had pummeled Tunney into near submission for six rounds when he landed a wicked left hook that knocked Tunney cold. But then Dempsey failed to back off to a neutral corner, violating a relatively new rule, thus preventing the referee from beginning the knockout count and buying Tunney as many as 15 to 17 seconds according to eyewitness accounts. Tunney used the time to collect himself, after which he reentered the brawl with a mission, eventually scoring a knockdown in the eighth round before going the distance to actually win a decision over the surprised Dempsey. Some said the "fix" had been in; others chalked it up to fate. Either way, a significant element of boxing history hinged upon a human judgment call over 70 years ago.

Such judgment calls are the bane of all sports, so much so that the NFL attempted to take the guesswork off the field with the phenomenon of instant replay. The replay concept was an attempt to install a judicial system of appeals into a dynamic game of speed, momentum, and quick decisions by coaches, players, and—yes—officials. For the most part it did not work because the premise was all wrong. The NFL had no business installing an appellate court system and then running it hastily during games. If the replay official upstairs saw a potential problem, he was to over-turn the field call or no-call if the error was deemed clear and con-vincing. But replay officials blew it, too, sometimes failing to overturn bad calls and occasionally negating good ones. The tell-tale sign was when the replay official studied the tapes for two or three minutes—how can something be "clear and convincing" and difficult to see all at the same time?

A better way to run the NFL replay system would be to use it for what it is: an available technological tool capable of helping field officials understand and make the right calls.[7] Refs are not reluc-tant to ask each other for help; they do so all the time. If they dis-agree, or none of them got a good look, they may decide on their own to view the replay tapes. It is just that simple. Trust the offi-cials to do their job well, and then trust them to review in good faith. Perhaps a ref knows the receiver caught the ball, but he did not observe whether the player was legally in bounds. He knows what to look for on the tape and should gladly do so. He doesn't have to make the call, then get reversed, or guess about the call and be embarrassed. If an official is good—and we assume most are—then the process should be easy: no more courts of appeals, no cumbersome rules about losing timeouts, no coach intervention.

These days sports manipulation is by no means confined to the field of play or even a replay booth, however. Even the viewers are manipulated with, for example, a new beast cleverly described as "virtual ads." While live fans at the stadium see nothing but a blank wall, television viewers see elaborate backdrop ads for Coke, Pennzoil, and Chevrolet. The possibilities are endless, for the walls of a baseball field could be "covered" with phantom ads directed toward the TV audience. Then the ads could change every other inning. There could even be "virtual signage" in places that would otherwise distract players in live games. The 1998 Brickyard 400 auto race displayed logos for Miller Beer and others in a manner that made them appear to have been mowed into the grass on the fourth turn, but no one present could see them at all.

Games and viewers have been manipulated for years by com-mercial timeouts and the hour that televised games are played. Now that audiences are subjected to these virtual ads, can virtual play be far behind? It is already here if one counts the innovative yellow first-down line artificially injected into some televised NFL games. That line is harmless, even helpful to home viewers. But it would not be difficult to imagine a pro wrestling venue with some type of virtual entertainment imaged in for the television audience. And one wonders how far behind the legitimate sports would then be. Hockey already experimented with a computerized "comet tail" streak behind rocketing pucks, a cartoonlike image that had no redeeming value. What could be next—a computer image blimp over the stadium? Or how about computer-inserted crowds to fill sparse arenas?

Some of the most sweeping manipulation is accomplished neither through television imagery nor on-court gamesmanship, but by owners and league commissioners. The NFL's longtime chief Pete Rozelle forged expansion teams, crafted television deals, and implemented player trade rules so restrictive that they unofficially bore his name with the infamous "Rozelle Rule." Peter Ueberroth was behind the baseball salary collusion among owners in the 1980s, and David Stern skillfully guided the NBA through the labor wars of 1997–1999. Sometimes those machinations are good business; sometimes they are improper or even unlawful manipulations of players, fairness, and money.

Even the money itself is manipulated. So long as Ted Turner owns both the Braves and the cable broadcast superstation WTBS, for example, he could easily manipulate the Braves' net income by tinkering with the amount paid by WTBS to broadcast games. Parking, concessions, luxury suites, stadium ad revenue, and local TV deals all greatly influence the revenue and net income of team franchises, which, in turn, has an effect upon player salaries, the salary cap effectiveness, and other trickle-down issues that influence games on the field. According to sports economist Andrew Zimbalist, "One of the major motivations in each of the sports for going into new stadiums is because most of those revenue sources are not shared with the players."[8] Result? Team income is often manipulated, usually downward.

Forbes did a study of 1997 team income, recalculating reported team revenues to accommodate artificial aberrations. It found that although 16 NBA teams claimed to have lost money, only 10 really did. But sometimes the rules can work against a team, too. The Chicago Bulls were on the short end of the financial stick every year of Michael Jordan's megasalaries in the $30 million to $40 million range. Although the Bulls sold out every home game year after year, and were the most popular road team and television draw, and the biggest contributor to NBA merchandise sales, they were not listed among the most profitable NBA franchises. They were not even in the top five, comprised of Portland, Detroit, the Lakers, Utah, and Houston—in that order. Not even a new stadium, luxury boxes, and concessions thrown into the mix could make the Bulls one of the most valuable teams in sports (including football, baseball, and hockey), notwithstanding that they were the most popular team nationwide for most of the 1990s. But even though they were not among the most profitable officially, the reconstituted franchise income is good enough to value the Bulls atop the NBA at an estimated $303 million, even though they were tied for eleventh in operating income.

Interestingly, the team they tied in the eleventh spot was Philadelphia, with both franchises showing reported operating income of $8.6 million. But the 76ers did it on just over half the team revenue—$69.9 million versus $112.2 million for Chicago. The difference? Michael Jordan's salary was greater than an entire team allocated salary cap. Plug his salary back in and the Bulls would have been the most lucrative, beating out Portland's $34.2 million. Of course, remove Jordan's salary and one removes Jordan, and therefore the demand and related revenue would suffer. But put back all but $14 million of Jordan's paycheck (hypothetically leaving the new cap limit for 10-year veterans on the table for MJ) and Bulls operating income still jumps from eleventh place to the second slot. (This certainly explains the logic behind the new cap system, and it might even explain, at least partially, Michael Jordan's 1998 retirement.)

Whether it is creative owners fudging the salary cap, a slow Cubs team growing the infield grass a little on the long side, or Tonya Harding's colleagues attempting to take out Nancy Kerrigan's knee, sports manipulation is pervasive—sometimes innocently or widely accepted, but often unfair, culpable, and even cruel. Either way, the history of sports manipulation is an alluring point-counterpoint of deceit, psych-jobs, cheating, and clever machinations. From Kenesaw Mountain Landis to Bowie Kuhn, Selig, and Stern, Tyson-Holyfield to Ali-Foreman, the NFL fog bowl, the 1963 expansion of the strike zone, Bill Veeck's midget hitters, or Michael Jordan's shake-and-bake traveling, the compelling story of sports manipulation is now a part of sports lore, helping to shape all big-time sports in America. But nowhere are the playmasters more effective or prevalent than the entertainment dynamo of today's National Basketball Association, where, at least for now, the owners are in control of television, the union, the money . . . and the game.

Indeed, in 1999, NBA conspiracy theorists emerged again as the draft lottery just happened to give the Chicago Bulls the number-one choice,[9] calling to mind the first NBA lottery, when the big-market, struggling Knicks just happened to land high-profile franchise player Patrick Ewing in 1985 even though two other teams (Indiana and Golden State) had worse records. Whether legitimate or not, the NBA lottery system is a blatant manipulation of the game, flying in the face of parity and the sports tradition of drafting in reverse order of team standings. Originally touted as a disincentive for poor teams to lose games near season's end, it still rewards losing by weighting the picks in favor of the worst teams—yet leaving the door open for teams other than the worst to sneak a top pick. Thus, the saga of manipulation comes full circle, with a manipulative artificial device intended to prevent manipulation. If such a scheme looks and sounds disingenuous, perhaps it flunks the cliché "quack-walk-look" duck test of life, business, and sports. But the facts are still the facts: the worst teams in 1985 ended up with picks Wayman Tisdale and Chris Mullin while the big-market Knicks got Ewing; and the 1999 Bulls (13–37) won the lottery ahead of lowly Vancouver (8–42) and the Clippers (9–41).

That 1999 draft was perhaps the culmination of a bizarre conspiracy of fate, blunders, and manipulation that began before the final Bulls title run of 1997–98. According to national commentator and former coach Hubie Brown, Krause and the Bulls then risked a team breakup when they attempted to trade Scottie Pippen to Boston for the third and sixth picks, but New Jersey beat them to the punch with a multiplayer deal that left the Bulls no alternative but to keep the team intact and go for championship number six.

So the 1999 Bulls needed a year-end dose of good luck—and they got it.

ENDNOTES

1. Even statements about manipulation can be manipulated, especially where statistics are concerned. The definition of *mediocre* is of course highly subjective, but in general we can think of it as teams hovering around the .500 level, or even a bit lower.

2. In the 1950s and 1960s there were incidents involving Jack Molinas and the Fort Wayne Pistons that spilled over to Connie Hawkins in later years. Although Hawkins's affiliation with Molinas cost him an NCAA career, that loss was probably unfair given Connie's limited involvement—and there is no record that Hawkins was connected to gambling during his eventual NBA career. Before his interim retirement in 1994, Michael Jordan experienced a great deal of heat over alleged gambling on golf and other contests, but not basketball. The matter blew over when he retired, and it never resurfaced again.

3. This is the same Leon Wood who was plaintiff in a famous basketball antitrust lawsuit as a player.

4. All of those events have been reported in the press over the years.

5. Home and away analysis was performed with statistics generated by Stats, Inc., Skokie, Illinois.

6. Aggregate averages were calculated by the arithmetic mean of home and away free throw percentages of each respective team, thus weighting each team's percentages equally.

7. The NFL implemented a modified approach for 1999, but it still misses the point.

8. Quoted originally in *Forbes*, December 14, 1998.

9. According to well-known *Chicago Tribune* sports columnist Bernie Lincicome, giving the Bulls and GM Jerry Krause the top pick now is rather like "handing a new hammer to the guy who knocked the nose off Michelangelo's *Pieta*."

15

SPREWELL AND THE PLAYER PSYCHE

Star athletes are by no means normal people, but as human beings they can neither be fully categorized or dismissed as aberrations. Still, they do carry plenty of baggage, ranging from pure fame to deep-rooted emotional needs to compete, excel, and win. No two are alike, of course, but on the whole they demonstrate various categories of predictable traits, and understanding their personality tendencies is necessary to truly knowing them as people.

I'm gonna foul out of this motherfucker.

—BIMBO COLES, GOLDEN STATE WARRIORS [REFERRING TO THE LOPSIDED LAKERS GAME OF NOVEMBER 9, 1997]

From the 1920s to the 1960s star athletes were not perceived as truly human. They were bigger than life, almost like movie stars in a world of make-believe. From Ruth to Mantle, the public believed athletes were as perfect off the field as they were on it. The press helped perpetuate the ruse, rarely reporting the off-field exploits with any detail, even though drinking and womanizing were invented long before 1920. The nonbaseball exploits of Babe Ruth were legendary—but in a way, that is just the point. They were "legendary" because, unlike today, there were no blow-by-blow details reported in the sports pages.

Former statesman Henry Kissinger, one of the more savvy leaders to emerge from the Washington quagmire in the past several decades, once observed that "power is an aphrodisiac." Fame produces similar results, probably because fame is often confused with power. When fame is achieved early, as it always is where athletes are concerned, the results can be explosive. So profound is the essence of fame that it has captured the attention of great philosophers for many centuries. Francis Bacon, for example, observed, "Fame is like a river, that beareth up things light and swollen, and drowns things weighty and solid." Truly genuine, steadfast people rarely seek out fame, a pursuit often reserved for the insecure or shallow souls among us. Literary thinker James Thorpe was more succinct but equally cynical on a different plane, possibly explaining the addictive qualities of adulation: "Fame creates earlier friends."

This is the essence of the pro athlete, a young person thrust into the spotlight of life. Perhaps the athlete did not seek fame, but notoriety finds the athlete anyway in an era of relentless television and burgeoning hero worship. The friends do come early and often, including bimbos and groupies, not to mention hangers-on who form the collective entourage of today's superstars. Fame produces a smorgasbord of temptations, from sex to drugs to outrageous partying, all excesses reminiscent of self-destructive rock stars, but applying equally well to contemporary pro sports.

Basketball players seem to have enjoyed more than their share. They are highly visible, and their fast-paced sport is made for television entertainment. They are also the beneficiaries (victims?) of a contemporary free press that is more than anxious to air any and all personal laundry, dirty or otherwise. Just as politicians from Roosevelt to Kennedy once received a free pass on their personal lives, no one looked too deeply into the nonpublic personas of Ted Williams, Willie Mays, or Hank Aaron. But basketball exploded onto the public consciousness at about the same time the press was spreading its voyeuristic wings. Basketball itself has also been the most visible sport of late with its colorful recent stars, from Bird and Magic to Jordan, Barkley, and Rodman.

It also requires a particularly cocky attitude to play basketball, a sport that rewards so many diverse qualities predicated upon supreme confidence: shake-and-bake dribbling, shooting, rebounding, steals, and blocks—in other words, lots of showcased individual effort in a team-sport setting. So by practice, if not definition, basketball is a forum for the egocentric, a sport that rewards a one-on-one attitude uniquely suited to the persona of its stars.

So unique are the personalities of prize athletes that a cottage industry of sports psychologists has sprung up, and at least one expert has made a career of counseling teams, coaches, and owners about the conscious and subconscious makeup of successful athletes. Jonathan P. Niednagel is so adept at reading player personalities that he has become a mainstay with some owners and other team insiders. Niednagel tracks four distinct personality traits, studying two variations of each, to size up what makes individual players tick. The Niednagel approach is reminiscent of the Myers-Brigg Personality Indicator. Although he does not refer to it as such, Niednagel does acknowledge the Jungian roots behind his work. He also has observed which playing positions demand certain personality combinations, helping to predict which players will succeed in different roles.

According to Niednagel, every player has one dominant trait among four pairs of different types. Specifically, the athlete is Sensitive or Intuitive; a Thinker or a Feeler; Perceptive or Judgmental; and Extrovert or Introvert. The traits that make up the best players are not necessarily those one would expect. Niednagel should know. The Phoenix Suns signed him to a three-year exclusive basketball contract; the Arizona Diamondbacks to a two-year baseball deal. He has also advised the Dallas Cowboys, Orlando Magic, and many others. He advised the Suns to pick up Jason Kidd, for example, whom Niednagel feels has an ideal point guard personality. He refers to Kidd as an ISTP: introverted, sensitive, thinker, perceptive. Point guards must above all be perceptive, quickly comprehending all movement on the court. They must also be sensitive to evolving situations and, remarkably, are not customarily extroverted. They preserve their energy, not burning themselves out unnecessarily. Michael Jordan, says Niednagel, is also an ISTP, demonstrating great perceptive qualities on and off the court, not to mention his obvious intelligence and even sensitivities.

In many ways societal beliefs and mores have helped mold the player psyche. Young athletes are treated preferentially. Even at seven or eight years of age, the budding stars who can run faster, dribble a basketball, or shoot a hockey puck enjoy an abundance of praise and even a taste of fame as they strike out batters or hit home runs for the traveling team before legions of proud parents. Athlete worship begins young, it appears, and perhaps most of us are guilty of elevating early athletics to unwarranted levels of importance, skewing the perceptions and priorities of our young people. Do we cut these young athletes a break too often, even subconsciously, giving them the wrong message about work ethics and responsibility? Many psychologists think so, for the athlete mentality is formed very early—and society may do these young stars a disservice.

But regardless of formal typing or how they got here, it is clear that NBA players are a unique breed. The excesses of Wilt Chamberlain's alleged twenty thousand sexual conquests and Magic Johnson's confrontation with HIV are eye-openers for society. And as unique as the players may be, their professional environment is at least as singular. Nowhere was that more obvious than the Latrell Sprewell melee, which found Warriors coach P. J. Carlesimo on the wrong end of Latrell's infamous choking grip. In the minds of many fans, the Sprewell affair was a watershed event, proving once and for all that sports and everyday reality may have officially parted company. When Latrell's suspension was reduced by an arbitrator, many fans could not relate to such multimillion-dollar foolishness, knowing full well that in no other industry can choking one's boss be even remotely justifiable.

But the Sprewell arbitrator considered just that: the basketball world is not normal, and perhaps it does not always benefit from "normal" logic. Where else do employees go into physical combat two or three nights a week, a job that not only tolerates aggressive behavior but rewards and even requires it? There is little normalcy in suiting up for an NBA contest; it is not a run-of-the-mill lunchbucket day at the jobsite. Never has that distinction been so real than when Sprewell the *assailant* filed a grievance alleging unfair treatment after he had physically attacked his coach.

The Sprewell grievance hearings took place over nine days at the end of 1997 and the beginning of 1998. Testimony from 21 witnesses was heard, including such notables as Tyrone Bogues, Felton Spencer, Joe Smith, Sprewell's agent Arn Tellem, Paul West-head, David Stern, and, of course, Sprewell and Carlesimo. At issue was Sprewell's one-year suspension by the NBA and the cancellation of his playing contract by the Warriors. Sprewell's representatives essentially argued that Stern's yearlong suspension was arbitrary and capricious, unjustified in view of past suspensions for violent conduct on the part of other players. The team's cancellation of the playing contract, although provided for under the rules, was argued in this case to comprise a double jeopardy of sorts, the issue being whether both the NBA and the team could sanction Sprewell at the same time for the same act.

The written findings and decision of the arbitrator covered 106 pages of text, revealing a remarkably candid glimpse of the NBA. The commissioner's power was derived in part from this provision of the NBA constitution:

> The Commissioner shall have the power to suspend for a definite or indefinite period, or to impose a fine not exceeding $25,000, or inflict both such suspension and fine upon any Player who, in his opinion, shall have been guilty of conduct that does not conform to standards of morality or fair play, that does not comply at all times with all federal, state, and local laws, or that is prejudicial or detrimental to the Association.

Sprewell's duties as a player on the Warriors team were spelled out in his uniform player contract, partially including the following:

> The Player agrees (i) to give his best services, as well as his loyalty, to the Team, and to play basketball only for the Team and its assignees; (ii) to be neatly and fully attired in public; (iii) to conduct himself on and off the court according to the highest standards of honesty, citizenship, and sportsmanship; and (iv) not to do anything that is materially detrimental or materially prejudicial to the best interest of the Team or of the League.

Perhaps those goals sound good on paper—no doubt they appealed to whatever committee thought them up in the first place—

but in practice they are a mudhole of vague ideals, begging for arbitrary interpretation and enforcement. Therein lies the opportunity, of course, for anyone about to represent Mr. Sprewell.

Warriors team rules elaborated on the possible consequences as set forth in the team handbook:

> . . . A FAILURE TO ABIDE BY THESE STANDARDS OR THE FAILURE TO COMPLY WITH THE SPECIFIC RULES SET FORTH IN THIS HANDBOOK MAY RESULT IN YOUR BEING FINED AND/OR SUSPENDED, AND REPEATED OR INTENTIONAL VIOLATIONS OF SIGNIFICANT RULES WILL BE CONSIDERED A MATERIAL BREACH OF YOUR INDIVIDUAL CONTRACT AND COULD RESULT IN THE TERMINATION OF YOUR PLAYER CONTRACT . . .

At the same time, the NBA had its own policies concerning violent behavior, including this one-sentence preamble: "Violence has no place in the game of basketball and violent behavior cannot be tolerated under any circumstances." After a series of admonitions about violence, the NBA policies address the issue of tempers.

> In addition to the above, it is the position of the Club that each professional athlete is expected to keep control of his temper, no matter what the provocation from opposing players, fans, officials, or others.

But this is the kicker, a remarkably naive instruction that in practice would have absolutely no pragmatic value whatsoever: "*If you think you are losing your ability to keep control of your temper, you should inform the Coach and you will be taken out of the game.*" If a player boils over during regulation play, is he rationally capable of summoning the coach, especially if it means he'll be yanked from the game? Certainly coaches have sat many players on the bench when tempers jeopardized performance, but one can hardly imagine a reasoned approach from any player who himself has "lost it" on the court. But this is the Sprewell arena, a land as foreign as *Alice in Wonderland*, full of goofy caterpillars, rules that make no sense, and expectations of fairyland proportions.

According to the transcript and findings of Sprewell's grievance hearing, "Spree" physically attacked Coach Carlesimo during a team practice on December 1, 1997, choked him, and shouted death threats. After returning to the locker room, Sprewell again emerged, fought his way through several players and coaches, and engaged in a premeditated attack on the coach. Again Sprewell threatened to kill him—and then demanded a trade that very day.

Later that same day, the Warriors informed Sprewell that he would be suspended at least 10 games by the team itself, pending a final team investigation and decision; all the while, the Warriors reserved the right to terminate Spree's contract altogether. Upon further review of the facts, the team decided not to accede to the trade demands and chose to terminate Spree's contract instead. The effect of such termination was to turn Sprewell into a free agent, essentially granting his freedom to go wherever he could land an NBA position. Commissioner Stern countered with a league imposed one-year suspension, thus giving teeth to the contract termination and not rewarding Sprewell with total free agency.

Sprewell was joined by the NBA Players Association in pursuit of his grievance. Together they contended the incident was not premeditated but, rather, Sprewell had never "cooled down" from the first attack sufficiently for him to premeditate the second assault. Instead, they argued, the whole episode resulted from a month of tension and confrontations between Carlesimo and Sprewell. Two of their best legal arguments included a challenge to the double jeopardy implications of both a team and a league sanction, arguing that one or the other could discipline him, but not both. There is no proscribed NBA "double jeopardy" analogous to criminal law, but the term sounded good and had some degree of validity from the language of the contracts and rules in question, which did imply that either the team or the league could impose sanctions.

The other good argument compared these sanctions to prior suspensions and other disciplinary action taken in response to other violent episodes. From a reasonably objective vantage, the

NBA had been remarkably tolerant of violent conduct for many years. By suddenly imposing a one-year suspension without warning, the NBA may have entered the world of "arbitrary and capricious" conduct, reviewable by a grievance arbitrator. (Dennis Rodman, by way of contrast, got 10 games off for kicking an innocent cameraman in full view on the court during a televised Bulls game.)

Although Sprewell had a history of obnoxious and occasionally violent behavior (as a rookie he fought with friend Byron Houston for throwing an elbow, and he once attacked and threatened teammate Jerome Kersey), his indiscretions rarely surfaced on the court in game situations. In five years as an NBA player, Sprewell had never been ejected from a game, and only received one technical foul—a very good, even exemplary, on-court record. As a Warriors player, he was an All-Star three times, and even received the team's "Most Inspirational Player" award from his prior coach Don Nelson, a coach Sprewell himself described as a hardnosed, in-your-face disciplinarian type. Although Spree was sometimes late for meetings and practices, he had never had run-ins with fans, referees, or other coaches. In fact, Sprewell found himself as team captain, hardly a no-confidence vote.

Sprewell had first met P. J. Carlesimo at Warriors training camp in October of 1997. He felt they had a good initial relationship, but things soured as the team began to lose games. According to Sprewell, Carlesimo took most of his frustration out on Spree and teammate Donyell Marshall. Spree testified later that P.J. was constantly in his face, cursing and swearing at him, on one occasion calling Sprewell a "fucking idiot." On November 3, Sprewell was stretching with player Joe Smith when Carlesimo accosted him and instigated a shouting match.

Six days later, the Warriors were being blown out by the Lakers when Spree heard frustrated teammate Bimbo Coles exclaim, "I'm gonna foul out of this motherfucker." When Sprewell laughed at Bimbo's rather excited utterance, Carlesimo benched him (not Coles, but Sprewell), inspiring Spree to call the coach a "fucking joke." On November 19, he was taken out of the Spurs game in the third quarter, a move Sprewell called "bullshit" because he was trying to get the coach to modify the pick-and-roll strategy because it was not working. Nine days later Spree "overslept" and missed the flight to Utah for a date with the Jazz.

The fateful blowup occurred at practice just 11 days later. Sprewell was involved in a three-man, two-ball shooting drill with teammates Bogues and Grabow. Spree's job was to pass in to Bogues, and the coach was on Sprewell to give sharper, crisper passes, even though Sprewell later insisted in sworn testimony that he was not "dogging it." As the coach persisted, a frustrated Spree slammed the ball down and addressed Carlesimo, "What the fuck do you want me to do?"

"Get the fuck out of here," was P.J.'s retort.

Throwing Sprewell out of practice that way was apparently the last straw. According to Spree's testimony later, he "just lost it" as a result of all the tension over the prior two months. Sprewell grabbed Carlesimo around the neck with his arms fully extended, exclaiming "I'll kill you," and the coach answered, "Do it."

Spree felt he had his hands around the coach's neck, not throat (a minor distinction?), but did admit his nails had scratched Carlesimo. Grabow yelled, "Don't do it," prompting Sprewell to let go. As he was led from the gym, Sprewell continued to fulminate, shouting "I'm gonna kill your ass" and "I hate you," knocking over the water cooler along the way. No one followed Spree to the locker room, where he remained by himself for some interval between 5 and 15 minutes. Upon his return, Spree was still angry, upset, and "pissed off" as he put it, intending to tell Carlesimo he wanted out but not thinking of attacking him again.

Pushing himself through players and others, Spree went for Carlesimo again. As a number of people grabbed him, Spree fought to free himself, triggering his anger all over again as he kicked and struggled. Cross-examination produced a vague if not evasive response from Sprewell. "I didn't draw back and punch P.J. in the face. I was trying to break away and I might have hit him."

Eventually the other players pushed Spree toward the exit, and on the way out he uttered such audible subtleties as "Trade me"; "Get me the fuck out of here"; and (perhaps—the testimony here is conflicting) "I'll kill you." He then stormed to the front office, again shrieking "Get me the fuck out of here." The team informed Spree's agent, Arn Tellem, to expect about a 10-day suspension from the whole affair, a penalty that would cost Sprewell about $1 million. Sprewell later apologized privately to Carlesimo, who also apologized to Spree; then Sprewell publicly apologized again at a press conference to let the public know he was not the villain being portrayed in the media.

When the team terminated his contract, Sprewell was surprised, but when the league also suspended him for one year, he was shocked. Eventually one of the biggest issues at the hearing was the level of punishment for other heinous basketball transgressions. Other fines for punching had been in the $25,000 range or less; for example, an upset Shaquille O'Neal was once nailed $10,000 for slapping another player in the face, but there was no injury involved. Before Sprewell, the longest suspension in NBA history belonged to Kermit Washington, who punched out and demolished player Rudy Tomjanovich (who would later win two rings as the Rockets coach), shattering his jaw, fracturing his nose and skull, cutting his face, and causing a leakage of spinal fluid from the brain cavity. Kermit was hit with a 60-day suspension for his part in the on-court melee, causing him to miss 26 games without pay. Suspensions are normally much more severe than fines, for the player's pay is docked for each game missed. Thus, a $25,000 fine pales when compared to losing $20,000 to $100,000 per game during a suspension of any duration.

Overall, NBA violence does seem to be on an upward trend. In addition to the travails of Rodman, Strickland, and Shaq, Robert Horry threw a towel in the face of his coach when taken out of a game and received a two-game suspension. Player Alvin Robertson once grabbed his team director of player personnel around the throat, causing both of them to tumble over a banister into a row of seats. Robertson received an indefinite suspension from the team, but was soon traded in a move approved by the commissioner's office. Tom Chambers once punched his strength and conditioning coach, inflicting a cut that required stitches; Chambers apologized but was traded from the team.

Vernon Maxwell took the problem to a new level when he attacked a fan in the stands, receiving both a 10-game suspension and a league fine of $20,000.[1] Such transgressions, however, were not reserved just for players. At another game the owner of the Utah Jazz also went after a fan in the stands and was suspended for two games by the league.

Incidents between players and officials seem also to be on the rise. In addition to Dennis Rodman's head-butt and related fine ($20,000) and league suspension (six games), Nick Van Exel exchanged words with another referee before pushing the official over the scorer's table. The league fined him $25,000 to go along with a seven-game suspension, but the team imposed no sanction. Even Seattle coach George Karl had an altercation with a ref. Although it did not escalate into a fight, Karl still wound up with a fine of $7,500. Other relatively minor incidents involved such stars as Isiah Thomas, Charles Barkley, and Clyde Drexler, generating little or no disciplinary action.

So with a rising tide of NBA violence as the backdrop, the Sprewell hearings were under way. Carlesimo himself testified that just before the altercation the team was performing a three-man, two-ball shooting drill: one player passes, one rebounds, and the other shoots. In the drill, each player goes for about a minute, then they change positions for a total rotation time of around six minutes. Carlesimo explained that one purpose of the drill is to shoot the ball quickly in rapid fire. Concerned that Bogues was not getting enough shots, P.J. turned to Latrell and said, "Get Muggsy some more shots, Spree." Hearing no response, Carlesimo repeated himself, whereupon Spree threw the ball down and exclaimed, "Get off my back, motherfucker." Carlesimo, apparently inspired by Latrell's colorful expressions, responded, "You're the fuck out of here."

At that point Sprewell approached P.J., grabbed him around the throat, choking and gripping him "extremely tight" while pushing the coach backwards. Carlesimo recounted that Spree was screaming threats during the course of the incident, which, according to his recollection, lasted perhaps seven to ten seconds. At that point, Carlesimo recalled, "It was difficult to breathe and getting more difficult." The following is excerpted verbatim from the grievance hearing transcript of findings:

> Carlesimo said that during the first incident he did not try to move his hands up to stop the choking in the beginning, believing that it would not last very long and that a fight would not be good. He said that he did raise his arms near the end, with his palms down. He also said that he was not dizzy from the grabbing of his neck, and that he did not know if the marks on his neck were from the Grievant's [Sprewell's] nails or from choking. He also said that he did not know how the Grievant's hands were extracted from his neck, and that the Grievant could have let go voluntarily.
>
> Carlesimo said that after the Grievant was removed the first time, he said, "I'm gonna kill ya" to which he replied, "I'm here." He said that he did not really believe that the Grievant was going to kill him and that the Grievant was still emotional when he returned to the practice the second time.
>
> Carlesimo said that he felt capable of continuing practice so he went on. He said that about 15 to 20 minutes[2] later, the Grievant came back through the door in street clothes and appeared emotional and in a highly agitated state. He said that he was upset and talking loudly. He testified that Grievant said "Get me the fuck out of here" or "I'm gonna fuck you up" and "I'm gonna kill you." He said that Grievant walked up the baseline where Staak tried to head him off, advanced through players, and when he got to him, he punched him with a closed hand, which hit the right side of his face. He said that the punch was deliberate and not the result of a flailing. He described the punch as being a little bit of a reach around as opposed to a straight jab. He said that the Grievant threw a second punch that could have landed anywhere from his mid chest area to the top of his back.

Over the course of 106 typed pages the arbitrator analyzed the whole event not only in historical context, but also in the purview of an NBA world of rough language, physical contact, and emotional personalities. The NBA itself was concerned about progressing violence, escalating the penalties in Latrell's case to unprecedented levels certainly to send a new message about such conduct, especially since the altercation received such wide media exposure and compelling public interest. In other words, perhaps the penalty was meant not only as a deterrent but also as a necessary public relations move to appease a surprisingly hostile fan base that was vocally appalled by the incident.

Ultimately the arbitrator reduced the suspension from one 82-game season down to 62 games, the number of contests already missed by the time the decision was rendered. The arbitrator also rescinded the cancellation of the Warriors playing contract, the effect of which was to reinstate Latrell as a Warrior. The public was dismayed at the outcome, for the decision appeared to be a victory for Sprewell. Indeed it was a win to a degree, but the suspension was really reduced only by 20 games down to 62, still costing Spree a quantum leap record in lost earnings. This is how the arbitrator saw it:

> As for a penalty of $6.4 million against a history of lesser penalties for misconduct not involving a coach, I find it justified by virtue of the singularity of the misconduct and the emphasis placed on combating violence by both the NBA and NBPA. A suspension of practically an entire season is one of great severity, to be sure, but appropriate given the fact that physical altercations with a head coach strike at the very core of a structure that provides stability for a team and an organized sport.
>
> Having so concluded, I should note the Grievant, on December 1, 1997, acted out of anger and passion, not a premeditated state, and despite some earlier acts of defiance by him with respect to his coach, he has had an honorable career in the NBA. He has worked hard and played hard; has won All-Star status on a number of occasions; carried the captaincy of the Team by its appointment through December 1, 1997; and won the Team's Most Inspirational Player Award during one of his playing seasons. At the hearings before me he conducted

himself in a calm and restrained manner, even at moments that would have challenged the most even-tempered individuals. The severity of the discipline, the commentary that has accompanied this matter, and the experience undergone by the Grievant may well equip him in the future years of his life to be an example of a person who can overcome adversity and be a role model. As Commissioner Stern noted at the conclusion of the testimonial portion of the hearings: "[Grievant] is a gifted athlete who has done well in the NBA . . . . We want Mr. Sprewell in the NBA. We expect him to be in the NBA during the '98/'99 season."

In 1999 Sprewell was traded to the New York Knicks, where he fought through injuries and rust before catching fire with significant contributions to the Knicks' surprising playoff run.

The contemporary NBA athlete is strong yet fragile, gifted but often insecure, confident but still fallible, and above all proud and very emotional. Both traits are readily observed in such diverse players as Sprewell, Dennis Rodman, Charles Barkley, John Starks, Patrick Ewing, Alonzo Mourning, and even Michael Jordan, whose on-court emotional persona was enough to make his teammates better. It is impossible to understand the NBA without a glimpse of the players who make it happen, for ultimately the game does not truly belong to the owners or even the fans—it belongs to them, the players, the heart and soul of the National Basketball Association.

The Sprewell incident was public and far-reaching, to be sure, but it was not and will not be the only transgression born of emotion on and off the court. And even though the arbitrator cut back the penalties, it still raised the bar for NBA retribution, no doubt sending the requisite message to players, fans, and owners: the NBA is a business dependent upon public perceptions and support, and aberrant behavior will be neither rewarded nor tolerated.

ENDNOTES

1. This was one example of sanctions by both the team and the league at the same time. It may also have influenced the Sprewell arbitrator, for, if anything, one would think that assaults on the fans would be more severely punished than anything. Yet Sprewell's one-year suspension amounted to 82 games, over eight times what Maxwell received.
2. Carlesimo remembered a slightly longer span than Sprewell, who had recalled a range of 5 to 15 minutes.

16

THE SUPERAGENTS

There are thousands of sports agents in America, some almost in name only as they hustle athletes from a portable office stationed in the trunks of their cars, usually with little success. Others are flashy agents long on glitz but short on reputation if not cash, draped in sunglasses, the appropriate Mercedes, and too much jewelry. But the top sports agents are not hangers-on looking just to snare a percentage of the big-league playing contract of an unsophisticated athlete—they are the movers and shakers of pro sports, power brokers of the elite athletes.

Some of the most successful agents are not especially high profile, such as Chicago's Herb Rudoy, who has represented players from the Artis Gilmore era to more contemporary basketball players in the mold of Toni Kukoc or Dee Brown. Rudoy has immense European connections and is known for successfully placing players in and out of Europe, but he is seldom a headliner himself. Others are very high profile, such as Mark McCormack, who invented the modern sports agent concept when he signed young emerging golfer Arnold Palmer to generate sports marketing and endorsements. That initial deal, followed by over three decades of effort by McCormack, produced Cleveland-based International Management Group (IMG), the world's largest sports representation firm.[1]

With the sports business about to explode in the 1960s, IMG's timing could not have been better. It began to handle the marketing and business affairs of such diverse clients as Greg Norman, Chris Evert, John Madden, violinist Itzhak Perlman, and even the Ringling Brothers Circus. Notwithstanding its successful representation of individuals, the lion's share of its contemporary business lies with IMG's event management and sports programming prowess. Many of those events are golf and figure skating competitions, although in 1982 it even promoted Pope John Paul II's tour of the British Isles.

But Mark McCormack was not the only burgeoning sports agent. A diminutive, youthful Leigh Steinberg represented roommate Steve Bartkowski when he was picked number-one in the NFL draft over 20 years ago as an emerging top quarterback. Steinberg quickly rose to become the dean of NFL agents, representing many of the big-name quarterbacks (including Joe Montana) on and off the field. With most sports agents recruiting, indeed hustling, prospective clients, Steinberg has the ability to work in reverse, picking and choosing among the legions of players already looking to wear the venerable Leigh Steinberg name on their sleeves.

Although both Steinberg and McCormack did much to reinvent the business, the original sports agent emerged from a different kind of representative—the talent agent. William Morris invented that notion in the 1890s, founding the entertainment monolith that still bears his name. Showman and hustler C. C. ("Cash and Carry") Pyle recognized the entertainment value of sports as early as the 1920s when he represented the original football superstar, Red Grange, the Illinois Galloping Ghost who barnstormed America and helped George Halas launch the Chicago Bears and the National Football League.

The 1920s also saw the growth of prizefight promoters, quasi-agents who represented a stable of boxers and also promoted the matches, many of which were spectacular affairs. The most prolific promoter of big-time matches during the Roaring Twenties was one Tex Rickard. Before Tex, no one had promoted a million-dollar-gate fight, but Tex himself did it five times between 1921 and 1927. The most spectacular was undoubtedly the 1927 "long count" rematch between heavyweights Gene Tunney and Jack Dempsey before a sea of 105,000 frantic fans shoehorned into Chicago's Soldier Field.

The $2.6 million gate was a stunner, but of course it pales against today's television and pay-per-view purses, a phenomenon launched by Don King nearly 50 years after the Dempsey-Tunney extravaganza. With little experience and less money, King promoted himself to the top in 1974 as he hustled the greatest fight of the last quarter century in which George Foreman met challenger Muhammad Ali in Zaire, Africa. Ali and Foreman were each guaranteed $5 million for the fight (backed by Zaire itself as almost a "sports marketing" investment promoting the whole country on worldwide television).

Still, with all his success, Don King is not really a sports agent in the pure sense. He is a promoter, a showman, and a hustler, and even though he maintains a stable of fighters, he uses them for his fights and promotions rather than representing their interests the way a football or basketball agent would. He is unique to be sure, including his identity as an African American, for it took black agents many years to establish a foothold in the sports agent arena.

The initial sports agents were all white lawyers and businessmen, from McCormack to Steinberg, Marvin Demoff, Herb Rudoy, Jack Childers, Jerry Kapstein, and many others. With the ranks of pro athletes filled with mostly nonwhite players, one would suspect black agents to have emerged sooner and in great numbers. They did not.[2] With fewer black lawyers to chose from, white team ownership almost across the board, and the foothold already obtained by white agents, there were many barriers to entry.

Norby Walters and Lloyd Bloom were two agents in the entertainment business who bridged the gap in a perverse way. Although they were white, their expertise was in black entertainment, representing such star clients as Patti Labelle, Luther Vandross, and Marvin Gaye. Walters was sly and crusty, sporting a distinguished gray coiffure that complemented his youthful partner, Lloyd Bloom, a dashing hustler still in his 30s.

With a stable of black superstar entertainers, Walters and Bloom had instant credibility, which they leveraged with a cache of under-the-table payments to lure young black athletes about to turn pro. While some prospective agents take years to penetrate the market, Walters and Bloom were an instant success. They signed 10 emerging college athletes in 1985, 2 of whom became first-round NFL draft picks (Tim McGee and Ronnie Harmon). Their 1986 crop was even better, producing 8 first-rounders from a field of 35 new clients, a spectacular number in the agent business. The agent duo quickly invested over $750,000 to assemble a full complement of 60 or so athletes, mostly football players with a few NBA prospects as well. They wore fancy rings and drove the best luxury cars, doling out money to hungry young athletes dazzled by the big show, many of whom affectionately referred to Walters as "Uncle Norby." But the bigger they become, the harder they often fall, and eventually the house of illicit cards came crashing down around Walters and Bloom.

One of the star players they had purchased with improper payments in violation of NCAA rules was running back Brent Fullwood, a high first-round pick of the Green Bay Packers. They had loaned the high-profile Auburn star $8,000 to induce him to sign on—a good deal for Walters and Bloom, who stood to make 5 percent of Fullwood's football earnings, equating to agent fees of $200,000 or more over the life of Fullwood's Green Bay contract. Unfortunately for them, Fullwood fired the pair and retained another agent before signing with the Packers. Walters and Bloom took exception to such anarchy and sued Fullwood for the return of the loans, plus their supposed share of his Green Bay contract. In addition to pursuing legal remedies, Walters and Bloom were known for making physical threats against player clients—such as leg breaking—an especially low approach given the athletes' reliance upon their physical abilities to pursue their respective livelihoods.

Once in court, Walters and Bloom discovered the ultimate problem in suing for the return of illicit funds: the whole sordid affair quickly becomes exposed in court. But by then the collective egos of Walters and Bloom had outgrown all rational proportions, trampling logic and discretion like a 50-ton tank grinding over a rose garden. Even in the face of their own "unclean hands," they could not resist filing suit in federal district court in Manhattan.

Not surprisingly, Walters and Bloom encountered a most unsympathetic judiciary that believed the unsanctioned nature of the Fullwood deal violated public policy and therefore was not an enforceable contract under New York law. Unimpressed with Fullwood's own ethics as well, the court chastised both sides and refused to act as "paymaster of the wages of crime, or referee between thieves." The practical effect, though, was a victory for Fullwood, for by not intervening the court effectively left the $8,000 in the hands of Fullwood to the direct detriment of Walters and Bloom.

But the adventure cost the agents much more than the eight grand, for soon they were on the wrong end of a criminal indictment for mail fraud stemming directly from their payola scheme in violation of NCAA rules. The government believed they had defrauded the universities involved, all of which paid scholarship tuition on behalf of those they thought were eligible amateur athletes. They were eventually convicted, but an appeals court overturned the verdict on grounds relating to the technical requirements of the federal mail fraud statutes. Still, exposed and depleted of cash, the Walters and Bloom agency had been dealt a fatal blow. Walters was thoroughly discredited, but the youthful Bloom mysteriously turned up dead. Although no one was convicted of a homicide, one might suspect that Bloom's unsavory financial backers were less than favorably impressed by the public demise of their investment.

With a potential financial plum of 3 to 5 percent of an athlete's team contract up for grabs, the agent business soon exploded with accountants, lawyers, and insurance salesmen vying for a piece of the action. With player salaries exploding from an average of about $25,000 per year to over $1 million, potential agent fees experienced an equivalent quantum leap, attracting a cadre of movers, shakers, and losers into the business. Not only was the money good, but sports agents grew to live and work in the fast lane, close to celebrities and money, if not sex and drugs in many cases.[3] But most agents were not the cause of these great financial gains—they just went for the ride. The biggest catalyst industrywide was the advent of the players union, which enabled the athletes to fight for and retain a fair piece of the burgeoning sports entertainment pie fueled by television dollars and a ravenous sports audience. Still, individual agents were and are necessary, ideally assuring individual players the optimum bargaining power for themselves, spurred by the experience and objectivity a good agent can provide. The essence of the business lies not in reviewing the player's contract, although that is eventually an important function, but rather is a function of savvy, guts, intuition, and bargaining prowess, allowing the agent to find the best opportunity and negotiate the best deal possible.

Good agents provide peace of mind and optimum economic security, fighting for guaranteed years, leveraging one team off another in a delicate negotiating contest that requires a most difficult brand of toughness to push the envelope, tempered by the necessary intuition to prevent both the deal and the client from going over the edge. Sometimes these agents come from nowhere, such as Dwight Manley, who simply befriended and then signed the impulsive NBA star Dennis Rodman, while others earn their own success and stardom the old-fashioned way with years of hard work, savvy, and adroit skill, such as the mega-agent of the '90s, David Falk.

To be sure, David Falk lucked out greatly by landing rookie Michael Jordan, but luck is an integral part of business that should not require apologies. If nothing else, as baseball icon Branch Rickey put it, "Luck is the residue of design." Certainly lucky things happen in business, but one must have the ability and prowess to recognize good fortune when it happens along and make something of it when it does. Leigh Steinberg "lucked out" with Steve Bartkowski, as did Falk with Jordan, but luck alone does not produce a 15-year relationship generating upwards of a billion dollars without a lot more in the formula than happenstance. Falk may have recognized the "specialness" of Jordan before most others, and in any event he exploited it better than probably anyone could have, a feat not lost upon Michael Jordan the businessman.

Although David Falk certainly rode the Jordan tidal wave as adroitly as anyone, he was much, much more than a hanger-on. Falk steered Jordan through shark-infested waters, honing a public persona built upon the Jordan smile and charisma as skillfully as any Madison Avenue effort could have hoped for. But the Falk agency was much more than a one-man show. It built a base of clients that turned an NBA All-Star team into a thriving representation business, which Falk eventually sold to media conglomerate SFX Entertainment, Inc., for a reported $100 million.

Certainly Falk's power rose with Jordan's star, but it continues to shine even in the face of MJ's retirement. In a display of power and influence greater than that of any other sports agent in history, Falk and Jordan had engineered years of player posturing to fight the NBA salary cap, eventually guiding the players through the 1998–99 NBA lockout.[4] Indeed, they may have caused the lockout in the first place, intimidating the owners into a first-strike defensive measure. Now that the labor action is over and Jordan the player is history, Falk continues to influence the NBA landscape, fueling critics, annoying owners, and positioning his high-profile players with cunning and unparalleled skill, such as his adroit handling of Minnesota star Stephon Marbury, prying him loose from the Timberwolves in a package that sent him near home to the New Jersey Nets during the spring of 1999.

Falk's obvious influence is, of course, generating more than his share of critics, many of whom make cogent arguments against the Falk factor. Still, no one accuses Falk of unfair conduct or criminal influence à la Walters and Bloom or otherwise. If nothing else, David Falk symbolizes a new era of the mega-agent, countering at least a portion of the power garnered by leagues and team owners over many, many years.

As of 1998 there were 252 agents duly registered with the National Basketball Players Association, rivaling the number of NBA players on active team rosters. With nearly one agent per player, the competition is fierce, especially since most of the credible agents represent far more than just one player, leaving too few athletes to go around. Although there are good, energetic, youthful agents with a special foothold,[5] many of the superagents are steering the industry toward a series of strategic alliances to replicate, even challenge, the IMG success formula. Until recently, one of the biggest independent agencies was Advantage International. Based near Washington, D.C., Ad International was founded in 1983 by Frank Craighill and Lee Fentress with an original client base of pro tennis players. By 1998 the firm had grown to 275 employees with a foothold in several sports, including basketball. Still, it felt bigger was better, selling out for $30 million to New York's Interpublic Group, an international advertising and public relations juggernaut with $3.4 billion in annual revenues.

Meanwhile the new centurion agencies keep coming, including Marquee Group, a newly formed industry player with $62 million in public capital backing up founder Robert Gutkowski, the former head of Madison Square Garden. Smaller, Chicago-based Kemper Sports resembles a small IMG, managing golf courses and administering a sophisticated corporate sports marketing practice from its posh offices at NBC Tower. Most recently, agent Arn Tellem (representing Latrell Sprewell, Kobe Bryant, and others) explored a business alliance with billionaire Herb Allen (Allen & Co.) to take on IMG, SFX Entertainment, and the other big boys before selling his business outright to SFX in a multimillion dollar transaction announced on September 29, 1999.

Still, IMG remains the world leader. With 2,000 employees and 77 worldwide offices, its own revenues top $1 billion per year. Not only does it represent Tiger Woods and Pete Sampras, it sports a host of corporate clients like Texaco and Nokia. Its event management and production capabilities are second to no other firm in its category, and it is well poised to maintain a huge chunk of the $15 billion sports marketing and event management industry.

As IMG maintains its worldwide corporate market share, however, the dogmatic David Falk has successfully established himself as the individual powerhouse of big-time sports. He moves players like chess pieces, all while positioning Michael Jordan as the most popular athlete of the current sports era. Jordan has retired twice, won six championships, and endured a foray into the world of gambling just before his first retirement to play AA baseball in the White Sox organization.

Indeed Falk and Jordan may still be posturing, either for an ownership position in Charlotte or otherwise. Time will ultimately tell, but the emerging question is whether there still is a semblance of "between the lines" warfare between Jordan and Falk (and Phil Jackson?) and the Bulls' Jerry Krause. Is Krause the best scapegoat and yes man in the NBA, or is he a loose cannon out to rebuild the Bulls in his own image? The answer may one day be clear, depending upon whether Krause or Jordan one day gets the pleasure of the last laugh.[6]

ENDNOTES

1. Perhaps IMG partly inspired the 1996 Sony/Tri-Star production *Jerry Maguire* which took aim at a fictional monolithic sports representation firm called SMI. IMG, like most success stories, is not without its critics, but whether the movie specifically intended the parallel is unclear. Still, the similarity in the look, sound, and cadence of the respective firm names suggests something other than sheer coincidence, at least from the movie's perspective—but whether IMG deserves the parallel is another matter.

2. Given the proliferation of black athletes, the eventual growth of black agents was inevitable. For example, Eugene Parker, a young black lawyer from Fort Wayne, Indiana, built a thriving practice around one of his first big name clients, Deion Sanders. Still, there are few black sports agents at the very top, although many blacks are now registered as agents with the various players associations.

3. One brochure I came across around 1990 unabashedly displayed a pile of gold and bikini-clad models on the cover.

4. As more fully addressed by the following chapter, the lockout was an event unto its own, an extravaganza battleground between the establishment owners and the superstar players, with Falk squarely in the middle.

5. Take for example Chicago-based Mark Bartelstein or attorney Steve Mandell, each with a growing base of established athletes, Mandell also representing a host of sportscasters from ESPN, Fox, and elsewhere.

6. Aside from the dubious wisdom of dismantling the Bulls in the first place, Krause got off to a good start in 1999 by winning the number-one lottery pick of the summer NBA draft.

17

BATTLE OF THE PLAYMASTERS

Money, egos, fortune, and fame—what greater fuel to stoke the flames of human emotions at any level, let alone the pinnacle of NBA basketball greatness?

The quickest way to end a war is to lose it.

—GEORGE ORWELL

The battle for control is likely as old as the league itself, but the closed-door battles of yesteryear have emerged from the shadows of smoke-filled rooms, engulfing the media and public with ever-increasing abandon. Whatever lingering struggles remain between the lines, the lofty stakes of pro sports warfare have by and large stripped the leagues of even the appearance of discretion. These days the NBA wars are fought in open fields for all to see, much like a white-hot family feud that finally boils over into the streets, drowning the remaining semblance of family dignity in favor of police cars, stun guns, and transfixed neighbors.

The first labor skirmish that boiled into public view occurred in 1964 when the players threatened a boycott of the All-Star Game in Boston. At issue was a dispute over owner contributions to a newly created player pension fund. The game was actually delayed for several minutes as negotiations continued in the locker room, but the owners soon relented and the game was begun. Other than those few minutes, the NBA had never experienced a formal labor stoppage until the 1998–99 lockout.[1]

Player discontent escalated, however, while the NBA wars intensified during the past 30 years, reaching raging levels of discord in the mid to late 1990s. The battles have been fought everywhere from coast to coast, in the courts and in the press, but much of the conflict is linked to the canyons of Manhattan and a pair of mercenary guns hired by the playmasters themselves. They are by no means household names, but attorneys Howard Ganz of New York's high-powered Proskauer Rose L.L.P. and Jeffrey Kessler from corporate giant Weil, Gotshal & Manges L.L.P. have taken aim at each other from opposite sides for years.

Ganz, who represents the NBA, is a graying corporate type with an engaging smile that belies his streetfighting savvy. Kessler, sporting a boyish round face, dark-rimmed glasses, and a youthful crop of dark hair extending over forehead and ears, is a determined warrior unafraid to take aim at the NBA's ivory towers. Kessler won a landmark sports victory in 1992 when he successfully represented football star Freeman McNeil and other plaintiffs, wresting free agency from the tight-fisted NFL owners. For a decade Kessler and Ganz have gone head to head, including the Sprewell-Carlesimo melee.

Both firms come with a long history of NBA connections. In fact, current commissioner David Stern hails from Ganz's Proskauer firm, where Stern himself practiced law in the 1970s before his appointment as NBA commissioner.[2] At that time the Stern counterpart at Weil, Gotshal was one James Quinn, who, among other things, won the historic Oscar Robertson antitrust suit, effectively creating legal free agency for NBA players.

In 1995, the contemporary Jeffrey Kessler filed his own antitrust lawsuit against the NBA on behalf of Knicks center Patrick Ewing. The action failed, and was doomed to be a tough uphill battle from the start, for there is a technical restriction exempting sports leagues from restraints of trade when a certified sports union is in place. The plan had been to file the action, then have the players decertify the union as the recognized labor bargaining arm of the players, a move supported by Michael Jordan at the time. The matter was put to a vote, but the players defeated it handily to keep the union intact, and the Ewing antitrust action collapsed.

But the stage was set for the greatest NBA battle of all as force vectors of greed and power, fueled by a three-way dynamo comprised of David Stern, the players union, and the Falk-Jordan wild card, exploded into the 1998 player lockout. On July 1, 1998, the owners exercised their federal labor rights by locking the players out, forcing something of an inverted strike. The players wanted to eliminate the NBA salary cap in general while the owners sought to dump the Larry Bird Rule in particular.[3] The entire structure of NBA labor economics was about to go on trial—if not literally then in the courts of public perception—stretching fundamental laws of supply and demand up to and perhaps beyond the limits of economic leverage.

Ironically, the salary cap had preserved labor peace for many years, providing a soft limit to team labor costs but concurrently committing the NBA to allocating a minimum percentage of league revenues to overall player payrolls. Stripping away a variety of technical nuances, at one time that mandatory share was calculated at 53 percent. As NBA television revenues, merchandising, and gate receipts soared, the players benefitted automatically. It was a great partnership of sorts, engineered by the master politician David Stern, but there were hidden flaws in the execution of the system. The players as a group were making money, but the average mean salary was shifting away from the mode—in other words, the arithmetic average salaries were going up, but most of the gain was in the hands of relatively few superstars. Most salaries languished, often at or near the minimums.

Thus, the NBA players were gradually rearranged into at least two classes: superstars, and everyone else. On the surface there was understandable tension between the union and NBA ownership, but there was a subplot brewing among players at the bottom of the food chain. The NBA likely recognized the disparity, for a labor lockout would be just the right strategy to exploit the rank-and-file weaknesses. Although the 1994 baseball strike was player induced, baseball began to experience similar problems as lesser players ran short of funds. This was not lost on the NBA owners, who proceeded to grab and retain control with the lockout device.

The players union also recognized that same Achilles' heel and pressed the owners to pay players even during the lockout. A victory on that front would have left the league reeling, but it was not to be. The owners fired a preemptive strike against the union, filing a federal action to force an early ruling on whether the players had to be paid under federal labor laws. The lockout occurred July 1, 1998, and within two weeks the owners were in court. The union opposed the move, of course, but lost its argument. A lockout properly invoked has many of the attributes of a strike action, and the owners were within their rights to withhold player payments. That was the beginning of the end for the players' cause, for all that remained was to wait them out.

Why were the owners so determined? The Larry Bird Rule had so softened the NBA salary cap that in some cases there was no cap at all. In Michael Jordan's last years as a Bull, he was paid a sum approximating the entire team cap. Because of Jordan, the Bulls enjoyed the highest operating revenues of any NBA team ($112.2 million in 1998), but Bulls ownership was only tied for eleventh place in profitability, with operating income of only $8.5 million. At around $32 million (or more) per year, Jordan was making almost four times as much as the whole organization.

Philadelphia was the team tied with the Bulls, but the 76ers made their $8.5 million on just $69.9 million in revenue—about $42 million less than the Bulls, roughly equal to the Jordan salary, goosed up a bit by the multimillion-dollar extras of Dennis Rodman and coach Phil Jackson (all then added on top of the Bulls regular team payroll). Essentially the Bulls went to a lot of trouble winning six championships, paying Jordan perennial fortunes, putting up with Dennis Rodman, building a new stadium, and helping catapult the NBA to new heights—all for the anticlimactic privilege of making less money than 10 other NBA teams. The Trail Blazers made four times as much ($34.2 million), Detroit almost three and a half ($30.0 million), and the Lakers three times the Bulls ($24.8 million). Even the Charlotte Hornets made more ($9.2 million), and they did it at half the Bulls' revenue at $56.4 million gross.[4]

Conventional wisdom attributes the breakup of the championship Bulls to age, rebuilding for the future, and even egos and personalities—but the economic reality of the Bulls' success is almost certainly an equal factor. As a team the Bulls decimated themselves in 1999, but in so doing they drastically cut player payroll to about $29 million total, the lowest in the league. With a sold-out house for the year and a constant share of television and merchandising revenue, the 1999 Bulls are a moneymaking machine.

At this writing the 1999 financial results are not yet in, but assuming revenues equal to 1998 on a pro rata basis (adjusting for 50 games instead of 82, and eliminating the effect of the playoffs, a thing of the past for the Bulls' immediate future), Chicago stands to net a pile of money, perhaps more than any NBA team in history. Possibly the Bulls can perpetuate that phenomenon one more year before the crowd catches on, but the gravy train will screech to an abrupt halt one day soon unless a credible winner is on the foreseeable horizon.

But with salaries spiraling out of control and no dynasty goodwill to fall back on, the day of reckoning was already upon the rest of the league, hence the lockout strategy to divide and control the union as a means to concretely cap superstar salaries. No fewer than 10 NBA teams actually lost money in the 1997–98 season. These included the mediocre teams such as the Clippers, Kings, and Mavericks, as well as better teams with big payrolls like Indiana, Miami, and Orlando.

The owners actually claim to be doing worse than published reports and estimates. According to the league, 16 NBA teams lost money. Why the difference? One side effect of mandatory revenue sharing with the players was to drive some of the revenue out of team coffers. If an owner also has an interest in the team stadium, revenue from parking, concessions, sky boxes, advertising, and stadium, sponsorship flows to the team owner(s) but not to the team itself. Yes, money was lost by 16 NBA teams, but not necessarily their owners. The same principle holds where the owner also controls team television packages. One of the best examples includes the Atlanta Hawks and Atlanta Braves—both owned by the Turner empire, both part of the Turner media conglomerate with games shown on WTBS and TNT for many years.

Regardless of the financial shenanigans that may have been at play, without any meaningful control on spending the owners nonetheless had a monster on their hands. That monster was themselves to a great degree, but it is overly simplistic to stop there. As Bulls managing partner Jerry Reinsdorf once remarked, he is in the only business where one is forced to spend what his dumbest competitor spends. Spice that up with a dash of monster egos from both players and owners, and the ingredients for financial chaos are in place.

The proof is in the economic pudding. As of the end of 1998, financial pundits estimated the values of all major sports team franchises. No NBA team was in the top 10. Not even the Bulls, not even the highly profitable Portland Trail Blazers. The top 3 franchises were, in fact, all football teams: Dallas, Washington, and Carolina.[5] The Yankees slipped in at fourth place, followed by four more football teams in the form of Tampa Bay, Miami, Baltimore, and Seattle. Two more baseball teams, the Orioles and Indians, rounded out the top 10.

However, with a new labor agreement and revised cap in place, NBA teams should begin to command more. Some of them are quite profitable, and that value should now begin to translate into higher team values without the same risk of financial Armageddon. But to achieve those objectives, the NBA ownership had to hold the union in check. They did so with sheer financial muscle, outwitting and outlasting the players. The league managed to wrangle television concessions before the lockout, requiring network payments even if games were canceled due to labor actions.[6] Although those payments would be treated later as advances against future games and not strictly "gifts" to the owners, still the deal preserved valuable owner cash flow at precisely the time most individual players needed cash flow—desperately in some cases.

A cave-in by the players was inevitable. The superstars like Patrick Ewing and Michael Jordan could afford a lockout, of course, but most players could not. Ironically, the superstars created this anomaly, for it was their gargantuan salaries that pushed the rank-and-file journeymen toward the depths of the minimum NBA wage in the first place. Since those players could not sustain a protracted labor action, the union house would soon be divided and the Bird exception was on a slippery slope to extinction.

When the smoke cleared and the lockout was relegated to history, the owners were the big winners, followed by the journeymen players. The superstars were stymied. The league nailed down a firm maximum veteran salary based upon years of service. The new labor agreement calls for a top annual salary of $14 million for 10-year veterans, $11 million for players with 5 to 9 years in the league, and $9 million for "maxed out" players in the league 5 or fewer years. The Bird exemption is gone. There will be no new $18 million to $35 million paydays like those of late for Ewing and Jordan.

The exceptions to the salary limitations are few, mostly tied to new NBA minimum player compensation rules. The old minimums were calculated for all players at a modestly increasing flat rate of under $300,000 per year. Under the new deal, 1-year veterans must make at least $350,000 each, $425,000 for 2-year players, and so on up to a $1 million annual minimum for 10-year veterans. At least on paper, the bench players may do much better. However, there is a veteran penalty phenomenon that has already appeared in other leagues, notably football. Journeymen veterans can easily price themselves out of a job, and they do it regularly in the NFL. Will NBA ownership really choose to pay an aging 10-year role player a million bucks when it can invest in a younger player at less than half that amount? Perhaps not, at least not all the time.

Did the lockout victory come with a price? Certainly. But it was a calculated risk openly taken by the owners. Still, the jury may be out on the true economic carnage wreaked by the labor action. The NBA lost goodwill among fans, and it lost Michael Jordan. MJ's coming retirement was inevitable, of course; but whether caused by the lockout or not, he is no longer a Bull. Even if the lockout was not a contributing cause of that retirement, his exit is not irrelevant to the overall equation. A Jordan retirement is a blow to the league all its own; but added to the animosity of a protracted labor action, the blow to fan interest is magnified geometrically.

Published reports show fan interest and attendance down. That is to be expected under the circumstances, but can the league rebound with a makeshift 50-game season followed by a Jordan-less playoff run? Reported midseason (1999), league attendance was down as much as 32 percent for Atlanta, 20 percent for Charlotte, and 17 percent for Cleveland. The 1999 Bulls were off something over 6 percent, but they benefited from an enormous base of presold season tickets. Some teams have better attendance figures, but estimates suggest that for the first 247 league games in early 1999, aggregate league attendance was down over 500,000 fans who otherwise would not only have bought tickets, but would have paid for parking, hot dogs, beers, and merchandise. And even those attendance figures are likely inflated, for many tickets were likely sold without a corresponding seat filled. Will new play-off interest with the Bulls clearly out of the picture spark enough genuine year-long interest in other cities like Detroit, Houston, Salt Lake City, San Antonio, Los Angeles, Miami, Orlando, and Indianapolis? Maybe. Maybe not.

The bigger question lies not with the first 1999 season, but with the second one. The interest generated by the 1999–2000 NBA season will be crucial. It may determine whether the playmasters are indeed masters of their own fate, if not the sports universe, or whether they have finally outsmarted themselves by killing basketball to rid themselves of the salary cap.

And lost amidst the diversion of the lockout and subsequent patchwork season is the overall Jordan effect. When he had briefly retired to pursue baseball, NBA merchandising and licensing revenues began to trail off. By the opening of the 1999 season, Jordan was gone again, but the first time he retired, the remainder of the Bulls were still intact and good enough for the playoffs. And this time there is the x-factor of labor fallout and possible fan discontent. Everywhere Jordan went, success was sure to follow, including North Carolina, where his team won the NCAA title. The year after Jordan was drafted, Reinsdorf's group bought a majority interest in the Bulls at a price that valued the whole team at around $15 million. Most estimates now place the value over $300 million, a great investment regardless of recent cash flow. But the Jordan effect did not stop there. The rising tide lifted all boats for 15 years as Michael brought the league to new levels of excellence, television exposure, and merchandising.

Even the Jordan *Space Jam* movie grossed nearly a quarter of a *billion* dollars. According to *Fortune* magazine, Jordan's sports videos have sold over four million copies and MJ has done, inspired, or been the subject of at least 70 books. And none of this counts payment for straight endorsements from Nike to Wheaties, Gatorade, and others. Michael has appeared on Wheaties boxes a record 13 times, and total Gatorade revenues have soared $837 million since Jordan signed on.

The effect upon the league as a whole is also stunning. Before Michael Jordan, the Bulls drew only a handful of fans for road games (well under ten thousand, less than the NBA average); with MJ the Bulls played to near sellouts everywhere with average road attendance over twenty thousand per game. Tellingly, the Bulls road draw dipped noticeably during Jordan's first retirement. Television revenues and player salaries have done well, too. The average NBA player salary rose about ten-fold during the Jordan era, although some of that was skewed in favor of the big-time superstars at the expense of lesser players. Still, the scent of success was everywhere—in the air, on the airwaves, on the court, off the court.

Will the NBA survive the Jordan exodus? Probably. Will it be the same? Obviously not. Without MJ, the league reduces itself to a predictable pick-and-roll season with little "motion" either on the court or outside the arena. To sustain even a portion of its continuous growth, the NBA must reinvent itself and/or hang its star on another icon. It will not be easy, especially in the face of the great labor carnage of 1998–99.

ENDNOTES

1. Baseball, by contrast, experienced its first threat of a strike in 1889, with numerous battles ensuing from 1912 through at least 1994.
2. The founder and longtime leader of the NBPA was Larry Fleisher, a sports agent. The 1975 settlement of the Oscar Robertson antitrust litigation (see Chapter 5) was engineered by Fleisher, league commissioner Larry O'Brien (former chairman of the Democratic Party), and NBA general counsel David Stern.
3. The Larry Bird Rule allowed owners to exceed the salary cap for purposes of retaining their own free agent veterans, the effect of which was to skyrocket superstar salaries at the expense of rank-and-file players squeezed by the cap rules and paucity of leftover team funds.

4. There is lots of room to make more money in Charlotte, which could be one reason behind a brief string of rumors about Jordan either buying or playing for the Hornets.

5. The Cowboys' worth was then pegged at $413 million, with the Redskins a close second at $403 million. Then suddenly, offers in the $600 million to $800 million range were made for the Washington franchise—lofty numbers, yet still attributable to football, not basketball.

6. The lockout cost NBC 9 regular season games plus the All-Star Game, whatever that was worth. TNT lost nearly 50 regular season games.

18

THE SEVEN SINS OF THE NBA

On or off the court, bull markets, to choose a pun, are susceptible to the gravity of business: what goes up must come down.

Fools rush in where angels fear to tread.

—ALEXANDER POPE

If the NBA leviathan were to maintain unbridled growth into perpetuity, it would be the first American industry to do so. In the wake of a double jolt in the form of Jordan's retirement and the great 1998–99 lockout, the NBA is vulnerable—not finished or dead by any means, but it can no longer afford to be arrogant.

The ultimate team-sports product is entertainment, but that description is too simplistic. The key is how the entertainment is manufactured: hope. Audiences do not watch sports just to see the best athletes perform. If they did, no one would watch high school or intercollegiate sports. No, the issue is credible sports complemented by excitement—and excitement is generated by a personal stake in the outcome. For some, the personal stake is quite literal, if derived from the rush of sports gambling; for most fans, though, the energy is fueled by hope. Nearly everyone identifies with a team, usually a home team or an adopted favorite team.

The Cowboys know the "adopted team" phenomenon—indeed, they were "America's team" for a number of years, meaning that people without a home NFL city had a propensity to follow the Dallas Cowboys. The Chicago Bears dethroned Dallas in 1985 two ways: first, by thrashing the Cowboys on the field 44–0, the worst defeat in Dallas history; second, by trotting out the most devastatingly entertaining football team in at least the last quarter century, if not all time. With Walter Payton, Jim McMahon, Willie Gault, Dennis McKinnon, and an All-Pro offensive line, the offense was cocky, fun, and successful. But the defense stole the show, crushing opponents, controlling games, and steamrolling through the playoffs with devastating shutouts of both the Giants and Rams before dismantling the Patriots in Super Bowl XX. Those Super Bowl Bears did not just beat teams, they left them decimated for years to come. They became "America's team" for two or three years, leading the NFL in merchandising sales as fans clamored for the cocky, tough attitude of the swaggering Bears and their colorful personalities, from McMahon to Steve McMichael, Richard Dent, Payton, Otis Wilson, William "Refrigerator" Perry, and the inimitable coach Mike Ditka. That team knew what business it was in: entertainment.[1]

Then came the Chicago Bulls, at that time a lesser team that first sparked fan curiosity with its new "phenom," Michael Jordan. They built an entertainment dynasty as America craved the Jordan heroics and engaging smile, six championships, the durable sidekick Scottie Pippen, and for a time the colorful, quirky genius of Dennis Rodman. Those Bulls were watched by nearly everyone, even worldwide, regardless of whether viewers had a favorite home team. But what about after 1999? There certainly is no Jordan in Chicago; Pippen signed on with Houston, then moved on to Portland; and Dennis took a strange, temporal fling with the Lakers before he flaked out completely.

More important, there is no apparent successor to the Bulls on the foreseeable NBA horizon, either in terms of success, color, attitude, personality, or, in summary, entertainment. Do those of us in non-NBA locales such as Montana, Alabama, Nebraska, Maine, or Tennessee crave a glimpse of the Rockets? The Knicks? The Magic? The Jazz? Once in awhile there is a glimmer for the Lakers with Shaq, Bryant, and a complement of stars (especially during Rodman's brief stay), but the Lakers do not seem to have a personality that engages the public. One thing the Lakers do have now is former Bulls coach and mentor Phil Jackson. Whether Jackson can build a perennial winner on the west coast remains to be seen, but he will bring a different style of play and coaching that could allow the Lakers talent to finally gel. The Jazz team has a chance with Malone and Stockton, but they are both aging and Utah has yet to go on a championship tear, even though its regular season records of late are stellar. The Knicks surprised everyone in the 1999 playoffs, but will America adopt them as their own? San Antonio looks good with Tim Duncan and David Robinson, but they are a small-market team still a couple of championships short of a national dynasty. Thus, we observe the first in the seven sins of the NBA: no America's team in the making.

1. AMERICA'S NON-TEAMS

Television drives the NBA, and full stadiums do not hurt, either. The Bulls dynasty certainly drew big television ratings, especially in the playoffs, including millions of viewers with no particular vested interest in the NBA, emotional or otherwise. When on top, Chicago also drew big crowds at home (sellouts all year every year, not just isolated games) and monster crowds on the road, packing stadiums with curious locals. In turn, NBA merchandising soared as hungry fans gobbled up "attitude" marketing in the form of Jordan, Rodman, and Pippen jerseys, shoes, and memorabilia.

Where have all the road crowds gone? Where are the TV ratings? There is no flagship team stepping up to carry the load. One might still do so, of course, but will it happen when it counts the most—soon?

2. DILUTION OF HOPE

With no universal star or team to transcend local loyalties and attract viewers and customers regardless of affiliation, the NBA must rely upon its entertainment ace-in-the-hole: hope.

Hope, though, is a fleeting commodity in view of league expansion. What teams have realistic hopes of winning the title? Very few, although there are more now than when Jordan & Company ruled the courts. Surely there was less broad-based hope to sell fans so long as the Bulls were gobbling up championships year after year. But the excited energy brought to the playoffs by those colorful Bulls made up for lost hope; indeed, many comers had their own shots to throw punches at Chicago throughout the play-offs year after year after year. Many fans temporarily adopted the Bulls as their own, even though they were not Chicagoans.

Still, to capitalize on the entertainment value of the NBA, every-one has to believe his team has a chance to win on any given night, and to "go all the way" as the season itself unfolds. All four major sports leagues have recognized the problem and managed to satisfy the latter by cleverly—and successfully—transferring cham-pionship hopes to playoff hopes. With divisional play, wild cards, conference championships, and all the rest, the expanded playoffs provide massive doses of hope for all but the worst teams. Each year mediocre clubs have renewed hope of making the playoffs, lending something of a promised land approach to postseason play. If mediocre to poor teams qualify for the playoffs, a suc-cessful season can be declared regardless of the first-round out-come. If that team wins the first round against a lower-seeded patsy, then it has successfully "gone deep into the playoffs," another moral victory disguised as a real triumph, leaving satisfied fans *hoping* for next year and all the great things it surely would bring.

Hope, however, may or may not spring eternal. League expan-sion has proven irresistible to sports owners, but for every team added, the elusive hope is diluted for all the rest. By 1999 the NBA had become a league of 29 teams. Even if championships were won precisely pro rata, each team would win the title only once every 29 years, much more than a generation. Indeed, winning twice would take nearly 60 years, the better part of an entire adult lifetime.

As discouraging as such hypotheticals may be, the reality is worse. Perfect winning distribution does not occur in the real world—the NBA is not a scientifically random event, and even if it were it could take a century or two to even out mathematically. In practice, good teams stay good for inordinate periods of time. Most recently the Bulls gobbled up six championships with a pair of threepeats sandwiching two Houston titles. Thus, only two different teams won during an eight-year run, skewing the winning distribution significantly. Other perennial winners in the last pair of decades included the Lakers and Celtics, both of which won a disproportionate share of championships.

With odds like that, some teams might only win once or twice per century (like baseball's Chicago Cubs and White Sox). The whole purpose of conducting a draft and allowing poor teams to choose first, not to mention the team salary caps, is to accelerate the arithmetic process of distributing wins more evenly. Perhaps it works to a small degree, but winning seems to be more contagious than anything, building upon some fortuitous combination of personalities, skill, and attitudes. The Celtics of old had Russell and Red Auerbach; the Bulls had Jordan and Phil Jackson to build upon. Unless tinkered with recklessly, success, once achieved, breeds upon itself. Going backward from 1998, the Bulls won three titles; before that Houston nailed two in a row; then the Bulls have three straight again; and before that the bad boys of Detroit snared a pair. Going still further, the Lakers won two in a row before Detroit. In other words, for 12 straight years each title winner repeated at least once before succumbing. The last one-time winners were the 1985–86 Celtics (not counting the Spurs of 1999), preceded by the Lakers again—but the Celtics had already won one the year before that, still supporting the proposition that winning is contagious in the NBA.

The infectious nature of winning is not difficult to dissect. Any rookie or promising free agent on the championship Celtics, Lakers, Pistons, or Bulls benefited immediately from team confidence, a formula that worked, a coach who knew his team, and team leaders like Bird, Magic, Thomas, and Jordan who commanded respect and demanded great things from the new players on the bench. This equation works more often than not, provided aging teams are allowed to evolve, optimizing the remaining intangibles as new blood is brought in. If a team is dismantled completely, of course, the synergies are no more, and success is much harder to sustain. The old Bears proved that, and the new Bulls seem to be trying.

Nonetheless, most success breeds more, at least for awhile, bringing great hope, even swagger, to a given city and its fans. There is a cost, though, in the form of diluted fan hope for the rest of the league. Adding one team does not exacerbate the problem noticeably, but tacking on a dozen does. What would happen if the NBA had 100 teams? Would fans lose so much interest that the practical size of the league would be 20 or 30 viable franchises? Probably. The NBA is on the brink of such a phenomenon now, aggravated by the great lockout followed by the "great retirement." The 1999 winner may always carry an implied asterisk given the abbreviated, strange season, and subsequent winners may not be able to command a national fan base so necessary for league prosperity.

3. RECESSION VULNERABILITY

The United States has enjoyed prosperity and mostly bull markets on Wall Street since at least 1982. When business is up while interest rates and unemployment are down, prosperity is inevitable and leisure spending goes up on fashion, entertainment, and luxury cars.

When business cycles go south, recessions result. But spending on entertainment during recessions can remain strong under the right circumstances. Movies were very popular during the Great Depression, for example, for two reasons: entertainment value and price tradeoffs. Offering both escapism and a dash of hope, the popular movies during the desperate Depression years were musicals (Fred Astaire and Busby Berkeley) and comedies (Marx Brothers and others). And the public could afford them. On the other hand, high-ticket spending dried up—few families bought cars and durable goods, but they traded down in their spending habits: ice cream and movies, both cheap and fun, were popular.

So what does all that have to do with basketball? Watch the business cycle. The end of the NBA as we know it will likely come during the next moderate to deep recession. With NBA tickets hovering around $75 each, prices are in the stratosphere. Factoring in parking, concessions, and souvenirs, a family of four can easily spend nearly $400 to attend one game. That is more than 10 times the cost of a first-run movie for the same family, even with all the trappings. It is *almost* 100 times the cost of ice cream and *more* than 100 times the cost of a movie rental.

When the recession hits, not only will family ticket buyers dry up, corporate spending will collapse. Big companies will retrench, and small and medium employers will regroup or go belly-up altogether. Either way, American business will look for more efficient ways to spend promotional dollars than season tickets and sky boxes, and families will spend a lot of time in movie theaters, at the rental store, and in front of the television. But they won't be in a $75 NBA seat.

The NBA is dangling on a long, shaky limb of ticket prices vulnerable to the laws of recession spending.

4. GUARANTEED CONTRACTS

Long-term guaranteed contracts for players can be an economic annoyance to owners when business is good, but they spell disaster for ownership in the event of a downturn. Those deals are very good for players, of course, but what happens to the salary cap and other issues if league revenues ever go down from one year to the next? Further, if attendance dries up and the owners are left staring at multiyear $70 million to $100 million player deals, the economic squeeze could jeopardize some teams.

By contrast, NFL contracts are not guaranteed. If a player is a bust, the player is cut. Period. Teams do not prefer that route with high draft picks, especially since football operates on a signing bonus system. NFL signees are paid lucrative bonuses up front, encouraging teams to keep them around; still, football owners have great flexibility with the nonguaranteed contracts. The NBA typically has no signing bonus provision, but it guarantees the contracts. If a player loses his abilities or the team chooses to cut him for whatever reason, the salary is still payable. Even violent insubordination was not enough to allow Golden State to cancel the Latrell Sprewell contract, so it is clear these deals are long term and airtight.

The rigidity of NBA contracts offers fewer problems during economic upturns and prosperity, but collectively those deals may cause material problems for all concerned if at any time teams simply cannot pay.

5. SUPPLY AND DEMAND

Not only are NBA ticket prices high and vulnerable to consumer demand swings, the NBA potentially has an overabundance of games. (Only baseball has more—a problem for the one-time national pastime, but at least baseball's ticket prices are not in the stratosphere.) All NBA teams normally play 41 regular season home games, plus preseason and playoff games, if any. The playoffs have been expanded over the years, with 15 postseason wins required for the championship over potentially a 26-game span. Most NBA aficionados realize that good NBA basketball often fails to occur before playoff time, and during the regular season the best play normally takes place in the fourth quarter.

With expensive tickets and an abundance of games, season ticket costs are extraordinary. Two tickets in normal seats will cost in the range of $7,000 annually—not exactly ice cream and a movie. But aside from the cost is the challenge of maintaining fan interest. Although it approaches heresy to suggest it, even during the latter Bulls title runs, season ticket holders began to find the regular season games tedious. Certainly the stadium was full all the time, for there was no shortage of interest by endless fans in the Chicago area—but many of them were corporate guests, friends or relatives of friends, tourists with tickets from brokers, and what have you. No matter how one slices it, driving to and attending over 40 games a year is a chore. It is especially arduous when one has a poor team to watch. Something may have to give even in good times, but certainly bad times will expose the over-abundance of games.

6. ANTITRUST

With all its shortcomings, baseball has one remarkable advantage: it is exempt from antitrust laws.[2] This exemption is an illogical legacy from a nearly senile U.S. Supreme Court decision in 1922 that declared baseball "not a business engaged in interstate commerce." Every other major sports league, though, has been subjected to the same legal scrutiny with the opposite result: the NFL, NHL, and NBA are all very much *non*exempt, for it is patently obvious that each is very much a thriving interstate business.

NBA owners have won the most recent legal skirmishes, but the players union has become increasingly hostile. It has already attempted to decertify itself to legally expose the NBA to greater antitrust scrutiny where players are concerned (antitrust activity is exempt when a certified bargaining unit is in place). But the league is open to attack from others, both as a conspiracy in restraint of trade and potentially as a monopoly over "championship basketball." The league has already had its nose bloodied by WGN television in Chicago. Owned by the Tribune entertainment conglomerate, WGN is a cable superstation that showed Bulls games across the country. When the NBA attempted to gain control over all game telecasts, the way the NFL packages its games, a six-year antitrust suit was launched by the Tribune subsidiary. WGN repeatedly won in the federal district court, with the Court of Appeals carving down the victories then sending the case back down to the lower courts again. After repeating this cycle several times over a half-dozen years, the case was finally settled, largely in favor of the plaintiff WGN.

With its draft lottery, new salary caps, and a ravenous appetite for control over television, stadium venues, women's pro basketball, and even its own team owners, the NBA is poised for antitrust trouble. Under the federal Sherman Act, NBA actions are vulnerable as potential conspiracies in restraint of trade. If the league experiences a financial downturn at any point, the economic pressures may inspire the league to take radical collective measures, exposing it to antitrust scrutiny, if not liability.

7. THE GAME

NBA games are boring. They are played with the best athletes and presumably the best coaches, but they still lack an intense excitement that was once present with Wilt Chamberlain, Magic, Bird, Dr. J, and the icon Jordan.

Why? The games are tedious and predictable. Isolation. Hit the low post. Hit the high post, run the pick-and-roll. Play a disguised zone on defense, assuming there is a defense. Limited pressing. Swing the ball six times, take a shot, no offensive rebound.[3] So why are games so uninspired? The great athletes neutralize each other; there are too many games, so players must conserve energy over the long haul, thus a reluctance to press often; a feeder system of one-on-one street players uninterested in games of motion, speed, and teamwork; mind-numbing salaries that render players uncoachable; and coaches are unable to relate to today's players—thus aggravating all the foregoing.

With all that, even the rote play of games is not the whole story. There are no personalities. No color. No character. No char-ac*ters*. Several years ago the National Football League slipped into an abyss appropriately summed up as "taking itself too seriously." At one point, the NFL had banned both player exuberance and crowd cheering when it interfered with certain action on the field. The NFL lost itself, forgetting it was in the *entertainment* business. When the press finally gave it the derisive moniker "No Fun League," the NFL relented. Now players leapfrog each other (New Orleans) and even jump into the stands (Green Bay). Crowds are allowed to cheer and annoy visiting teams. And teams still manage a few colorful players and coaches, from Mike Ditka to Neon Deion Sanders, Doug Flutie, Barry Sanders (assuming his retirement is temporary), Randy Moss, recently retired John Elway, and even color broadcasters who actually are colorful, such as John Madden.

What do we have in basketball? Corporate coaches dressed like they escaped from a board meeting; games played as predictably as a board meeting; and players with tattoos, hairdos, and phony attitudes—everything necessary to create personality, except personality.

If it is not on the court, where has all the entertainment gone?

Sadly, it seems to have traversed from the hardwood floors to the hard-headed front office. And solutions are hard to come by. The Celtics tried capturing the energy of Kentucky's basketball program by putting an NCAA team on the floor. At least they tried something different, but even with Kentucky icon Rick Pitino at the helm, the athletes are less than responsive. Boston players are reluctant to press for 82 games, and there just isn't the energy of the NCAA and all its built-in trappings of student fans with a psychotic investment of personal energy in their home team. And one more thing: dubious under-the-table stipends aside, all NBA players are more than well paid and many are less than impressed with the team spirit phenomenon.

Numerous front offices, even coaches, are simply out of touch. There are few icon coaches left in the NBA: No Red Holzman, no Red Auerbach. There are no Shulas, Walshes, Ditkas; no Dean Smith, no Bobby Knight, no Coach K. Even promoting an icon to the NBA fails to do the trick, as with Rick Pitino. No, it takes a thinking coach, a battle-tested former NBA player with a nose for the game and a knack for people—just the presence brought by former Bulls and now Lakers coach Phil Jackson. Cerebral, witty, eccentric, tweaking management, loving his players as people. Perhaps the youthful Laker Kurt Rambis could have been such a coach, but his Lakers team responded poorly in spite of its talent, prompting management to sign the older, cerebral Jackson. Perhaps Larry Bird is such a coach already. Maybe Jerry Sloan is, too, as is Rudy "T" in Houston. Chuck Daly was one of the elite, but he retired in May of 1999. Overall there are too few of their breed, and the NBA as a whole pays the price.

If history one day brings both the rise and fall of the NBA, perhaps the beginning of the end will be traced to the front offices, bastions of self-anointed basketball genius, mired in their own press clippings, both real and imagined. We have thus come full circle. Egos. The problem is, there are no geniuses in the NBA, and if there are, that is a waste. Our geniuses need to be in medicine and science; economics and art; literature; politics; business. Geniuses cure polio, fly the space shuttle, build Microsoft, reinvent communications and news in the form of CNN, fly packages in quantum leaps via Federal Express.

Maybe Michael Jordan was a genius ball player. Maybe he was and is a genius entertainer. At his basketball zenith, MJ certainly was no less successful in the entertainment business than the likes of the Smashing Pumpkins, Rolling Stones, Steven Spielberg, Jack Nicholson, Robert DeNiro, Michael Eisner. On the other hand, there was never much message in his delivery, although the stark delivery was a quantum leap on the court. Still, genius might be more than that—more than just skill, more than just a flair for the near-supernatural defiance of basketball logic, wisdom, and even gravity.

Either way, there are few in basketball to match Jordan's skill, savvy, and addictive grace. But many would try, and more will feign genius, strutting on the court and off. And now we have come full circle twice. For the path of Jordan's genius, if it may be called that, leads the argument straight to the Bulls and erstwhile GM Jerry Krause.

Mr. Krause has to be given credit for two things: he managed not to screw up the Bulls dynasty by accident, a real challenge in today's sports world; and in dismantling the Bulls on purpose, he took a major chance, stranding himself at the far, far end on a limb of public scrutiny. But his willingness to stand out, be different, and take the ultimate chance is nothing if not refreshing in the increasingly predictable world of professional sports. If Krause succeeds and rebuilds a champion from the ashes of ruin, some pundits will fall victim to the genius trap, possibly confusing foresight with a flawed ego and blind luck.

The Seven Sins of the NBA | 237

Having said that, Bulls ownership was probably right to pursue a rebuilding phase, even a radical one. The short-term economics made sense—for the first time in years, the ownership partners could make a competitive return without the salaries of Jordan, Rodman, and Jackson. It made business sense, and after a story-book title run, the team of the '90s yielded to the ownership of the '90s.

But there is something in the transition that defies the logic of business. Some hidden bug nags at the public gut, tormenting Bulls fans and other followers of basketball, fueled by hints in the printed word—stories published of inner strife, peculiar sensitivities, and egos run amuck. Fact: Jerry Krause did not draft Michael Jordan, he inherited him. Fact: Jerry Krause handpicked every other piece of the six championship puzzles. Fact: Krause and Phil Jackson did not get along, especially during the latter years. Jackson says that before the last title year, Krause heatedly admonished Phil, insisting the embattled coach would never, ever get another year from the Bulls. A year later, the spin was put on Jackson's retirement, with management making an alleged last-ditch effort in coaxing Phil out of retirement even as it was hiring Krause's anointed coach of the present and future, Tim Floyd.

Many basketball observers believe Jackson was run out of town, but lost in the ambiguities of spin is a larger question: did Krause really run Jordan out of town? The circumstantial evidence supports the proposition.[4] Jordan had been very clear he would play in Chicago for no coach other than Phil Jackson, probably buying Phil one last title run by the graces of Jerry Reinsdorf, consistent with the deep-rooted respect Reinsdorf harbored for the Jordan phenomenon, if not Michael the man. But business is business, and so perhaps the Bulls owner could stand in the way of "progress" no longer, stepping back to let GM Jerry run (demolish) the show.

Again, rebuilding was not a bad idea. Total decimation, however, could prove a mistake and, either way, appears to have been born as much from animosity as the result of business planning. If the result is the same, maybe the motives do not matter; on the other hand, how could the motives be immaterial to the result?

Although clearly disliked by Krause, Jackson could have been more the pawn in the middle of the larger carnage, perhaps a tool in the larger picture: ridding Krause of the Jordan legacy. Jordan's public ultimatum in support of Jackson bought Phil time, but it also landed MJ squarely in the proverbial corner. All Krause had to do was push Jackson out of town. Checkmate. The chances of Michael Jordan playing for a rookie coach with an average NCAA career were nil to zero. Whether MJ would have retired anyway is speculation, of course, but with Jackson and Michael still around, the transition with young players would not only have been more successful, but probably more fun.

It was not to be. The team was understandably reluctant to bear the financial burden of Michael Jordan on its shoulders so the rest of the league could free-ride on MJ's popularity. Enough was enough, harsh as that may be for the fans. But the alternative is not without profound risks. Will the NBA survive Jordan's exodus? Will the Bulls survive Krause's vision?

The risks are compounded by the labor lockout and shortened season. History may one day dismiss the 1999 season as a lost cause, perhaps leaving 1999–2000 as the real test. If 1999 proves the season of fan discontent, will 2000 fare better? NBA franchises, on paper at least, are up about 25 times in value over the last 15 years. That "value" is real, of course, only if there is a willing buyer at that price. NFL franchises are experiencing an explosion of growth, with some team prices soaring past the half-billion mark. If the NBA is reduced to a starless pick-and-roll with little excitement and hostile players, it is at risk of sliding into a 1970s abyss.

Either way, America's team, the Bulls of Jordan & Company, is no more. The league, at least for now, has been reduced from a frenzy of sellouts to one near-fatal lockout. The playmasters have played their riskiest hand. Whether they win, lose, or draw will be up to the fans, the customers, the true lifeblood of the NBA— unless fate intervenes with a sudden new superstar capable of again elevating the league to the promised land of eternal success. Eternal, that is, until some unbridled playmaster loses a battle of egos and internal demons. If "Colonel Krause" fails, he will be run out of town; if he succeeds, he will be crowned a genius—a great loss to medicine, science, and the arts, but perhaps a sports genius all the same.

Whatever the Bulls' tribulations may be, they are strangely symbolic of the league's problems as a whole. Jordan not only propped up those Bulls—he salvaged and then built the entire league, mostly on his own. Will Jerry Krause succeed or will he reduce the once proud Bulls to shambles for years to come? By the same token, has the NBA finally shot itself in the foot, or will it rise from the ashes of labor strife and Chicago's superstar follies to soar once again?

The superlative Spurs and overachieving Knicks met for the 1999 championship, a refreshing start that pitted the newcomers against the battleworn New Yorkers. But will it be enough to launch a wounded NBA?

All the excuses and all the rationales are meaningless, for many arguments can be made to sound good by NBA spin doctors—even the devil can cite Scripture for his own purpose—but in the end, only time and history will tell. Just remember in the meantime: what goes up must come down.

ENDNOTES

1. Perhaps the owner did not recognize as much, for Mike McCaskey quickly dismantled the team, losing more games every year until it collapsed altogether, culminating in the unceremonious firing of Ditka. Ironically, those Bears could have aced the Bulls as Chicago's team, if not America's, for many years. The whole team was made up of Rodman types, punky players and loose cannons who came together as one great cohesive wrecking ball—in short, an entertainment dynamo.

2. Congress has chipped away at the exemption of late, essentially removing it where player issues are concerned—but that means little, for there already is a legal exemption when a certified union is in place. For practical purposes, baseball is still very much exempt on all fronts.

3. Three-quarters of the way through the 1999 season, an NBA graphic popped up on the television screen displaying the league-leading percentage shooters. Only seven players in the league were above 50 percent, most of them just barely.

4. Mr. Krause was asked to comment on that precise issue for this book. He declined.

EPILOGUE

The future is here. Phil Jackson has re-emerged at the helm of the talented, heretofore underachieving Los Angeles Lakers, and Tim Duncan, of the San Antonio Spurs, has asserted himself as a legitimate NBA force.

Will the post-lockout new guard be enough? Perhaps. But the future of the NBA is in the hands of ego and greed more than ever. True, Major League Baseball recovered from its own labor debacle of 1994, benefiting from the home run deluge of 1998 and 1999. Will basketball find its own fortuitous shot in the arm to dispel the demons of a lockout, shortened season, and repeat retirement of the one and only Michael Jordan? It can if new stars emerge and if motion basketball based on teamwork, defense, and speed is allowed to flourish in the image of the valiant undermanned Knicks of 1999 or Jackson's Bulls of old.

The new NBA millennium begins with both the NBA union and superstar salaries under control, a good sign for the intermediate future of the league. The owner playmasters clearly won the 1999 battle of the NBA; if they can control their enhanced power and temper their egos with reason, the league has a shot at winning back its fans in great numbers. But it still must contend with dilution—not of talent, but of hope. Will very bad teams continue to draw fans? Will a new "America's Team" emerge to interest fans from coast to coast? Will the league allow new personalities to emerge—if not the likes of Dennis Rodman, then at least enough for teams to develop their own personalities? The NFL once became the "No Fun League" until fans went to sleep and owners woke up. The NBA could meet the same fate if it takes itself too seriously.

Hustle, speed, confidence, personality, and success—these are the ingredients to a healthy NBA future. Chamberlain was mean and strong, Jordan relentlessly determined. Magic made his team better, while Bird's passes were breathtaking—and all were winners. Tim Duncan proved he can carry the Spurs on his back, but can he elevate an entire league? It would appear unlikely. His lunch-bucket, effective approach to the game is wondrous à la football's Walter Payton, but supporting an entire league requires charisma. Winning is not enough; winning dramatically keeps fans coming back.

Tim Duncan is very good, but he doesn't smile much on the court, his play lacks electricity and the Spurs have a robot-like, albeit effective, approach to basketball. Their legend will grow if they can repeat the NBA title, but there remain plenty of teams with grudges and good memories, from Miami to New York, Los Angeles to Portland. In defeat, the 1999 Knicks were much more entertaining. Undermanned from the get-go, the Knickerbockers ran, shot, and hustled their way through the playoffs behind the shooting of Allan Houston and the wide-open flurry of none other than Latrell Sprewell.

Although he was good before, Sprewell emerged as a legitimate NBA star during the 1999 playoffs. In the finals against the superior Spurs, Latrell cut, slashed, and hustled his way to stardom before a national television audience. His relentless drive for the basket was matched only by his fearless, full-throttle approach to basketball, his obvious stamina defying both physics and biology as each game wore on.

Is there enough drama left in the NBA to matter? The answer lies in a full 82-game season, and will depend upon whether the playmasters can bring themselves to take positive, productive risks and not rest on the laurels of their renewed power. The old Bulls took a risk on Rodman and won, and it appears the Knicks won their bet on Sprewell. The Bulls organization also took a big chance by dismantling the team and running off not only Phil Jackson but perhaps Michael Jordan as well. That bold move may not have been positive or productive, but it could still pay off if the obvious animosity in its execution did not take too large a toll. If powerbroker egos take all the entertainment off the floor in favor of enhanced control, they may very well break the heart of the league and alienate its breadth of fans.

How will the playmasters handle the spoils of 1999 victory? Did they win the battle but lose the war? The 2000 season will be a watershed year in the annals of the embattled NBA, but most of all it will be a referendum on the playmaster egos that have reshaped the playing field for the next decade and beyond.

SOURCES

Araton, Harvey, "Jordan Proves It Takes More than Legs," *New York Times*, 16 June 1998.

Bagnato, Andrew, "Rule Could Aid Athletes—If It Survives in Court," *Chicago Tribune*, 11 August 1998.

Bagnato, Andrew, "$67 Million Hit Spurs Talk of Breaking Up NCAA," *Chicago Tribune*, 11 August 1998.

Banks, Lacy, "Labor Battle Hinges on Hard Salary Cap," *Chicago Sun-Times*, 3 April 1998.

Berkow, Ira, "Dynasties of a Different Day," *The New York Times*, 16 June 1998.

Bjarkman, Peter C., *The Encyclopedia of Pro-Basketball Team Histories* (New York: Carroll & Graf, 1994).

Brennan, Lisa, "Tark the Shark Has a Shark of His Own," *The National Law Journal*, 20 April 1998.

Carter, Craig, and Alex Sachare, ed., NBA *Guide, 1992–93 Edition* (St. Louis, Missouri: The Sporting News, 1992).

Carter, Craig, and Alex Sachare, ed., *Official* NBA *Guide, 1993–94 Edition* (St. Louis, Missouri: The Sporting News, 1993).

Cohen, J. M., and M. J. Cohen, *The New Penguin Dictionary of Quotations* (New York: Penguin Books USA, 1993).

Cotts, Cynthia, "Proskauer, Weil Gotshal: They Love this Game," *The National Law Journal*, 2 February 1998.

Dickson, Paul, *Baseball's Greatest Quotations* (New York: HarperCollins, 1991).

Dugard, Martin, "Head Games," *American Way*, 15 December 1998.

Feerick, John D., Grievance Arbitrator, Opinion and Award, *In the Matter of NBA Players Association on behalf of player Latrell Sprewell, and Warriors Basketball Club and National Basketball Association*, 4 March 1998.

Foster, William T., "An Indictment of Intercollegiate Athletics," *The Atlantic Monthly*, November 1915.

Fox, Larry, *Illustrated History of Basketball*, (USA: Larry Fox, 1974).

Gotthelf, Josh, "Early Concession Cost Union in End," *Street & Smith's Sports Business Journal*, 11 January 1999.

Gotthelf, Josh, "NBA's No-shows Threaten Bottom Line," *Street & Smith's Sports Business Journal*, 15 March 1999.

Hassan, John, ed., *The 1997 Information Please® Sports Almanac* (New York: Houghton Mifflin, 1996).

Heimer, Mel, *The Long Count* (New York: Atheneum, 1969).

Hickok, Ralph, *A Who's Who of Sports Champions: Their Stories and Records* (New York: Houghton Mifflin Company, 1995).

Ho, Rodney, "Entrepreneurs Aim to Elbow NCAA with New Leagues," *The Wall Street Journal*, 18 August 1998.

Johnson, Roy S., "The Jordan Effect," *Fortune*, 22 June 1998.

Jordan, Michael, *For the Love of the Game: My Story* (Crown Publishers, 1998), quoted in *Chicago Tribune*, 9 November 1998.

Kaplan, Daniel, "Big Apple Takes NBA Lockout Hit," *Street & Smith's Sports Business Journal*, 21 December 1998.

Lazenby, Roland, *Blood on the Horns* (Lenexa, Kansas: Addax Publishing Group, 1998).

Lewis, Pamela, "Sparkling Comet," *Basketball News*, September 1998.

Lincicome, Bernie, "In the Wake of the News," *Chicago Tribune*, 23 May 1999.

Mariotti, Jay, "Order Is Restored to Bulls' Chaotic World," *Chicago Sun-Times*, 28 May 1998.

Milbert, Neil, "IRS Agent: Referees Who Gamble Could Be Easy Targets for Fixers," *Chicago Tribune*, 6 October 1998.

Pluto, Terry, *Loose Balls: The Short, Wild Life of the American Basketball Association* (New York: Simon & Schuster, 1990).

Power, William, "The Virtual Ad: On TV You See It, at Games You Don't," *The Wall Street Journal*, 30 July 1998.

O'Donnell, Jim, "An Official Inquiry," *Chicago Sun-Times*, 8 May 1998.

O'Donnell, Jim, "O'Donnell's Tipoff," *Chicago Sun-Times*, 3 April 1998.

Ozanian, Michael K., "Selective Accounting," *Forbes*, 14 December 1998.

Rosenberg, Michael, "Losing Home-Court Edge Could Mean Losing, Period," *Chicago Tribune*, 3 June 1998.

Sachare, Alex, and David Sloan, ed., *Official NBA Guide, 1990–91 Edition* (St. Louis, Missouri: The Sporting News, 1990).

Sachare, Alex, and David Sloan, ed., *NBA Register*, 1990-91 Edition (St. Louis, Missouri: The Sporting News, 1990).

Smith, Sam, "Houston Just Missed Dynasty," *Chicago Tribune*, 11 June 1998.

Smith, Sam, *The Jordan Rules* (New York: Simon & Schuster, 1992).

Smith, Sam, "Labor Peace at Hand After 6-Month Wait," *Chicago Tribune*, 7 January 1999.

Spiegel, Peter, "Flesh Peddlers Go Global," *Forbes*, 9 March 1998.

Taylor, Phil, "The Resolution of the NBA Labor Dispute Poses Many Questions," *Sports Illustrated*, 18 January 1999.

Telander, Rick, "These Point Shavers Offer Many Valuable Lessons," *Chicago Sun-Times*, 13 April 1998.

Thurow, Roger, "A Sports Icon Regains its Footing by Using the Moves of the Past," *The Wall Street Journal*, 21 January 1998.

Uberstine, Gary A., ed., *Law of Professional and Amateur Sports* (St. Paul, Minn.: West Group/Clark Boardman Callaghan, 1998).

Weiler, Paul, and Gary Roberts, *Sports and the Law: Text, Cases, Problems* (St. Paul, Minnesota: West Group, 1998).

Published Court Opinions:

Boston Celtics v. Brian Shaw, 908 F.2d 1041 (First Cir., 1990).

Central New York Basketball v. Barnett, 181 NE2d 506 (Ohio, 1961).

Chicago Professional Sports Limited Partnership & WGN v. NBA, 754 F.Supp. 1336 (N.D.Ill., 1991).

Chicago Professional Sports Limited Partnership & WGN v. NBA, 961 F.2d 667 (Seventh Cir., 1992).

Cohen v. Brown University, 991 F.2d 888 (First Cir., 1993).

Collins v. NBPA and Grantham, 976 F.2d 740 (Tenth Cir., 1992).

Federal Baseball Club of Baltimore v. National League, 42 Sup.Ct. 465 (1922).

Haywood v. Denver Rockets, 325 F.Supp. 1049 (C.D.Cal., 1971).

Molinas v. NBA, 190 F.Supp. 241 (S.D.N.Y., 1961).

Munchak Corporation v. Cunningham, 457 F.2d 721 (Fourth Cir., 1972).

Parish v. NCAA, 361 F.Supp. 1220 (W.D. La., 1973).

Robertson v. National Basketball Association, 389 F.Supp. 867 (S.D.N.Y., 1975).

Wood v. NBA, 809 F.2d 954 (Second Cir., 1987).

INDEX